The Art of Economic Catch-Up

In his previous Schumpeter Prize-winning work, Lee analysed the "middle-income trap," in which a developing country grows strongly only to plateau at a certain point. Yet certain developing countries, most significantly China, have managed to escape this trap. Building on the conception of the ladder from developing to developed countries being kicked way, this book suggests alternative ways, such as "leapfrogging," in which latecomers can catch up with their forerunners. Providing policy solutions for development challenges in nontechnical terms, Lee frames his theories with insightful and inventive allegories. In doing so, he also accounts for the catch-up paradox, in which one cannot conclusively catch up if they are continually trying to follow the path of those ahead. Lee argues that eventual catch-up and overtaking require pursuing a path that differs from that taken by forerunners. This highly original and accessible book will appeal to students, scholars, practitioners, and anyone interested in economic development and innovation.

KEUN LEE is Professor of Economics at the Seoul National University, and the founding director of the Center for Economic Catch-up. He was also the President of the International Schumpeter Society, and a member of the UN Committee for Development Policy, and currently an editor of *Research Policy*, a council member of the World Economic Forum, and a member of the governing board of Globelics. He was awarded the 2014 Schumpeter Prize for his book on *Schumpeterian Analysis of Economic Catch-up: Knowledge, Path-creation and the Middle Income Trap* (Cambridge University Press, 2013).

T0349196

Economists and policy makers all over the world are eager to understand better the remarkable technological and economic development of Korea, Taiwan, and more recently China from poor backward economies to economies supporting a number of world class sophisticated industries. In my view the writings over the past decade of Keun Lee have provided great illumination regarding how this progress has been achieved. This book provides a coherent and accessible review of his analyses and takes it further to consider how these countries have been able to reach the technological and economic frontiers despite increasing resistance from firms and countries who have not welcomed this new competition. This book is essential reading for those interested in economic development.

– Richard R. Nelson, Columbia University

Only a few middle-income economies have been able to cross the hurdle to reach high-income status since the end of World War II. Drawing from the experiences of those few economies, the book not only identifies the key for the success to sustain dynamic, technological innovation but also provides practical advice to the enterprises and the government in a middle-income economy about how to do it. This is an impeccably researched and very readable book. A must read for anyone who is concerned about the middle-income trap and how to overcome it.

– Justin Yifu Lin, Dean, the Institute of New Structural Economics and Institute of South-South Cooperation and Development, Peking University; Former Chief Economist, the World Bank

Building on his mastery of state-of-the-art economic theories and drawing on his unparalleled knowledge of how firms and nations develop, Keun Lee has produced an invaluable guide to economic catch-up. The book provides very pragmatic but highly sophisticated advice to policy makers and firm-managers in developing nations that want to develop their economies. It is simply a remarkable book.

With the technological frontier changing as fast as it is now, a must-read to better understand the past and the future of development. Lee provides compelling evidence that catching up is an "art" with no predetermined path and makes societies and policy makers accountable for their choices.

– Annalisa Primi, Head, Structural Policies and Innovation,

Development Center, OECD

Keun Lee's new book proposes strategies for industrial development that are current, feasible, and well argued. He brings a welcome recognition of the scale of China's industrialization and its implications for the greening of development strategies.

– Professor John Mathews, Macquarie University, Sydney

In this book, one of the forefront thinkers today derives an attractive argument for the closing of the development gap between latecomer and leading countries. Framed along the catch-up paradox, the argument is based on the concept that one is not able to catch up if s/he just keeps catching up. In the author's words, eventual catch-up and overtaking require economies to pursue a path that differs from that taken by the forerunners. The important concepts here are building capabilities and leapfrogging by swiftly exploiting windows of opportunity. Keun Lee uses his virtuosity and deep understanding of the development process to put forward a very exciting book. A must-read for development economists in the field of technology upgrading and economic convergence.

– Nick Vonortas, Professor, the George Washington

University and Editor, *Science and Public Policy*

This lucidly written book is a seminal research work that recognizes narrow pathways with high risks and uncertainty, but shows alternative ways to move ahead on the sustainable path of economic development and transformation both in developed and developing countries. Keun Lee ignited hope for developing countries to catch up and shape economic thinking and public policy for a new and better world. This book is a must-read for public policy makers and scholars of development economics and innovation studies.

– Lakhwinder Singh, Professor of Economics, Punjabi
University, India

The Art of Economic Catch-Up

Barriers, Detours, and Leapfrogging In Innovation Systems

KEUN LEE

Seoul National University

CAMBRIDGE
UNIVERSITY PRESS

University Printing House, Cambridge CB2 8BS, United Kingdom

One Liberty Plaza, 20th Floor, New York, NY 10006, USA

477 Williamstown Road, Port Melbourne, VIC 3207, Australia

314–321, 3rd Floor, Plot 3, Splendor Forum, Jasola District Centre,
New Delhi – 110025, India

79 Anson Road, #06–04/06, Singapore 079906

Cambridge University Press is part of the University of Cambridge.

It furthers the University's mission by disseminating knowledge in the pursuit of
education, learning, and research at the highest international levels of excellence.

www.cambridge.org
Information on this title: www.cambridge.org/9781108472876
DOI: 10.1017/9781108588232

© Keun Lee 2019

First published 2019
3rd Printing 2020

Printed in the United Kingdom by TJ International Ltd. Padstow Cornwall

A catalogue record for this publication is available from the British Library.

Library of Congress Cataloging-in-Publication Data
Names: Lee, Keun, 1960– author.
Title: The art of economic catch-up : barriers, detours and leapfrogging / Keun
Lee, Seoul National University.
Description: Cambridge, United Kingdom ; New York, NY : Cambridge
University Press, 2018. | Includes bibliographical references and index.
Identifiers: LCCN 2018059086 | ISBN 9781108472876 (hardback : alk. paper)
Subjects: LCSH: Technological innovations – Developing countries. |
Economic development – Developing countries. | Endogenous growth
(Economics) – Developing countries.
Classification: LCC HC59.72.T4 L368 2013 | DDC 338.9009172/4–dc23
LC record available at https://lccn.loc.gov/2018059086

ISBN 978-1-108-47287-6 Hardback
ISBN 978-1-108-46070-5 Paperback

Contents

Tables

Figures

Preface

I published my book on economic catch-up five years ago. Although the book attracted recognition, won the Schumpeter Prize, and is getting a rapidly and increasing amount of citations, I have always felt that it is overly technical for a large audience. Furthermore, my personal research has continually progressed and has touched more aspects than those covered in the first book, urging me to write the current book.

Compared with the 2013 book, the current one is less technical than the first as it features no regression tables. The current book attempts to be more insightful than the previous by being framed along such terms as catch-up paradoxes and by employing several metaphors, such as kicking away the ladder, taking detours, and flying on a balloon. While catch up means closing the gap between latecomer and forerunner economies, the catch-up paradox posits that catching up cannot be attained if one merely continues to "catch up" or imitate the forerunners. The previous and current books discuss economic problems latecomer countries face as they attempt to go beyond the development trap. However, these books also differ in certain aspects. The first book focuses on sectoral specialization to go beyond the middle-income trap, whereas the second book discusses several other dimensions, namely, three detours and three paradoxes that are necessary to overcome the two failures and one barrier that latecomer economies face. In his bestselling book, *Kicking Away the Ladder*, Ha-Joon Chang observed that the passage (ladder) from poor to rich nations is either blocked or kicked away. In contrast, this book argues that transitioning from being a latecomer to a rich economy remains possible if economies were to take detours and then fly on a balloon, namely, leapfrog into new technologies.

Enhancing the welfare of humankind is vital. Yet achieving sustained economic growth, especially in developing countries, remains unknown and has been a longstanding topic in economic research. The economic literature endeavors to find a universal factor for economic growth that will bind all countries, regardless of income level and structural differences. As a point of departure, this book contends that the growth mechanisms of rich and poor nations differ and that a very narrow passage exists between those nations. Therefore, an economy must be very careful when crossing this passage, otherwise it may fall into a middle-income trap or face decelerated growth at the middle-income stage. I have entitled this book not as the science but as the art of catching up, because a successful catch-up rarely occurs and because navigating the narrow passage requires sophisticated mobilization of resources and strategic thinking. The book also delves into smart strategies and economic policy implementation more than it does scientific discovery. However, the prescribed arts are derived from various quantitative evidence cited in the book.

Recognizing the concept of growth mechanisms at various stages drives the exploration of key "transition" variables that facilitate the passage of countries from middle- to high-income stage growths. This book illustrates that such a transition is possible by taking detours and leapfrogging. Accordingly, this book first discusses why latecomers should take detours and leapfrog and then how latecomers can take three detours in building innovation capabilities and one detour in generating big businesses in the form of business groups. Finally, this book discusses leapfrogging into newly emerging sectors.

Latecomer economies must take detours because of the presence of two failures and one barrier: firm capability and size failures and intellectual property rights (IPR) protection from the incumbent North, respectively. Firm capability failure refers to the intrinsic difficulty of building innovation capabilities in developing countries. This type of failure radically differs from conventional market failure, which states that R&D subsidies help achieve optimal (or increased) R&D. This view is valid only under the hidden assumption that firms are already capable of conducting R&D. Otherwise, nothing will happen even with increased incentives or subsidies. A similar criticism applies to the notion that strong IPR protection leads to further innovation, which is true only under the assumption that the firm is already equipped with innovation capabilities. Size failure refers to the lack of world-class businesses in developing countries that are currently filled with small- to medium-sized enterprises, which are considered insufficient in leading a country toward a high-income status.

The existence of these "two failures and one barrier" has necessitated latecomer economies to explore a new path in building their innovation capabilities instead of replicating practices employed by advanced economies. Although consolidating technological capabilities has long been suggested by many as a vital component of economic catch-up, guiding details for this process are lacking. This book explains the three detours in building capabilities.

The first detour promotes imitative innovation under a loose IPR regime in the form of petit patents and trademarks instead of promoting and strengthening regular patent rights. The second detour focuses on global value chains (GVCs), specifically, a nonlinear sequence of the first increasing, then reducing, and increasing again the GVC participation. In contrast to Baldwin (2016), who states that increased GVC participation is preferable, the current book warns against such a linear view. Instead, the book suggests a GVC-related detour, in which an economy should initially learn by participating at the GVC but should later reduce its reliance on these chains at a certain point by building increased domestic value chains in sequential entries into high-end segments. Otherwise, the latecomers would remain at low value-added segments, which is a middle income trap (MIT) symptom. For instance, Mexico's per capita income has declined from 45% to 33% of the US level over the last decades, despite NAFTA (North America Free Trade Agreement).

The third detour means specializing first in short-cycle technology-based sectors and products (i.e., ITs) and, only at a later stage, in long-cycle sectors and segments (i.e., pharmaceuticals). Long-cycle technologies mean that previous knowledge remains useful and important for a long period of time. Such technologies act as entry barriers against latecomers, although they denote high profitability and thus desirable attributes. Therefore, latecomers are advised to target short-cycle technologies, where entry barriers are low but growth prospect is good because of high innovation frequency that often disrupts the dominance of the incumbent.

Aside from these detours, this book elucidates leapfrogging as the final stage of catching up or overtaking. Leapfrogging involves latecomers accomplishing something ahead of the forerunners, thereby leaping over them. This technique becomes necessary as a means of bypassing the IPR that forerunners hold by jumping ahead into new generations of technologies. Thus, leapfrogging is highly likely to succeed when executed during a shift in paradigm or generation or during exogenous moments of disruption, which early Schumpeterians such as Perez and Soete (1988) coined "windows of opportunity." Finding ways to overcome entry barriers is one of the key motivations for utilizing leapfrogging, as the subtitle of their article suggests. A window of opportunity is a moment in time in which the entry barriers for latecomers recede. Meanwhile, Hidalgo et al.'s (2007) concept of product spaces and economic complexity does not consider entry barriers and related competition with the incumbent.

Latecomers tend to experience difficulties because of entry barriers existing in many product areas, and because they have to compete with the incumbents to be able to enter and occupy spaces. Thus, in our dynamics of economic catch-up, the role of leapfrogging is similar to "flying on a balloon when the conventional ladder used to catch up is kicked away." As we can only fly balloons under favorable weather conditions, economic leapfrogging becomes successful only when exogenous windows of opportunity are available. Certain preconditions for flying also exist, such as having built-up capabilities, meaning driving skills. Otherwise, we may fall to the ground instead of flying into the sky.

Leapfrogging involves both intersectoral and intrasectoral dimensions. Inter-sectoral leapfrogging is, to a certain extent, similar to the "long jump" in Hidalgo et al. (2007), which argues that latecomer economies must shift to core product spaces that are located far away from their current or periphery position. By contrast, intrasectoral leapfrogging, which is our main concern, involves jumping across generations of technologies within the same sector. Intrasectoral leapfrogging is easier than the intersectoral long jump, as long as latecomers have already built certain absorptive capabilities such as manufacturing experiences in the given sectors. Although Hidalgo and his colleagues (2007) do not provide suggestions on how to achieve such long jumps, Chapter 5 in this book discusses several cases of leapfrogging and elaborates a number of strategies and conditions for that purpose.

Detour and leapfrogging are the two core theoretical concepts in economic catch-up. The third core concept, which is important, especially at early stages of development, is points of entry to the established international division of labor. Given their late entry, these economies generally enter through low-end segments or sectors freed from firms in advanced economies in the form of the own-equipment manufacturing processing type or the FDI. By combining the three core concepts, we devise a comprehensive theory of economic catch-up comprising entry → detours → leapfrogging. Such sequential dynamics are essential to overcoming the previously mentioned two failures and one barrier. Despite its inherent risks, leapfrogging is also necessary because it remains the sole means for economies to forge ahead and to overtake forerunners. Thus, leapfrogging is an insufficient yet necessary condition allowing the transition of latecomers to advanced economies.

Although this book shares Abramovitz's (1986) vision in his article, "Catching-Up, Forging Ahead, And Falling Behind," the key message of this book is rather paradoxical because a latecomer can never catch up unless they create a new path that is different from that of a forerunner. Such a paradoxical aspect of economic catch-up can be attributed to its nature as chasing not a fixed but moving target. Given that the target (i.e., the forerunner) is constantly moving, a latecomer cannot overtake if they merely follow footsteps. As an alternative, the latecomer should eventually create a new path, shortcut, or detour upon reaching a certain point on the road although it may start by imitating, following, and learning from the forerunner. This issue, which was introduced in the previous book, is comprehensively analyzed in the current book.

The catch-up theory presented in the current book is framed along three paradoxes. The first paradox is "to be similar, be different," which means that to reach and achieve similar income levels as their forerunners, a latecomer must take a path that is different from that of the forerunner. The second paradox is "taking a detour can be faster than taking a direct road," which means that given the traffic in the direct road, a latecomer may take a detour and reach their destination faster than others. The final paradox is "you may either fly or fall through a window," which means that only those who are ready to fly with strong wings can attempt leapfrogging; others will be faced with many risks. This book also discusses the role of firm organization, such as big businesses in the form of business groups, another aspect of the detour strategy that is necessary to overcome size failure or the lack of such businesses in latecomer economies. This book therefore establishes both technological and organizational innovation as the two black boxes in the Schumpeterian economic catch-up.

This manuscript has benefited from diverse sources of intellectual ideas, insights, and mutual interactions. First, the detailed stories of leapfrogging in Chapter 5 originated from collected works in a special issue on "Catch-up Cycles in Research Policy" (2017), to which Franco Malerba and I contributed as guest editor and coordinator. The project was jointly funded by Bocconi University in

Milan and the National Research Foundation of Korea, and the issue covered six sectors: memory chips (Jang-Sup Shin), mobile phones (Claudio Giachetti), steel (Jeehoon Ki and me), mid-sized jets (Daniel Vértesy), wines (Andrea Morrison and Roberta Rabellotti), and cameras (Hyo Kang and Jaeyong Song). The overall framework of catch-up cycles and the role of leapfrogging have also benefited from several rounds of feedback from Martin Bell, the lead editor of the special issue.

Successful catch-up requires not only capability-building but also smart specialization across sectors and technologies. This argument first emerged from my interaction with and feedback from Richard Nelson during the process of my writing a chapter on "Economic Catch-up as Evolutionary Process," which he edited for the volume entitled *Modern Evolutionary Economics* (2018). This chapter also discussed the two black boxes in economic catch-up, namely, technological and organizational innovation. I also acknowledge Bengt-Åke Lundvall for his recent initiative to integrate the two branches of literature, namely, innovation systems and GVCs, from which certain parts of this book also benefited. I thank several colleagues and former students of mine as certain parts of the book relied heavily on our joint work. These people include Wonkyu Shin on policy space under the WTO regime, as well as Raeyoon Kang on the role of trademarks and Zhuqing Mao on the role of GVC.

The actual writing and rewriting of the manuscript underwent several rounds of feedback from John Mathews, who also played such a role in the publication of my previous book. His input helped me refine various parts of the book, especially the concept of green development in Chapter 7 and restructure the last two chapters. Nicholas Vonortas, Lakhwinder Singh, and Eduardo Albuquerque also provided detailed feedback for the manuscript. The early draft of this book was presented in various places and thus benefited from feedback. The seminar held at the World Bank in February 2018 was a valuable opportunity to present the book. I thank William Maloney who arranged the seminar, as well as Xavier Cirera and Gonzalo Rivas Gomez. I also received feedback from Annalisa Primi, Benjamin

Coriat, and Ambassador Jong-Won Yoon in a seminar held at the OECD during the same month.

I would like to acknowledge the various seminars and conferences in which parts of this book were presented in their early versions. Such occasions include the Globelics Conference held in Athens in October 2017, and the innovation seminars held in several universities in Brazil, such as those in Campinas (organized by Nick Vonortas), Rio (Jose Cassiolato and Marina Szapiro), and Bello Horizonte (Eduardo Albuquerque) in August 2017. The contents on Africa in Chapter 7 has benefited from several seminars held on that continent, such as the Africa Development Bank in Abidjan and the Africa Economics Conference in Addis. I also thank the chief economist of the Africa Development Bank, Célestin Monga, and his colleague, Abebe Shimeles. Input was also received during the same conference from the Africa Ex-Im Bank in Kigali, Rwanda and at the World Bank Conference in Uganda. Justin Lin provided me with various input and opportunities to discuss my ideas in several meetings organized by the Center for New Structural Economics held in Beijing in 2016 and 2017, and a recent one in Addis Ababa in December 2017. Furthermore, I thank Slavo Radosevic for providing me with feedback and inviting me to various seminars in Europe, such as those held in Belarus, Brussels, London, and St. Petersburg. I also owe similar thanks to Sebastien Lechevalier, Clemente Duran, and Alenka Guzman, for the interactive seminars held in Paris and Mexico City. I learned tremendously by participating in the Babbage Symposium held at Cambridge University and by interacting with Lord David Sainsbury, Mike Gregory, Antonio Andreoni, and Ha-Joon Chang. The workshops held in the UNU-MERIT paved the way for interesting interactions with Bart Verspagen, Eddi Szirmai, Jan Fagerberg, Clovis Freire, Ludo Alcorta, and Nobuya Haraguchi.

For numerous other occasions and feedback, which I cannot specify here, I would like to thank Mario Pianta, Reiko Aoki, Hyeogug Kwon, David Kaplan, Jose Ocampo, Namsuk Kim, Georg Licht,

Philipp Boeing, Fink Carsten, Eva Paus, Sadao Nagaoka, Chen Jin, Xiaobu Wu, Xudong Gao, Xiaobo Li, Chong-En Bai, Javier Diez, Kamhon Kan, Wan-wen Chu, Mario Cimoli, Tilman Altenberg, Henry Yeung, Thomas Clark, Jose Alonso, Khuong Vu, Bronwen Dalton, and Yong Wang. My recent involvement as a member of the World Economic Forum also helped me update my ideas on recent trends in innovation, or the fourth Industrial Revolution, and their impacts on emerging economies. I thank Francisco Betti and Helena Leurent of the forum for the opportunity.

I would also like to acknowledge several academic associations I have been involved with, such as the Global Network for the Economics of Learning, Innovation, and Competence Building Systems (www.globelics.org) led by Lundvall and their regional networks in Africa, Asia, and Latin America; the International Schumpeter Society; the Asia-Pacific Innovation Network; and the European Association of Evolutionary Political Economy (EAEPE). My interactions with all these people have tremendously helped me.

I would like to thank the Hanssem DBEW Research Foundation, particularly Chairman Chang Gul Cho, for financially supporting this project. The team at Cambridge University Press, namely, Phil Good and Toby Ginsberg, provided effective support for this project. Lastly, my heartfelt thanks to my family, namely, Soyeon, Hyung-sok, and Jiwon, for their support and love, which keeps me going in this endless pursuit to uncover secrets of economic catch-up and the rise and fall of nations and firms.

Keun Lee

I   Introduction

While enhancing the welfare of humankind is a vital issue, how to achieve sustained economic growth remains unknown and has been a longstanding topic in economic research (North, 2005). Studies on economic growth all attempt to find one universal factor for economic growth that binds for all countries at all stages regardless of their income levels and structural differences. This observation is not surprising given that economics always attempts to find a "general" rather than a "specific" factor for economic growth. The field assumes a simple production function, with labor and capital as the primary factors of production and with their elasticities, and the associated technologies are also assumed to be the same across all countries. In this old growth model, which allows a gap in capital accumulation, the catch-up by the latecomer is treated as an issue of rapid capital accumulation without the consideration of different technologies. In line with this, developing countries strive for economic growth by copying the practices and institutions of advanced economies. An example is the so-called Washington Consensus, which promotes policy packages with minimal government intervention and privatization, trade and financial liberalization, foreign direct investments (FDIs) by multinational corporations (MNCs) over indigenous companies, and strong property rights.[1] However, given its poor performance, the Washington Consensus was declared dead by Rodrik, who called for a search for an alternative.[2] Against this background,

---

[1]   This consensus was first proposed by Williamson (1990).   [2]   See Rodrik (2006).

the research interest in industrial policy was reignited by Nobel Laureate Joseph Stiglitz and other alternatives, such as the new structural economics concept proposed by former World Bank Vice President Justin Lin, have appeared.[3]

As a point of departure, this book suggests that advanced economies and latecomer economies at the middle- or lower-income stages have different growth mechanisms, and that a very "narrow passage" exists among these countries. Thus, one must be very careful when crossing such passage in order to avoid falling into MIT,[4] or a situation where middle-income economies tend to face a decelerated growth and consequently fail to join the ranks of high-income economies. Several studies have verified the idea that different countries adopt varying growth mechanisms, such that the economic growth at the lower-income stages is correlated with basic political institutions and basic human capital, while the economic growth at the higher-income stages (upper-middle and high-income) is correlated with innovation capabilities and tertiary education.[5] Such an observation is consistent with that of other researchers who have found that various countries take different convergent paths, with the first path converging to a low-income steady state, the second path converging to a middle-income steady state, and the third path converging to a high-income steady state.[6]

The division of the world into two or three groups at different stages is consistent with the idea of MIT. However, some economists have doubted the existence of such a trap, saying that no theory explains why and how middle-income economies adopt different

[3]   On the revival of industrial policy, see Stiglitz, Lin, and Monga (2013); on the new structural economics, see Lin (2013).

[4]   The MIT phenomenon was first mentioned in Gill et al. (2007) and has become a subject of research for Eichengreen, Park, and Shin (2012, 2013), Lee (2013a), and the World Bank (2010).

[5]   Lee and Kim (2009) and Bulman, Eden, and Nguyen (2014) provide some examples.

[6]   These three paths were confirmed by Ito (2017), who found that the growth of Asian economies has decelerated over time and may fall to advanced economy levels before their income fully catches up with that of the advanced economies. He also uses the same example to define MIT.

growth mechanisms.[7] Thus, the existence of MIT itself has been debated in the field of economics over the last decade or so since its introduction in 2007. Diverse or conflicting answers regarding this issue have been generated because the related studies have adopted different definitions of the trap and different methodologies to test its existence.

This book does not attempt to try another answer to this issue of the existence or nonexistence of MIT, but instead just notes some broad consensus to which this book subscribes. First, regardless of whether MIT exists or not, many countries are struggling at the middle-income stage or are experiencing a very slow transition from middle- to high-income status.[8] A study by the World Bank found that only twelve out of 101 middle-income economies have joined the club of high-income economies since 1960.[9] Among these countries, nine were reported to be upper-middle-income economies (20% to 40% of the US per capita income, including Greece, Portugal, Spain, Ireland, Hong Kong, Israel, Japan, Mauritius, Puerto Rico, and Singapore). Only two were reported to be low- or lower-middle-income countries (Korea and Taiwan, respectively), and one was an oil-exporting country (Equatorial Guinea).

Actually, Figure 1–1 shows clearly that typical emerging economies have not closed the gap with the US, remaining below the 40% of the US per capita, except Malaysia. For instance, Mexico declined from the higher than 40% level in the mid-1980s to 32.8% in 2015. Brazil also dropped from the above 30% level in the 1980s to lower than the 30% level in 2015. South Africa was worse, at the 23% level in 2015.

---

[7]   Aiyar et al. (2013) expressed a similar view. Im and Rosenblatt (2013) and Han and Wei (2015) conducted a transition matrix analysis and rejected the existence of MIT.

[8]   By performing probit regressions, Aiyar et al. (2013) found that middle-income economies are disproportionately likely to experience growth slowdowns, and this result is robust for a wide range of income thresholds for defining "middle income." Felipe, Kumar, and Galope (2014) examined the transition of economies across income groups and found some evidence to support the slow transition of economies from middle- to high-income status.

[9]   See World Bank (2012).

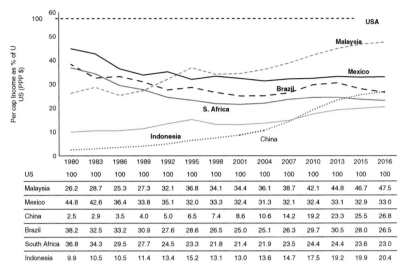

	1980	1983	1986	1989	1992	1995	1998	2001	2004	2007	2010	2013	2015	2016
US	100	100	100	100	100	100	100	100	100	100	100	100	100	100
Malaysia	26.2	28.7	25.3	27.3	32.1	36.8	34.1	34.4	36.1	38.7	42.1	44.8	46.7	47.5
Mexico	44.8	42.6	36.4	33.8	35.1	32.0	33.3	32.4	31.3	32.1	32.4	33.1	32.9	33.0
China	2.5	2.9	3.5	4.0	5.0	6.5	7.4	8.6	10.6	14.2	19.2	23.3	25.5	26.8
Brazil	38.2	32.5	33.2	30.9	27.6	28.6	26.5	25.0	25.1	26.3	29.7	30.5	28.0	26.5
South Africa	36.8	34.3	29.5	27.7	24.5	23.3	21.8	21.4	21.9	23.5	24.4	24.4	23.6	23.0
Indonesia	9.9	10.5	10.5	11.4	13.4	15.2	13.1	13.0	13.6	14.7	17.5	19.2	19.9	20.4

FIGURE 1–1. Per Capita Income Levels of Countries as % of the United States
(Source: author's work using IMF data)

Second, most studies highlight the need for these countries to reform or take exogenous actions to free themselves from MIT, inefficient equilibrium, or economic growth slowdown. For instance, some researchers view MIT not as a trap but rather as a failure to adapt to innovation or other required reform.

These two consensuses may lead to an understanding of MIT as a symptom of failing to jump from low- or middle-income economies to high-income economies, probably due to the lack of necessary reform. Then, the belief in the idea of having different growth mechanisms at different stages and the MIT motivate us to identify the key "transition" variables that are necessary to realize a transition from the middle-income stage growth to the higher-income stage growth. In line with this, innovation capability has been increasingly recognized as the key solution for an economy to free itself from MIT, which will be discussed in detail in the following chapter. The critical importance of innovation capability is consistent with the earlier observation of the World Bank, which suggests that middle-income economies tend

to fall into MIT because they get caught between low-wage manufacturers and high-wage innovators. Their wage rates are too high to
compete with low-wage exporters and the level of their technological
capability is too low to enable them to compete with advanced
countries.[10]

THE TWO FAILURES AND ONE BARRIER

Although the importance of innovation has been widely recognized,
enhancing innovation capabilities and overcoming MIT are not easy.
Chapter 2 argues that achieving such upward transition is rare and
difficult due to "two failures and one barrier," which make the transition path very narrow. In fact, only a very small number of East Asian
economies, such as Korea and Taiwan, have successfully traversed
this path.

The first failure, namely, capabilities failure, refers to the intrinsic difficulty of building innovation capabilities in developing countries. This type of failure radically differs from the conventional
market failure. The market failure in innovation stems from the
externality of knowledge as a public good. Thus, subsidies for R&D
are prescribed to induce an optimal amount of R&D. In the market
failure approach, the common and hidden presumption is that firms
and other economic actors are already capable of innovation, and that
monetary incentives act as both a problem and a solution. However,
the stark reality in developing countries is that economic actors,
especially firms, have extremely weak levels of capability and are
unable to pursue and conduct in-house R&D, which they consider
an uncertain endeavor with uncertain returns. Thus, the problem is
not one of less or more R&D but of "zero" R&D. In developing
countries where firms have a low R&D or technological capability, a
safe way of doing business has thus been to buy or borrow external
technologies or production facilities as well as to specialize in less-
technical methods or assembly manufacturing. Thus, our answer to

---

[10]   This view is expressed in World Bank (2010) and is shared by many, including Lee
(2013a).

the so-called "innovation paradox," such that developing countries do not do enough R&D despite its high return, is simply that they do not know how or lack such capabilities of doing innovation.[11]

To move beyond such states (which lead to MIT), effective forms of intervention must include not the simple provision of R&D funds but various ways for cultivating R&D capability. Thus, instead of the concept of market failure, this book focuses on the issue of "capability failure" and the need to enhance the capabilities of firms, sectors, and nations. According to this view, learning failure occurs because of the lack of opportunity for effective learning and capability-building. Thus, more effective and alternative forms of intervention may include the transfer of R&D outcomes performed by public research institutes, as well as public–private R&D consortiums that have gained success in Korea and Taiwan, and other modes of learning, which are discussed in Chapter 2.[12]

The second type of failure, namely, size failure, refers to the difficulty of generating big business (BBs), which is often required when jumping from middle- to high-income economies. While small and medium-sized enterprises (SMEs) are typically prevalent forms of businesses in developing countries, they cannot be relied upon to lead economies to reach the high-income status. Although the World Bank has provided a huge amount of monetary assistance to SMEs in developing countries,[13] a World Bank study tried but failed to establish a causal and robust relationship between SMEs and per capita income growth or poverty alleviation.[14] Rather, having too many microbusinesses in services is considered a bad symptom that leads to premature

---

[11] The term "innovation paradox" is discussed in Cirera and Maloney (2017). In a sense, the problems are intertwined. Given their low R&D capabilities, a return to doing R&D for themselves must be low rather than high; it would be high only when it is assumed that R&D is simply a matter of adoption of available technologies.

[12] For more details, see Mathews (2002b); Lee and Lim (2001); Lee, Lim, and Song (2005); and OECD (1996).

[13] The World Bank has provided more than 10 billion and 1.3 billion USD of targeted assistance to SMEs in developing countries from 1998 to 2001 and in 2003, respectively (World Bank 2002, 2004).

[14] Beck et al. (2005) find some positive yet weak correlations when controlling for endogeneity.

servicization (or deindustrialization). Instead, BBs are badly needed when making a transition from low- to high-income economies because these businesses tend to enjoy scale externalities and are better positioned to be in charge of higher-value-added activities of R&D and marketing. An econometric study has shown that having a certain number of BBs, specifically more than that predicted by economy size, may indicate whether or not an economy is stuck in MIT.[15] Moreover, many emerging economies, except for the more successful cases of Korea, Taiwan, and China, are shown to have a smaller number of BBs than that predicted by their sizes. For instance, Thailand and Turkey only had one or zero Global Fortune 500 companies over the last two decades, whereas the number of these companies in Korea and Taiwan increased from three and one in the early 1990s to fourteen and eight in the early 2010s, respectively.

The "one barrier" is associated with the negative impacts of strong intellectual property rights (IPR) protection in advanced economies on the exports from emerging economies, which often show up in IPR disputes between late entrants and incumbent firms. While IPR is increasingly recognized, owing to the activities of patent trolls, as the barrier to innovation even in advanced economies, such a harmful impact is more serious in latecomer economies.[16] A recent empirical study of mine verifies that the strong IPR protection in forerunning economies such as the US often acts as a barrier to exports for catching-up countries, such as the past Korea or present-day China.[17] As will be discussed in the next chapter, many latecomer firms, including a Korean firm, Samsung, in the 1980s and a Chinese firm, Huawei, in the 2010s, have been involved in IPR litigation brought by incumbent firms.

If we take a broader perspective, the barriers should also include the World Trade Organization (WTO) regime, which reduced the

---

[15]   See Lee et al. (2013) in the *Journal of Comparative Economics*.

[16]   Discussion of such harmful impacts of IPRs and how to remedy such situations is well reviewed in Coriat (2016).

[17]   Shin et al. (2016).

policy space by latecomer countries. This is often called the act of "kicking away the ladder" by Ha-Joon Chang (2002). This book discusses this issue in the concluding chapter on policy issues.

THE DETOURS TO OVERCOME THE CAPABILITY FAILURE

The existence of "two failures and one barrier," which has made economic transitions rare and difficult to achieve, necessitates catching-up economies to find a detour to build their innovation capabilities as well as to avoid replicating or emulating the practices of advanced economies. In other words, while the consolidation of technological capabilities at the firm level has long been suggested as a vital requirement for economic catch-up, this book posits that capability-building must be carefully designed and implemented within the broad framework of national innovation systems (NIS) proposed by Schumpeterian scholars, such as Nelson and Lundvall. The NIS is defined as the various elements and relationships that interact in the production, diffusion, and use of new and economically useful knowledge.[18] Otherwise, the process of capability-building becomes derailed and delayed. For instance, capability-building becomes less effective if a latecomer economy simply imitates the advanced economies and thus provides a very high level of IPR protection even at its early stage of development.

Moreover, the idea of sectoral innovation systems suggests that not all sectors are the same in terms of learning and catch-up possibilities, which raises the key issue of choices over technologies. In this case, the process of capability-building becomes derailed if a latecomer tries to enter sectors/segments with slow or difficult learning possibilities that are associated with long-cycle times or high entry barriers. In this sense, one of the distinctive orientations of this book, for instance, compared to the innovation paradox view, is that it

---

[18]   One of the early discussions about NIS can be found in Lundvall (2012) and Malerba and Nelson (2012). The discussions on national innovation systems have been extended to the sectoral innovation system in Malerba (2005) and to firm-level innovation systems in Lee (2013a) and others.

considers economic catch-up as not only a matter of building capabilities but also a matter of choice or specialization in certain technologies, sectors, or activities to find niches for entry and survival.[19] This issue of choice and specialization is less important and critical at the low- or lower-middle-income stage where latecomers are just to inherit the leftover sectors and businesses but becomes a critical issue at the upper-middle-income stages, where the latecomers are getting close to the frontier and increasingly competing with incumbent firms and countries in world markets. In sum, the differences in innovation systems at the firm, sector, and national levels lead to differences in learning and innovation performance and, consequently, to differences in economic performance, specifically at the middle-income stage, which is the primary concern of this work.

While following the Schumpeterian tradition, this book also shares Abramovitz's (1986) vision of economic "catching up, forging ahead, and falling behind" and defines catch up as "reducing the gap between the forerunning and latecomer economies." However, our key message is rather paradoxical because we propose that one can never catch up if they keep catching up, where the former "catch up" means closing the gap or overtaking and the latter "catching up" means imitation. Another way of illustrating this catch-up paradox is that "to be similar, you've got to be different," which means that while catch-up means trying to be similar, long-term success requires taking a path that differs from that taken by advanced countries.

The decision for a latecomer to create a new path that differs from that taken by the forerunner can be attributed to the nature of economic catch-up as a game of chasing a moving rather than a fixed target. Given that the target is constantly moving ahead, one can never overtake this target if they keep following in the footsteps of their forerunners. Therefore, one may start by imitating, following,

---

[19] This double focus is emphasized in Lee and Malerba (2018). In comparison, Xavier and Maloney (2017) focus on capability-building, setting aside the issue of specialization and choices over sectors, activities, or technologies. This difference comes partly from their book, which is more concerned with lower- or lower-middle-income economies.

and learning from their forerunners, but at some point on the road they must create a new path, shortcut, or detour to avoid colliding with the forerunners.

Whether a latecomer must "follow the similar path" of their forerunners or "create or take a different or new path" is among the most fundamental issues in the economics of catch-up introduced in my earlier book. Traditional and early studies have observed that latecomers try to catch up with advanced countries by assimilating and adapting the more-or-less obsolete technology of the incumbents. In one of the early articles, I argue that latecomers do not simply follow the advanced countries' path of technological development; they sometimes skip certain stages or even create their own path, which differs from that taken by the forerunners.[20] For instance, one of the reasons why Korean consumer electronics, led by Samsung, were able to take over the Japanese incumbent Sony was that the former leapfrogged into digital technologies ahead of the latter, which used to be the lead in the manufacturing of analogue products. From a Schumpeterian perspective, I argue in my previous book that the successful catching-up economies of Korea and Taiwan went through a different path by specializing in sectors with "short-cycle" technologies in contrast to advanced economies that specialize in "long-cycle" technology-based sectors.

Korea and Taiwan reached the middle-income stage by the mid-1980s, and then decided to upgrade their industrial structure to match that of emerging or close-to-frontier sectors, or the so-called high-tech sectors. However, when moving into these sectors, their latecomer firms engaged in a direct competition with companies that are at the technological frontier of other countries and that have a much greater amount of experience in a specific field. To overcome this situation, or MIT, these indigenous firms chose those sectors/products that are based on short-cycle technologies, such as the information technology sector where specific knowledge and technologies tend to be outdated

---

[20] This idea, introduced in Lee and Lim (2001), stands in contrast to the traditional view proposed by Lall (2000), Kim (1980), and Hobday (1995).

quickly and frequently. Thus, in such sectors, the extensive experience of firms in the frontier countries is no longer considered a great advantage because frontier technologies tend to be disrupted and to change radically and frequently. Therefore, such sectors tend to have lower entry barriers from the perspective of latecomers. By contrast, since the 2000s Korean firms such as Samsung have started to enter long-cycle sectors, such as pharmaceuticals (bio-similar) and medical equipment, in order to avoid being caught up in short-cycle sectors by the Chinese firms. In other words, although catching up with forerunners is less difficult with certain level of absorptive capacity in the short-cycle sectors, a country may also be caught up by the next emerging latecomers. In this case, Korea has taken a detour to reach high-entry barrier sectors with long cycles by first going through the transitionary stage of the short-cycle sectors with low entry barriers. This "short cycle first and long cycle later" detour is one of the three detours that will be elaborated in Chapter 3.

Another detour involves IPR protection and the switch from imitation to innovation. This book proposes that increasing the level of IPR protection at an early stage may not help to build innovation capabilities, given the trade-off between its impacts on diffusion and innovation; that is, despite stimulating innovation, strong IPR protection may hurt the diffusion of knowledge and imitative learning by the latecomers. In the Korean experience, weaker forms of IPRs, such as petit patents (also called utility models), had been more widely used than regular invention patents until the early 1990s, while strong and wider protection of IPRs was delayed until the late 1980s.[21] The idea of increasing the IPR protection level, which is often suggested as a solution to MIT, is based on the hidden assumption that the firms and economies in the developing world are already equipped with innovation capabilities. However, if that is not the case, then just providing stronger incentives associated with IPR would result in no change in innovations. We thus propose a detour with a lower level of

---

[21]   The econometric verification was performed in Kim et al. (2012).

IPR protection during the transition stages because higher IPR protection cannot stimulate innovation under the condition of capability failure. In other words, learn and build capabilities first, and then collect incentives later to correct market failures.

The third detour can be conceived in terms of participating in global value chains (GVC) and learning from such participation. Although participation in GVCs has been increasingly prescribed for developing countries to achieve economic growth (Baldwin, 2016), many of these countries remain stuck in low value-added activities or segments, thereby casting doubt on the effectiveness of GVCs as vehicles to upgrading and becoming rich economies. In other words, the fact that high-income economies all have a high degree of international integration and participation in GVCs does not necessarily mean that opening up the economy further will help a country traverse the narrow passage between latecomer and forerunning economies. Thus, our detour view on GVCs is dynamic or nonlinear.

We propose this "more-less-more-again" hypothesis, which posits that while at the initial stage of growth countries must actively participate in GVCs to learn from the outside. Upgrading to higher value-added requires a country to exert additional effort or to increase its domestic value-added, thereby prompting some countries to reduce their GVC participation or to seek separation and independence from foreign-dominated GVCs. Then, only at the later stage or after building their own domestic value chains, the latecomer firms and economies may have to reintegrate themselves back into GVCs.[22] This dynamic sequence of "first in, then out, and then in again" generates a nonlinear curve reflecting a country's degree of participation in GVCs, as measured by foreign value-added (FVA), that is, share of FVA in the gross exports of an economy. Therefore, as shown in the actual data for Asian economies, we hypothesize that FVA will initially increase at the low-income and lower-middle income stages. It should then decrease at the upper-middle and middle-income stages,

[22] This in-out-in-again hypothesis was verified by the data and regressions in Lee, Szapiro, and Mao (2017).

when countries attempt to create more domestic value-added (by relying less on GVC). FVA should increase again at the high-income stage when these countries reintegrate themselves back into GVCs with their enhanced innovation capabilities.[23] Thus, in terms of GVC participation, the passage between latecomer and forerunning countries is so narrow that only a few economies, such as Korea, Taiwan, and China, have experienced a period of increasing domestic value-added. The others have simply participated in GVCs yet failed to increase their share of domestic value-added in their gross exports.

In sum, Chapter 3 discusses the three detours in building technological capabilities. The first detour aims to promote imitative innovations under a loose IPR regime in the form of petit patents and trademarks instead of trying to build a higher level of innovation capabilities by promoting and strengthening regular patent rights from the early stage. The second detour aims to specialize in short-cycle technology-based sectors/products rather than in long-cycle technology-based sectors/segments that are considered the hallmarks of advanced economies. The third detour aims to promote domestic value-added and reduce a country's reliance on GVCs.

THE DETOUR TO OVERCOME SIZE FAILURE

Chapter 4 addresses the issue of "size failure" and discusses how to overcome this failure by growing BBs aside from SMEs. While BBs are considered important elements in realizing a transition to high-income economies, how to promote or grow BBs warrants further discussion. This question can be answered by looking at past catch-up episodes around the world where BBs in emerging economies tend to take the form of business groups (BGs). A BG is a collection of firms bound together in some formal and/or informal way and is characterized by an intermediate level of binding (i.e., neither bound merely by short-term

---

[23]   For instance, the Korean experience indicates that before becoming an open economy such as a typical advanced economy, a country may need to go through a period of being strategically closed to enhance the capabilities of its domestic firms (Shin & Lee, 2012).

strategic alliances nor legally consolidated into a single entity).[24] Apart from an early example of a BG in Japan called *keiretsu*, these groups have a heavy presence in several successful latecomer economies such as Korea, Taiwan, China, and India.[25] In Korea, BGs, or *chaebols*, such as Samsung have been regarded as symbols of economic growth although they were once criticized as one of the causes of the 1997 Asian financial crisis. In today's postcrisis world of radical globalization and market liberalization, we are still seeing the continuing importance of BGs. Although some of these groups went bankrupt during the crisis, the surviving and prevailing ones are equipped with high technological capabilities.

Since being analyzed by Williamson from the perspective of transaction cost economics, conglomerates or BGs have been naturally considered to be one of the forms that firms take to save on transaction costs when operating in an environment with a high degree of market failure or "institutional voids." Thus, BGs are unsurprisingly more prevalent in developing countries where transaction costs are high because of their less-developed market institutions.[26] However, if we see BGs simply as an evolutionary response to the institutional environment of an economy, then no interesting policies or strategic issues are involved.

Instead, we see BGs as organizational devices for economic catch-up and suggest that these groups not only emerge in response to market failure but also may serve as vehicles for economic catch-up. In this light, we have noted how BGs help affiliate firms to enter new markets by providing cross-subsidies during their initial phase of business, often under losses. Also noted was how BG firms enjoy the advantages of resource sharing and knowledge spillover among

---

[24]   This definition is from Granovetter (1995).

[25]   *Keiretsus* is similar to BGs in Korea, Taiwan, China, and India. They, are discussed in collected volumes, such as Chang (2003) and Colpan, Hikino, and Lincoln (2010), as well as in articles, such as Choo et al. (2009), Lee and Jin (2009), and Khanna and Palepu (2000).

[26]   Starting from Williamson (1975), we refer to the market failure view of BGs in Leff (1978) and Goto (1982). BGs also exist to fill "institutional voids" in emerging economies (Khana & Palepu, 2000a, 2000b; Khana, 2000a).

themselves, both of which can aid in their innovation. For example, Samsung suffered seven years of losses from its memory chip ventures after its entry in the 1980s, and these losses were offset by their profits from their other affiliates. Such ventures can be financed by capital markets in advanced economies, such as in the case of Tesla in the US. However, developing economies are full of such market failure. Thus, firms often resort to visible hands of the government or financing from the internal capital market of BGs. The promotion or prevalence of business firms that take the form of family-owned BGs during their transition stage can be considered another detour. This is because the firms in many advanced economies, such as those in the US, typically have a dispersed type of ownership and are operated by professional managers rather than by families. By contrast, family-owned BGs can be effective during the catching-up stages given their long time horizon, prompt decision making, and aggressive investments.

FLYING ON A BALLOON OF LEAPFROGGING

Apart from detours, other key concepts proposed in this book are the Schumpeterian ideas of leapfrogging and windows of opportunity.[27] The leapfrogging thesis posits that the rise of new generations of technologies or new techno-economic paradigms, specifically, the competence-destroying innovations, allow latecomer countries to have a head start in their catch-up. In the competition within a new techno-economic paradigm, both incumbents and latecomers start from the same starting line, and incumbents often fall into the "trap" of sticking to their existing technologies from which they derive their supremacy. Leapfrogging beyond detours is necessary because detours only involve building capabilities, which is insufficient to induce a radical reversal of market shares and leadership changes. The changes in industrial leadership from the incumbents to the late entrants in emerging economies often require not only a firm-level effort but also exogenous moments of disruption, which we

---

[27]   These two concepts are introduced in Perez and Soete (1988).

call "windows of opportunity"; otherwise, the chance for hegemonic changes is often very low. One may say that Korean latecomer firms built up a certain level of capabilities by the end of the 1980s at the hands of big chaebols. However, these latecomer firms would not have surpassed the Japanese incumbent if they had no window of opportunity associated with the rise of digital technologies. Nor could they have done so if no Japanese firms had fallen into the incumbent trap of sticking to their analogue technologies.

In many consumer product cases, such as those involving digital televisions or cell phones, the replacement of analogue technologies by digital ones provided a window of opportunity for some latecomers, especially Korea, to leapfrog ahead of Japan.[28] The digitalization of products and production processes entails few disadvantages for latecomers. This is because the functions and quality of these products are determined by electronic chips rather than by the accumulated tacit skills of engineers, which are critical in the production of analogue products and where the Japanese incumbent holds the advantage.

Chapter 5 discusses the role of leapfrogging as the final stage of catching up or overtaking. In our framework of economic catch-up, the role of leapfrogging is described as "flying on a balloon when the conventional ladder to catch up is kicked away." Given that we can only fly balloons under favorable weather conditions, an economy can successfully leapfrog only when attempted upon the arrival of exogenous windows of opportunity. Moreover, as a precondition for flying on a balloon, economies must have built up their capabilities; otherwise, they may fall through "windows" instead of flying upward.

Chapter 5 also discusses the role of leapfrogging along the framework of catch-up cycles, which refers to the successive changes in industry leadership across countries. In doing so, this chapter takes into account three types of windows of opportunity, such as technological windows, those that are associated with the demand or market side, as well as business cycles, and finally the roles of government

---

[28]   This is discussed in Lee, Lim, and Song (2005) and Lee (2013a) and in Chapter 7.

regulations and industrial policies. This chapter also reflects the find-ings of recent literature on catch-up cycles in diverse sectors—semi-conductors, shipbuilding, steels, wines, mid-sized jets, cameras, mobile phones, and others—to explain the frequent changes in their leadership.[29]

THE THREE PARADOXES IN ECONOMIC CATCH-UP

The two concepts of detour and leapfrogging are placed at the core of the "paradoxical art" of economic catch-up in this book. While detour refers to the latecomers doing things that differ from the previous practices of the forerunners, leapfrogging refers to the latecomers doing something new ahead of their forerunners and thereby over-taking their leadership. In other words, detour is consistent with the stage-based theory of economic development, which emphasizes the need to have a period or stage of building capabilities. Then, as a next step, leapfrogging means utilizing the built-up capabilities, often in BBs, to forge ahead or rapidly catch up with the forerunners while taking advantage of the emerging windows of opportunity.

We also consider "entry point" as another supplementary con-cept in addition to detour and leapfrogging. This concept, which is particularly relevant at the early stage of development, refers to the situation where the latecomers begin their manufacturing activities, and where the value chain of production is already well established in the market segment that they enter and is already occupied by firms from advanced countries.[30] Thus, given their late entry, the latecomer firms have no choice but to either inherit low-end segments or sectors that are left free by firms from advanced economies, or to start from original equipment manufacturing (OEM) while relying on FDIs rather than on indigenous firms. The OEM is a specific form of sub-contracting under which a complete, finished product is made to the

---

[29]   Refer to Lee and Malerba (2017) and the related articles on catch-up cycles in diverse sectors, such as semiconductors (Shin, 2017), steels (Lee & Ki, 2017), and mobile phones.

[30]   See Ernst and Guerrieri (1998) and Sturgeon and Gereffi (2009).

exact specifications of contracting firms and the latecomer firms do not add much value and only get processing fees (wages). Therefore, this stage of entry involves the latecomers learning or following the path of their forerunners. At the later stage, these firms may move to own design manufacturing (ODM) and own brand manufacturing (OBM), both of which correspond to the creation of more value-added in a domestic economy, including production, R&D, marketing, and branding.[31]

If we combine the three concepts discussed so far, then we obtain an overall picture of the long-term process of economic catch-up, which consists of "entry → detour → leapfrogging." Chapter 6 summarizes this process while focusing on the concepts of "two failures and one barrier" and "three detours and leapfrogging with several windows of opportunity." The theory is framed with three paradoxes. The first paradox is "to be similar, be different," which means that in order to catch up with and be similar to their forerunners, a latecomer must take a path that differs from that of its forerunners. The second paradox is "a detour can be faster than a straight road," which means that because of the traffic jam on the straight road, a firm must take a detour to reach its target faster than the others. The third paradox is "you may fly through the open window or fall through the window," which means that only those who are ready to fly with strong wings can attempt to leapfrog, while the others are exposed to high risk.

This paradox of catch-up can be understood through Xenon's paradox. In this paradox, a sophist in ancient Greece named Zenon predicted that Achilles, a famous marathoner at the time, would never be able to outrace a turtle if the latter started the race 100 meters ahead of the former. The paradoxical reasoning is that if Achilles reached the starting point of the turtle, then the turtle would have made some advances, thereby leaving some gap between him and Achilles. Then, when Achilles reaches this new point, the turtle would have made

---

[31]   The role of OEM at the earlier stage is discussed in Amsden (1989) and Hobday (1995), while the role of upgrading to ODM and OBM is discussed in Lee, Song, and Kwak (2015) and in Chapter 4 of this book.

some more advances, thereby still leaving some gap between him and Achilles. This fable clearly illustrates catch-up as a game of "chasing a moving target," which means that in order to catch up, the latecomer must run faster than its target or leap over the forerunner.

If interpreted in terms of the catch-up effect (i.e., the farther you are from the frontier, the faster you can grow owing to this effect), this paradox can no longer be considered impossible. The catch-up effect will disappear as soon as the latecomer approaches the target, and then the latecomer will slow down eventually. In this case, to outrace the target, the latecomer must find an alternative path to free themselves from the exhaustion of the catch-up effect that is associated with the decision to follow the same path as that taken by the forerunners. Actually, another effect is involved here to slow down the latecomers, namely, the competition effect. In other words, as the latecomers get close to the forerunners, the latter feel the potential threat of being overtaken and find ways to deter the catch-up by the latecomers. They do this by mobilizing entry barriers in the form of IPR disputes and anti-dumping litigations, besides declining technical transfers or licensing. These circumstances are the sources of the "one barrier" mentioned earlier and are discussed in detail in Chapter 2.

The second paradox of catch-up can also be explained using the aforementioned analogy. Suppose you are racing with many runners in a marathon. The road becomes jammed, thereby preventing you from running fast enough. Here, the jammed road represents a conventional (or easy) way of achieving economic growth in the developing countries that rely on cheap labor or mineral resources along with the modes of OEM and FDI. This way of doing similar things has been identified as one of the major growth problems in the South and has been labeled the "adding up problem" or the fallacy of composition (Spence, 2011). For example, when latecomer economies try to export the same or similar low-end products, the market becomes flooded and these economies are forced to charge low prices.

While Ha-Joon Chang (2002) highlights the difficulty of catch-up by using the "kicking away the ladder" metaphor, this book suggests

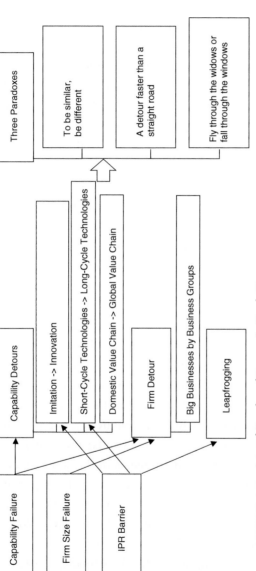

FIGURE I-2. Art and Paradox of Economic Catch-Up

that catch-up is difficult yet possible because one may take a detour and fly on a balloon when the ladder is kicked away. Here, flying on a balloon means leapfrogging through a window of opportunity after building up capabilities via detours. Although leapfrogging involves some risk, this technique presents the only way for a latecomer to forge ahead and overtake their forerunners. Given that leapfrogging may result in failure when attempted without preparation, this technique is denoted as the third paradox mentioned previously. To illustrate these ideas of detours and leapfrogging at the firm, sector, and country levels, this book analyzes the experiences of successful catching-up economies in Asia from a comparative perspective.

The ideas discussed so far can be summarized in Figure 1–2.

2 Different Mechanisms of Growth in Poor and Rich Nations and the Narrow Pathway in Between

2.1 INTRODUCTION

The determinants of economic growth still remain an important issue in economics. Previous studies have identified several factors for economic growth, such as policies, institutions, and geography. Among these factors, policies are often represented by the policies for economic integration and openness, with the so-called Washington Consensus serving as a prime example. Since then, as a partial effort to remedy the unsatisfactory performance of the Washington Consensus, a group of scholars led by Acemoglu observed that favorable policy prescriptions (such as the Washington Consensus) tend to fail because of poor institutional conditions, such as insecure property rights and weak rule of law, and added that none of the traditional factors would affect economic performance if a stable and trustworthy institutional environment was not present to sustain the economy.[1] Meanwhile, by questioning the robustness of institutions as a variable, Glaeser argued that institutions do not induce growth but rather economic growth brings in favorable institutions, such as democracy, as in the case of formerly authoritarian states such as South Korea, and highlighted the importance of human capital instead.[2]

The aforementioned studies of economic growth all attempt to find one universal factor for economic growth that binds all countries, regardless of their income levels and structural differences. By contrast, some scholars such as Rodrik (2006) go to the extremes

---

[1] Refer to the early work of Knack and Keefer (1995), Acemoglu et al. (2001, 2002), Rodrik et al. (2004), and Easterly (2001).

[2] Glaeser et al. (2004).

of finding "different binding factors" for each country. Meanwhile, this book takes a compromising view to find binding factors for two or three different groups of countries, such as low- and lower-middle-income countries and upper-middle- and high-income countries. It shows that (political) institutions are significant only in low- and lower-middle-income countries, whereas innovation and higher education are significant in upper-middle- and higher-income countries.[3] Such findings are consistent with the idea of the different determinants of growth at low- and high-income levels.[4] Such division of countries into two or three groups leads to the idea of MIT, which reflects the problem of economic growth slowdown being faced by middle-income countries. Over the last decade since its introduction, the existence of sources and policies for getting out of MIT have been subjected to heated debates.

For now, two broad compromises seem feasible. First, regardless of the existence or absence of MIT, many notable countries are struggling at the middle-income stage or are experiencing a very slow transition from middle- to high-income status. Second, most studies show that economies must take reform or exogenous actions to address MIT, inefficient equilibrium, or growth slowdown; those researchers who have doubted the existence of MIT have described it not as a trap but rather as a failure to adapt to innovation or other required reform.[5]

The preceding examples establish a favorable ground for this chapter, which aims to discuss the sources, nature, and ways to get out of MIT. In other words, the focus will be on the key "transition" variables for an economy to move from the lower- or middle-income to the higher-income stage growth. These variables will be discussed in terms of the conditions that are necessary for achieving such transition.

---

[3]   This is the results of an econometric study by Lee and Kim (2009).

[4]   Bulman, Eden, and Nguyen (2014) present an example of a compromise. Growth theories all assume one production function associated with the same technologies and are considered too unrealistic to be applied to developing countries that face different production functions and technologies.

[5]   Cited from Itoh (2017).

Section 2 discusses the sources of MIT and emphasizes innovation capability as the key variable for enabling the transition. Section 3 differentiates two aspects of innovation, namely, technological capabilities and scientific knowledge, while focusing on the decisive role of the former. Section 4 discusses the sources of difficulties when making an upward transition, especially from the middle- to high-income stage, in terms of the two failures and one barrier. Capability failure refers to the intrinsic difficulty in building up innovation capabilities in developing countries, while size failure refers to the difficulty in generating world-class BBs (big business) that are often required when jumping from middle- to high-income status. The one barrier refers to the barriers associated with the negative impacts of strong IPR protection in advanced economies on the exports from emerging economies.

Such existence of two failures and one barrier, which makes a successful transition rare and difficult to achieve, requires economies to find a detour to build their innovation capabilities and to avoid replicating or emulating the practices of advanced economies. The final section of this chapter focuses on this issue, while the next chapter discusses how economies can take a detour or path that differs from that taken by advanced economies.

2.2   DIVERSE SOURCES OF MIT (MIDDLE INCOME TRAP) WITH INNOVATION AS THE KEY HURDLE AND SOLUTION

When searching for the variables responsible for MIT, an International Monetary Fund (IMF) study considered as broad a range of factors as possible, including demographic conditions, institutions, industry and trade structures, diversification, physical infrastructure, and macro-financial developments.[6] Through an econometric analysis of growth equations, the IMF study has tested whether each of these variables is binding for middle-income countries and has identified different factors for each income group of countries. The findings of

---

[6]   See Aiyar et al. (2013).

the IMF study help us understand why only a selected number of countries have been able to jump from middle- to high-income status over the last five decades. Therefore, the primary question here is what key "transition" variables are needed to realize a successful transition. These variables will also be discussed in terms of the necessary or sufficient conditions for achieving such a transition.

Political Institutions

One of the most widely considered variables in economic growth is "institution." An increasingly large body of research has identified institution as an important factor for economic growth. However, this variable has been criticized for its robustness and endogeneity, and some studies, for instance, the one by Glaeser, have verified the robustness of human capital rather than institution. Moreover, institution can be measured in diverse aspects, such as rule of law, democracy, or political stability (order). The different aspects of institution may be binding only for a particular stage of development. In this regard, several studies consider certain institutions unimportant for middle-income countries. For instance, the IMF study also finds rule of law as an important factor for slowdown in economic growth in all countries but an insignificant factor for middle-income countries. Other researchers also highlight the insignificance of democracy for middle-income countries and the significance of political stability (order) for low-, middle-, and high-income countries.[7] These findings are consistent with our observations that the political institution (checks and balances against rulers) is significant only for low- and lower-middle-income countries. In sum, all these studies find that neither rule of law nor democracy is particularly binding for middle-income countries, whereas political stability matters for all countries.

Therefore, one may conclude that while democratic institutions and rule of law seem to be a common feature of high-income

---

[7] See Huang et al. (2013) and also Lee and Kim (2009).

countries, and thus necessary conditions for becoming a high-income country, pursuing a democratic institution does not guarantee a successful transition from low-income to high-income status. Many countries in Latin America have already achieved the highest index of political institutions, but many of them are stuck in MIT. However, this observation does not mean that low-income countries must not strive to become democratic but must do so because their political institutions greatly vary and serve as a binding factor for their economic growth. Therefore, low-income countries must improve their political institutions to reach middle-income status but doing so may not help them reach high-income status.

Trade and Industrial Structure and Openness

Other important factors may include trade and industrial structure as well as trade and financial liberalization. However, the same IMF study finds that the industry structure variables and export diversification become insignificant when the sample is restricted to middle-income countries, but they are considered significant for the entire sample. Financial liberalization is problematic because the IMF study finds that a high level of financial inflow to GDP increases the probability for middle-income countries to face a growth slowdown, and this finding is consistent with the liberalization-crisis story observed in some countries. Other countries, such as Korea, reached the high-income status by the mid-1990s to join the rich country club of the Organisation for Economic Cooperation and Development (OECD), while their financial system remained under government control and without external financial liberalization. The irrelevance of financial liberalization or privatization as a prerequisite for growth beyond the middle-income stage has also been highlighted by Rodrik, who found that the East Asian economies of Korea and Taiwan reached the high-income status without such liberalization, whereas Latin American countries embraced such liberalization yet failed to sustain growth.[8]

[8]   See Rodrik (1996).

Thus, financial openness or liberalization cannot be considered a robust variable for economic growth in upper-middle-income countries or a key transition variable for jumping to high-income status.

We then consider the variable of openness to trade or FDIs. Although the benefits of economic integration and openness have been widely recognized in the literature, the actual effects of openness and the question of which variable represents the best international integration are still being debated. While some studies find a positive correlation between economic growth and trade openness,[9] others find that trade openness is not robust as a factor for economic growth.[10] Similar controversies exist over the FDI variable as scholars are divided between pro- and skeptical-FDI groups.[11] Export diversification is another variable that is subject to debate because some researchers find this concept significant for economic growth in the South, while others find export specialization to have significant effects on growth.[12]

Apart from trade openness, FDI, and export diversification, one recent study verifies export growth (sustaining exports) as an alternative variable for representing economic integration and openness,[13] which is consistent with the findings of the emerging literature on export survival.[14] In a sense, the importance of export growth is not surprising or new as the economic growth of many successful emerging economies, particularly those in East Asia, has been

---

[9] See Frankel and Romer (1999), Rodriguez and Rodrik (2000), and Yanikkaya (2003).

[10] Rodriguez and Rodrik (2000), Vamvakidis (2002), and Lee and Kim (2009).

[11] The pro-FDI group includes, Hermes and Lensink (2003), Alfaro et al. (2004), Balasubramanyam et al. (1996), Durham (2004), Doytch and Uctum (2011), Borensztein et al. (1998), Hsiao and Shen (2003), and Makki and Somwaru (2004), while the skeptical-FDI group includes Carkovic and Levine (2002) and Adams (2009).

[12] The pro-diversification view includes Hesse (2009), Amurgo–Pacheco and Pierola (2008), and Dennis and Shepherd (2007), while the pro-specialization view includes Plümper and Graff (2001), Dalum et al. (1999), Greenaway et al. (1999), and Fosu (1990).

[13] Ramanayake and Lee (2015) found that aside from export specialization, export growth is highly robust, while the traditional variables of trade openness and FDI are not robust. This result is based on econometric estimations using not only cross-section and fixed-effect panel estimations but also system–GMM estimations.

[14] Export survival has been discussed in terms of several variables, such as the comparative advantage of products, competitiveness of exports, export diversification, learning through exporting, and export composition (Brenton et al., 2010; Besedes and Prusa, 2006; Nitsch, 2009; Fugazza and Molina, 2009; Hausman et al., 2007).

characterized as export-led since the early works by Krueger, Cline, and Balassa in the 1980s. Thus, the emerging literature argues that sustaining, rather than starting, exports is crucial for driving economic growth. Export growth (sustaining exports) is one of the most binding factors for economic growth in the South because developing countries must earn hard currencies through exporting to pay for the imported capital goods that are required for sustaining economic growth. In other words, export growth promotes economic growth by generating the foreign exchange that enables the importation of machinery and intermediate goods that are necessary for investment.

This aggregate-level evidence on the importance of export growth is consistent with the findings of the firm-level analysis,[15] which shows the robust impact of export orientation on firm growth in a large sample of developing countries that are included in the World Bank data set, in contrast to the weak impact of firms engaged in FDI. The findings of this work warn against the traditional emphasis on simple trade openness and FDI as policy prescriptions for developing countries. A similar warning can also be made with regard to the participation of developing economies in GVCs as a prescription for economic growth given that many of these countries are still stuck in low-value-added activities or segments, as discussed in the next chapter. In other words, opening an economy for international integration and GVCs or inviting FDIs into a host country does not guarantee sustained economic growth unless these actions lead to export growth, which requires capability-building in indigenous firms and investments in innovation. This observation is consistent with the experiences of successful catching-up economies in Asia, such as Korea, Taiwan, and China.

Therefore, while openness seems to be an important feature of many high-income countries and a necessary condition for jumping to high-income status, the sufficiency of openness as a condition remains unknown, and whether opening up the economy to more

---

[15]   See Lee and Temesgen (2009), who used firm data from the World Bank.

trade and FDIs will help middle-income economies reach high-income status warrants further research.

Innovation Capabilities to Sustain Export Growth

As discussed above, sustaining export growth seems to be important in all stages of development. In this case, how to sustain exports tends to be different across each stage of development. In high-income countries, being innovative seems to be the most binding factor for sustaining exports. Meanwhile, low- and middle-income countries tend to compete with each other based on prices rather than on innovation, thereby leading to the so-called "adding up" problem of flooding the market with the same or similar products and the related decrease in the price of goods.[16] Thus, these countries must be equipped with innovation capability and base their export growth not on price competitiveness (undervaluation or low wages) but on product differentiation.

The importance of innovation capability as a key transition variable is consistent with the findings of the World Bank and Asian Development Bank (ADB) works involving Eichengreen, and my own work.[17] The ADB study finds that human capital and innovation, especially tertiary education, are important for upper-middle-income countries. The emphasis on innovation is consistent with the original concern raised in World Bank reports and numerous studies which show that the MIT tends to occur as middle-income countries become caught between low-wage manufacturers and high-wage innovators. This occurs because their wage rates are too high to compete with low-wage exporters and their level of technological capability is too low to enable them to compete with advanced countries. Such concern is unsurprising because even the World Bank assessment of the reform

---

[16] This adding-up problem is noted in Spence (2011) and is often called a fallacy of composition.

[17] The "ADB study" refers to Eichengreen et al. (2013), while "my own work" refers to Lee (2013a). The World Bank studies include the original concern expressed in Yusuf and Nabeshima (2009) and World Bank (2010, 2012), as well as that echoed in Lin (2012a) and Williamson (2012).

decade of the 1990s shows that growth-oriented actions, such as technological catch-up and encouragement of risk taking, may be necessary; this assessment also recognizes technological innovation as one of the most serious bottlenecks of growth in many countries, especially in the middle-income countries of Latin America.[18]

In sum, MIT is a problem of economic growth slowdown resulting from weak innovation. Thus, by comparing the East Asian experience with the elements of the Washington Consensus, we find that the mixed results of the Consensus do not result from poor institutions but rather from missing or neglected policies, such as technological policies and revolutions in higher education. The preceding discussion identifies innovation, including high education, as the most important binding factor for economies to free themselves from MIT and to achieve an upward transition. However, innovation itself is a broad term, and we need to narrow down its scope. We discuss this issue in the next section.

2.3 BETWEEN THE TWO ASPECTS OF INNOVATION: TECHNOLOGIES VS. SCIENCES

As mentioned in the previous section, the improvements in innovation and higher education are two important factors when jumping from low- to high-income status. This section distinguishes the roles and contributions of these two factors in the transition. Both firms that generate patents and academic communities that generate articles are important elements of NIS, which is composed of elements and relationships that interact in the production, diffusion, and use of new and economically useful knowledge.

Schumpeterian scholars, such as Lundvall and Nelson, advocate the NIS concept and argue that the differences in NIS across countries lead to differences in innovation and economic performance, especially for countries in the middle-income stage, which is the primary concern in this work. However, many countries in the South lack an

---

[18] See World Bank (2005: 11), which provides an assessment of the reform decade of the 1990s.

effective system of translating scientific knowledge into technological knowledge and thus scientific knowledge tends not to be commercialized but remains within the ivory tower (academia). The so-called linear model of innovation linking science to innovation often does not work because the science sector in the South lacks the ability to identify the technologies needed by the industrial sector. Given the low demand from the industrial sector, the science sector tends to focus on basic academic research that is irrelevant to the needs of the industrial sector. Thus, focusing on the science sector without aiming to develop the industrial sector will only cause problems. Some volume of the literature tends to argue that this is the case of NIS in typical countries in Latin America.[19] If the literature is right, the performance difference between East Asia and Latin America can also be explained from this NIS perspective.

The divergent economic performance of East Asia and Latin America presents a key issue that has been widely explored in the development literature. The question is why the "Asian style" of catching up has not been observed in Latin America. In the 1950s, Latin American countries were much better "endowed" and developed than East Asian countries. Korea and Taiwan were less developed than Brazil and Mexico during the 1960s and early 1970s. Korea and Taiwan began catching up to other countries in the 1960s, overtook Brazil and Mexico by the 1980s, and finally reached high-income status by the late 1990s. By contrast, many Latin American countries failed to sustain their growth despite or because of the implementation of policy prescriptions by the so-called Washington Consensus, which emphasized economic liberalization over the promotion of the domestic industry. Rodrik observed that the difference in the performances of East Asian and Latin American countries can be explained in terms of the simultaneous adoption of the ten policy suggestions mentioned in the Washington Consensus in Latin America versus the sequential or gradual adoption of the ten policies in East Asia.[20]

---

[19]   See Pack (2001), Alcorta and Peres (1998), Katz (2001), and Velho (2004).
[20]   See Rodrik (1994, 2006).

By contrast, we contend that the economic difference between East Asia and Latin America can be explained not only by the difference in sequencing but also by the difference in their NIS and science and technology policy orientation.

In the Latin American NIS, the industrial sector of local firms tends to be weak, and successful exporting firms are subsidiaries of MNCs or have established relationship with firms in advanced economies.[21] Only those indigenous firms that face innovation challenges but lack in-house R&D capabilities would seek collaboration with public institutions or universities. Given that the industrial sector is a consumer of scientific knowledge, the underdevelopment of this sector implies that the science sector may function ineffectively given its inability to identify the technologies needed by the industrial sector. Instead, given the low demand from the industrial sector, the science sector tends to focus on basic academic research that is irrelevant to the industrial sector. Consequentially, a viable co-evolution is not achieved, and a vicious circle consisting of an ivory-tower style of scientific community and a weak industrial sector is observed.

Further, many have observed that in Latin America, identifying research priorities has traditionally been a task left to the research community, with little being negotiated to potential users although some cases of successful collaboration do exist.[22] As such, taking the lead from international science, research themes tend to be selected on the basis of their scientific importance rather than on local industrial needs. Universities and public research institutes, which together perform almost 70% of R&D activities, have not created mechanisms to identify the needs of users. Instead, their research agenda is selected based on the scientific criteria of international mainstream science, and the reward system for R&D activities is related to scientific advancements over technological

---

[21]   See Pack (2001), Alcorta and Peres (1998), Katz (2001), and Velho (2004).
[22]   The arguments in this paragraph are made in Arocena and Sutz (2001), Velho (2004), Hanson (2008), and Cimoli (2000: 123).

achievements.[23] In the meantime, while there do exist some success-ful cases of university–industry interaction, such as in sectors of soybean, steel, and aircraft (Embraer), the issue is then why they are so limited.[24]

In contrast, East Asian policy makers favor technological poli-cies over scientific ones by emphasizing the technological develop-ment in private industrial sectors, and the domestic firms in East Asia invest in their own R&D activities after adapting and assimilating foreign technologies.[25] As a result, the increasing demand of the industrial sector for research on applied science has enabled its co-evolution with the science sector. Thus, the prevalence of industrial technology sectors over science sectors in East Asia can be a key factor in explaining the difference in the economic performances of East Asia and Latin America. Actually, a recent study conducted a country-panel econometric analysis to prove that technological knowledge (patents), rather than scientific knowledge (academic articles), mat-ters directly for economic growth in the latecomer countries, the NIS of which is not mature enough to facilitate the mutual transformation of these two types of knowledge.[26]

The same study finds that science does not have a significant impact on either technology generation or economic growth; instead, it finds that corporate patents tend to contribute to the generation of scientific knowledge and the promotion of economic growth. The empirical findings suggest that the linear model of innovation that emphasizes the role of scientific knowledge as an input for indus-trial innovation is not supported, especially when the NIS of countries is not effective or mature enough to facilitate the transformation of

[23]   In the meantime, there is also a view, like that of Bernardes and Albuquerque (2003), that the failure of Latin America to uplift its scientific capacity has also resulted in its failure in the aspect of technological capacity. They also point toward a threshold level in scientific production, beyond which the efficiency in the use of scientific output by the technological sector increases. Then, it can be argued that a combination of reaching such a threshold and a strong industrial sector is needed to realize an effective interaction between the science and technological sectors.

[24]   On this point and the cases, see Suzigan and Albuquerque (2011).

[25]   Kim and Lee (2015).   [26]   Kim and Lee (2015).

knowledge. Kim and Lee find that technological knowledge is primarily generated not by scientific knowledge but by corporate R&D efforts, which Latin American countries greatly lack compared with East Asian countries. An important policy implication is that, without implementing a technology policy that emphasizes the role of corporate R&D in invigorating the industrial sector, a policy that only emphasizes science may not generate tangible economic benefits.

The preceding discussion leads us to conclude that between the innovation capabilities and scientific knowledge from higher education institutions, the former is a more important and binding variable in the transition of countries to high-income status. Figure 2–1 shows the R&D–GDP ratio of countries at different income levels. Although this figure indicates a positive correlation between income levels and R&D–GDP ratio, the latter suddenly becomes flat among middle-income countries or those countries with per capita incomes ranging from 1,000 to 10,000 USD. In other words, this ratio does not increase proportionally with per capita income in this group of countries, thereby indicating that the flat relationship is a root cause of MIT as noted by Lee (2013a).

A similar conclusion can be derived by examining the number of US patents filed by countries.[27] In the early 1980s, when the income level of Korea was similar to that of Brazil and Argentina, the number of US patent applications by Koreans reached approximately fifty, which was within the range of that of other middle-income countries, such as Brazil and Argentina. In the 1980s and 1990s, the Korean patent applications rapidly increased to more than ten times the average of that of other middle-income countries, the incomes of which remained relatively flat. In 2000, Korea and Taiwan filed approximately 5,000 US patent applications, while other middle- or lower-income countries, including Brazil and Argentina, filed less than 500 patents per year. In other words, the difference between the

---

[27]   The data here are taken from Table 1 in Lee and Kim (2009).

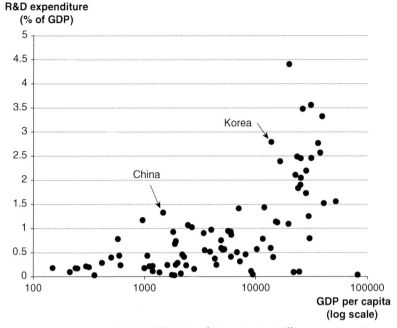

FIGURE 2-1. R&D–GDP Ratio of Countries in Different Income Groups
Note: Drawn by the author using the R&D figures from UNESCO and
World Development Indicators (WDI) data from the World Bank.
The average values for years 2001–2005 are used.

more successful Asian economies and the less successful Latin
American economies (or the reversal of fortune between these two
groups) can be explained by the priority they allocate to the enhancement of their long-term growth potential, particularly innovation
capability.

2.4 TWO FAILURES AND ONE BARRIER TO UPWARD TRANSITION: CAPABILITIES, SCALE, AND IPR

The preceding discussions have singled out innovation as the most
important factor in enabling an upward transition from middle- to
high-income status. However, several factors can make a successful
transition rare and difficult to achieve. This section discusses the

specific sources of these difficulties in terms of two failures and one barrier. The first failure is the capability failure, which is associated with the difficulty in building up innovation capabilities, while the second failure is the size failure, which is associated with the difficulty in generating world-class BBs. The one barrier refers to the negative impacts of strong IPR protection in the North and the related disputes with the incumbent firms.

Capability Failure Compared with Market and System Failures

The difficulties facing the upward transition of latecomers can be attributed to several important intrinsic sources. Among the most fundamental sources is the fact that building innovation capabilities involves much risk and failure. Such risk can be called "capability failure," which differs from the conventional market failure.

In the traditional neoclassical approach, "market failure" stems from the fact that knowledge is a public good. Therefore, an industrial policy is necessary due to the possible underinvestment in R&D expenditure when some flaws exist in capital and risk markets, in addition to the market failure associated with imperfectly competitive industries and with knowledge spillover. From this perspective, the actual amount of R&D is often less than the optimal amount that prevails when market failure is not present. Therefore, the government subsidies for supporting R&D are justified by the externality involved in the production of knowledge and the differences in learning possibilities across sectors (Greenwald and Stiglitz, 2014).

In the "market failure" approach, the common and hidden presumption is that the firms and other economic actors are already capable of production and innovation and that the government must simply try to modify the extent of their activities. Thus, in the market failure view, the reasons for failures are sought outside the firm; these are the areas where corrective actions from the government are recommended. However, the stark reality in developing countries is that economic actors, especially firms, have extremely weak levels of capability. In several developing countries, private firms are unable to pursue and conduct in-house R&D, which they consider an uncertain endeavor with uncertain returns. Thus, the problem is not one of less or more R&D, but of "zero" R&D. In contrast to the concept of market failure, this chapter emphasizes "capability failure" and the need to improve the innovation capabilities of firms, sectors, and nations. According to this view, learning failure occurs because of the lack of opportunity for effective learning and capability-building. Thus, capability failure emphasizes the difficulty and importance of increasing the level of capability of firms.[28]

The Schumpeterian concept of "system failure" becomes highly relevant after an economy builds up a certain level of capabilities for those actors that are involved in innovation. System failure refers to the failure in the functions of the NIS of countries, which consist of firms, universities, public research laboratories, government agencies, and financial institutions. Such failure may occur when the missing or weak connections (and synergies) among actors tend to result in the poor performance of the system.[29] These problems arise due to the cognitive distance (Nooteboom, 2009) among these actors, which is associated with the tacitness of knowledge resulting in cognition failure. In a failure situation, the virtuous cycles related to the workings of dynamic complementarities cannot take place, thereby trapping agents in vicious cycles of low interaction and learning. Failures may also occur due to the lack of information about the presence of other actors or because of the bounded rationality that constrains the actions of agents. Then, policy intervention may be justified by the mismatches or misalignments among actors within an established system that is undergoing transformation or by the failure of a new innovation system to emerge and develop.

---

[28]   See Lee (2013c) for a discussion on capability failure, and see Metcalfe (2005), Bergek et al. (2008), Malerba (2009), and Dodgson et al. (2011) for a discussion on evolutionary economics and system failures.

[29]   In particular, see arguments by some scholars (i.e., Bergek et al., 2008; Dodgson et al., 2011).

In contrast to the typical argument for government activism that is based on market or system failure, this chapter emphasizes "capability failure" as a justification for government activism and the need for promoting specific ways to raise the capabilities of firms in developing countries. In developing countries where firms have a low R&D capability, a safe way of doing business is to buy or borrow external technologies or production facilities as well as to specialize in less technical methods or assembly manufacturing. To move beyond such states (which lead to MIT), effective forms of government activism must include not the simple provision of R&D funds but various ways to cultivate R&D capability. The innovation survey of Chaminade et al. (2012) in Thailand identifies one related problem, namely, the tendency for government policies to be limited only to tax incentives without implementing explicit measures to encourage Thai firms to take greater risks in innovation. More effective and alternative forms of intervention may include the transfer of R&D outcomes by public research institutes and a public–private R&D consortium, which has achieved success in Korea and Taiwan.[30]

Such direct intervention is important because learning failure happens not only due to the fact that knowledge is a public good but also because of the lack of opportunity for effective learning resulting from historically inherited conditions or policy failure. From this perspective, industrial policy is not about choosing winners but about choosing good students and matching them with good teachers or bringing them to excellent schools. These schools may take the form of licensing-based learning (of tacit knowledge) or public–private joint R&D projects, in which direct and cooperative learning takes place. Meanwhile, the public sector or banks that merely supply R&D money may not serve as excellent schools.

Based on this analogy, the market failure view can be expressed as "I will pay for your school so that you may take more classes," whereas the system failure view may be expressed as "go to school

---

[30]   See Mathews (2002b), Lee and Lim (2001), Lee et al. (2005), and OECD (1996) for more details.

and make more friends." However, neither view pays enough attention to factors such as the initial aptitude of students, what is taught to them in schools, who their teachers are, and how they teach their students. From the capability view, these aspects are crucial to the successful upgrading of economies beyond MIT. Thus, the capability failure view essentially believes in the importance of raising the level of capabilities of firms (students) and the various learning methods to be provided over their dynamic course of learning. In sum, we need both tuition (R&D money) and friends (linkages to other components in the system) in schools. Besides, critical factors include the students themselves, an excellent curriculum, knowledgeable teachers, and effective teaching methods. Table 2–1 summarizes the aforementioned arguments.

In sum, catching up and economic development are processes of capability-building and innovation system creation. The difference in the income level of countries results from the differences in their capabilities and system development in many aspects, including their capability to produce and sell internationally competitive products for a prolonged period. Neo-classical economics cannot be "good development economics" because it is all about the optimization or optimal use of (existing) resources, with an implicit assumption that all resources are already present and that we only have to think about how to utilize these resources most efficiently in well-functioning markets. In reality, most developing countries do not have to worry about the optimal use of resources because they do not have these resources at hand. A more critical issue is how to build up such capabilities and how to develop the innovation systems that support the firms' catching up in learning and innovation.

Size Failure: Difficulty of Generating World-Class BBs

SMEs have long been promoted as vehicles for job creation, economic growth, and helping the poor in developing countries. The World Bank has provided the SMEs in developing countries with targeted assistance worth more than 10 billion USD from 1998 to 2002 and

Table 2–1. *Three Types of Failures and Economic Development*

	Market failure	System failure	Capability failure
Focus	Market institutions	Firms and non-firm actors Interaction among actors	Actors (firms)
Source	Knowledge as a public good	Lack of capabilities of actors	Lack of firms' capabilities
	Lack of incentives	Lack of linkages and interactive learning	No learning opportunity
Problem	Suboptimal R&D	Lack of capable non-firm actors. Blocks to interactive learning	No R&D
Solutions	R&D subsidies	Creation of new actors Fostering interfaces and interactions	Access to knowledge and help in learning
Relevance	Developing and advanced countries	Developing and advanced countries	Unique to developing countries

(*Source:* Lee 2013c)

1.3 billion USD in 2003.[31] Previous studies have considered subsidizing SMEs as a tool to alleviate poverty because of its labor intensiveness. However, by applying cross-country regressions while using instrumental variables to control endogeneity, a World Bank study failed to confirm a robust relationship between SMEs and per capita income growth as well as poverty alleviation, although it found some positive yet weak correlations.[32]

In this case, the next question will be, "how about the BBs?" The importance of large firms in the process of economic development has been analyzed by several scholars in various ways. An influential

---

[31] These figures are from the World Bank (2002, 2004) cited in a study done by Beck et al. (2005). Here BBs are an abbreviation of big businesses.

[32] See Beck et al. (2005).

book by Chandler (1990), *Scale and Scope*, showed how BBs in the United States and Germany have contributed to these countries' economic growth. While Schumpeter emphasized in his earlier work entrepreneurship, which is mostly associated with startups or SMEs, in his later work Schumpeter (1943: 71–72) also discussed the contribution of BB in generating innovation by large R&D investment and thereby enhancing the living standard of people.[33] In addition to the traditionally recognized merits of BBs such as scale economies, the importance of BBs in national economic growth can also be discussed in the context of a new economic environment.[34] For example, BBs have become very important in the era of globalization, during which small or formerly domestically oriented firms tend to be directly exposed to competition with global companies and imports. Given that traditional SMEs are having difficulties in surviving independently, the umbrella, networking, and learning-hub roles of BBs in outsourcing and providing learning opportunities to SMEs can now be recognized. Despite the increasing renewed importance of BBs, this issue has received limited empirical attention.

One exception is my own work (Lee et al., 2013), which verified that BBs, represented by Fortune's Global 500 or Businessweek's 1000 firms, have a significant positive effect on economic growth;[35] the elasticity of Fortune's BBs with respect to GDP per capita growth rate is about 0.01, and such elasticity increases to more than 0.02 when the industrial structure is controlled. In other words, if the number of

---

[33] Schumpeter (1932, originally 1911 in German) discussed the role of entrepreneurs in economic development. This changing emphasis from entrepreneurship to BBs is called the Schumpeter mark I and mark II.

[34] Other recent studies that provide evidence on the positive role of large firms in the development of nations include Chandler et al. (1997), Kozul–Wright and Rowthorn (1998), Pagano and Schivardi (2003), Blackford (1998), Cassis (1997), and Wardley (1991). Nolan (2003) points out their roles in the era of globalization.

[35] Lee et al. (2013) used two databases, namely, Fortune's 500 and Businessweek's 1000 largest companies in the world, which covered many developing countries for more than 16 years. The endogeneity or two-way causality presents another issue. One cannot be sure whether BBs cause national growth or national growth causes these BBs to grow. To control for these fundamental problems, Lee et al. used several econometric techniques; specifically, they not only applied residuals from growth regressions with country size as regressors but also panel data techniques, including GMM.

Fortune 500 companies in a country increases by 10% (e.g., from 10 to 11 or from 40 to 44), then the GDP per capita growth rate of that country increases by 0.1% points (e.g., from a 3% growth rate to 3.1%). Furthermore, when the share of SME employment is included in the estimations and the possible endogeneity of both BBs and SMEs is controlled simultaneously, the role of BBs still has a positive and significant impact and the SME variable becomes negative. The same finding holds when national dependence on BBs is added as a variable. When using the standard deviation of annual GDP per capita growth rates in constant purchasing power parity (PPP) terms as a dependent variable, the number of BBs becomes positively associated with more stable economic growth.

Lee et al. (2013) also showed that having or not having a certain number of BBs may indicate whether or not an economy is stuck in MIT. Many emerging economies, except the more successful cases of Korea, Taiwan, China, and India, are shown to have a smaller number of BBs than that predicted by their sizes, while many rich countries tend to have a larger number of BBs than that predicted by their sizes. For instance, a country such as Thailand, Turkey, or South Africa has one or zero Fortune 500 companies over the last two decades, whereas the number of these firms in Korea and Taiwan increased to fourteen and to eight by 2010, respectively. Also, rapid rise of BRIC countries (Brazil, Russia, India, and China) is consistent with the rapid increase of the number of BBs in these economies, as shown by Table 2–2; for instance, from 3 in 1994 to 109 in 2016 in China, and from 1 in 1994 to 7 in 2016 in India. In contrast, the last two decades of Japan is shown by the decrease of its world-class BBs from 149 in 1994 to 51 in 2016. While economic development depends on firms of all sizes in a given nation, these results suggest that BBs, rather than SMEs, have an independent and robust impact on economic growth, especially at the middle-income stage.

Therefore, the best scenario is to have a combination of world-class BBs and a large number of SMEs. The latter play an important role, especially in job creation, but these firms may not be able to

Table 2–2. *Number of Global Fortune 500 Firms by Selected Countries*

Country	1994	1997	1998	2001	2005	2008	2009	2010	2014	2015	2016
UNITED STATES	149	175	185	196	170	140	139	133	128	134	132
CHINA	3	4	6	11	20	37	46	61	98	103	109
JAPAN	149	112	100	89	70	68	71	68	54	52	51
FRANCE	42	39	39	37	38	40	39	35	31	29	29
GERMANY	44	42	42	35	35	39	37	34	28	28	29
UNITED KINGDOM	33	35	38	33	38	26	29	30	28	25	23
KOREA, REP.	8	12	9	12	12	14	10	14	17	15	15
NETHERLANDS	8	9	7	9	14	12	13	12	13	12	14
AUSTRALIA	3	7	7	6	8	9	8	8	8	8	7
BRAZIL	2	5	4	4	4	6	7	7	7	7	7
INDIA	1	1	1	1	6	7	8	8	7	7	7
ITALY	11	13	11	8	10	10	11	10	9	9	7
TAIWAN	2	2	2	2	3	6	8	8	8	7	6

Table 2–2. (cont.)

Country	1994	1997	1998	2001	2005	2008	2009	2010	2014	2015	2016
RUSSIA	0	1	1	2	5	8	6	7	5	5	4
MEXICO	2	1	1	2	5	4	2	3	3	2	2
INDONESIA	0	0	0	0	0	0	0	0	2	1	1
MALAYSIA	0	1	1	1	1	1	1	1	1	1	1
THAILAND	0	0	0	0	1	1	1	1	1	1	1
TURKEY	1	0	0	0	1	1	1	1	1	1	1
SOUTH AFRICA	0	0	0	0	0	0	0	0	0	0	0

(*Source:* Author's compilation of the data released by *Fortune* magazine.)

trigger economic growth and tend to be promoted by economic growth triggered by BBs.

BBs tend to have a global presence in many countries as they conduct FDIs in their host countries. While many studies have examined the impact of FDIs or the production locations of BBs, Lee et al. (2013) verified the importance of the hosting headquarters of BBs. BBs drive growth not by locating their production hubs in a recipient country but by locating their headquarters in their home countries to conduct R&D and marketing, which are more high-value-added activities than assembly or low-end-based manufacturing. In other words, BBs are more likely to be in charge of innovation and can generate "rents" or extra profits to support higher levels of incomes, whereas working in production factories may only generate wages for paying living expenses without upgrading. This finding is consistent with the original insights of Schumpeter when he emphasized the important role of BBs in R&D and innovation, which can be verified by the very high correlations between the number of BBs and US patents in each country.

Therefore, scale failure, or the inability of developing countries to generate world-class BBs, has been identified as a source of difficulty in making the transition from a poor country to a rich country. Consequently, policy makers from middle-income and developing countries who have recognized the importance of SMEs must now focus on the importance of BBs. Otherwise, they may remain stuck in MIT and fail to reach high-income status. Chapter 4 discusses how to promote or grow BBs.

Barrier of IPR Protection and Predatory Pricing by the North

The previous sections have pointed out that building a higher level of human capabilities that enable innovation is a key element in the upward transition of low- and middle-income economies to high-income economies. However, such upgrading rarely occurs, thereby leading some researchers to ask whether there are barriers that hinder such transition. This subsection discusses this issue while focusing on the role of IPR protection in advanced countries against the exports from catching-up economies, which intensifies the difficulty of achieving innovation-based catch-up.[36]

Under the auspices of the WTO, free trade has been promoted as a vehicle for world economic development. The WTO also regulates and provides guidelines for IPRs through the Trade-Related Aspects of Intellectual Property Rights (TRIPS) agreement, which represents the most extensive multilateral agreement toward the global harmonization of IPRs by setting out minimum standards for protection across member countries. One impact of TRIPS is that developing countries increased their level of IPR protection to reduce the gap in the IPR protection level of developed and developing countries by 2005, which is the last year for the implementation of the TRIPS agreement by the committed developing countries.

The research that links trade and IPRs have focused on the extent to which IPRs in the destination (or importing) country can attract exports from the source country while controlling for the other determinants of trade.[37] However, determining the extent to which the expansion and enforcement of global IPRs contribute to export growth requires one to break down the impacts of IPRs by economic development. This is because developed and developing countries correspond to different stages and mechanisms of economic development. Specifically, many exporting firms in the developing world tend to incur high costs when adapting to TRIPS obligations, and the strict enforcement of IPR laws in developed countries may curb the imports from developing countries because the latter's exports are negatively affected when they are too imitative in nature or are invented around existing products.

The WTO's dispute settlement body has overseen numerous TRIPS-related disputes, and thirty-two official cases have been filed

[36]   The following three paragraphs rely heavily on Shin et al. (2015), which was co written
       by the author of this work.
[37]   For the literature, see Maskus and Penubarti (1995), Smith (1999, 2001), McCalman
       (2005), Awokuse and Yin (2010), and Ivus (2010).

since the inception of the WTO by 2013, with the majority of cases (twenty-six disputes) filed by developed countries, primarily the United States.[38] According to Shin et al. (2015), the US International Trade Commission (USITC) has witnessed a fourfold increase in IPR-related disputes involving foreign imports over the past two decades. Interestingly, more US firms have complained about IPR violations than about unfair dumping, thereby highlighting the increasing importance of IPRs as a measure of trade protection. In fact, the entry of Korean firms into the US market has been marred by the patent disputes between US and Korean firms since the mid-1980s. One of the most noteworthy cases is the ban on Samsung's computer chip exports imposed by the USITC for violating the patent rights of Texas Instruments.[39] A leading high-tech firm from China, Huawei, recently had a serious patent dispute with Cisco in 2011, thereby explaining the weak performance of Huawei's main product (telecommunication switches) in the US market.

Although Samsung and Huawei are BBs with many resources to handle such disputes, solving them can be a matter of life or death for SMEs, as shown by the examples from Korea.[40] An interesting case in this regard is a Korean company called Sunstar, which has indigenously developed a computer-controlled automatic embroidery machine. Sunstar entered the market in 1997, much later than the incumbent Japanese firm, Tokai, which has been the unchallenged leader in the embroidery machine market since the 1990s. Tokai became alarmed and filed a lawsuit against Sunstar in March 1998, arguing that the communicational input tool used by the latter violated its patent. Sunstar was thus ordered by the court to stop selling the product until the charges were cleared. The company barely managed this crisis by presenting critical evidence that the technology had

---

[38]   These cases are from Shin et al. (2015); unlike those that targeted developed countries, all cases (ten) that targeted developing countries were settled out of court or ruled against the developing countries. Firms in developing countries prefer out-of-court settlements or summary judgments due to concerns about litigation and legal costs.

[39]   For details, see Lee and Kim (2010).

[40]   These SME cases are taken from Kim and Lee (2009).

already been in use in the industry even before Tokai adopted it for manufacturing its products. This lawsuit obviously marked a critical moment in the history of Sunstar.

The case of Jusung Engineering presents another example.[41] Established in 1996, Jusung Engineering manufactures equipment for semiconductors and liquid crystal displays (LCDs), such as those used in chemical vapor deposition (CVD) machines. CVD is a process of plating chemicals on a wafer substrate that is imported to Korean user firms. Mr. Hwang, the founder and CEO of Jusung Engineering, used to work as an after-sales service engineer and local agent for ASM, a semiconductor machine company in the Netherlands that used to do business with Samsung Electronics. After leaving ASM, Hwang established his own company and developed equipment for front-end processes. Since 2002, Jusung Engineering has expanded its production scope to plasma-enhanced CVD for LCDs and branched its sales to the United States, Japan, Taiwan, and other countries. Applied Material Inc. filed a lawsuit against Jusung Engineering for its patent violations in Korea and another lawsuit in a Taiwanese court for provisional disposition. These legal actions ordered a sudden halt in all of Jusung Engineering's commercial activities in the emerging LCD machine market in Taiwan. Yearlong litigations took place, with the company eventually being cleared of all charges. Despite these advancements, Jusung Engineering gained a negative image as a "patent robber" in the Taiwanese market.

If SMEs are entangled in IPR lawsuits, then the litigation usually hurts these firms in many ways and not only in terms of sales. Prohibitive patent license fees and marketing channels can be lost during the extended lawsuit period. Given these difficulties, most SMEs are highly concerned with patent lawsuits, especially during the stage when they are starting to develop a new technology. A survey of Korean SMEs in the semiconductor equipment sector found that while the localization of intermediate materials and goods is not difficult (the feasibility of which they estimated as "very high"

---

[41]   These SME cases are taken from Kim and Lee (2009).

[40.9%] and "high" [59.1%]), they regarded "IPR-related legal disputes" (64.3%) as the biggest obstacle to localization.[42]

Since the 1980s, the patent lawsuits filed by US firms have caused enormous losses or fees for rising Japanese firms. Through these experiences, the CEOs of Japanese firms have learned the importance of IPRs. In the same fashion, the extent to which litigation filed by Japanese firms that export products coincides with that of Korean firms has dramatically increased.[43] For instance, in 2004, Japanese firms filed lawsuits against Samsung SDI, Samsung Electronics, LG Electronics (April), Kiryung Electronics (May), Daewoo Electronics (September), LG Electronics in Korea (November), Nanya Technology (February), AUO (July), and E&E in Taiwan (July). Japan has strengthened its IPR protection after revising its Custom Tariff Law in 2003 to enable the government to request from the Customs Office the suspension of the importation of products after the patent or rights of Japanese firms have been violated. Once requiring a request from the Industrial Property Office, Japanese authorities can now investigate the imported product themselves and, if found to infringe on patent rights, it is banned immediately. This measure is definitely a strong one, and only upon the domestic firms' request can a custom clearance be retained. In general, technologically advanced countries have strengthened their IPR protection policies and rules, which has emerged as one of the important challenges that need to be addressed by catching-up firms.

An implication of these incidents is that the possibly negative impact of the levels of IPR protection in the North may be greater for rapidly catching-up developing countries than for low-income countries with very low technological capabilities, weak export performance, or exports that are arranged by inter-firm trade in the form of contract manufacturing and FDIs. Such reasoning has been verified by the extensive econometric analysis in Shin et al. (2015), who found

---

[42]   A survey conducted by the Center for Corporate Competitiveness of Seoul National University in 2004 (Kim, 2006).
[43]   This information is also from Kim and Lee (2009).

that as the IPR level of an importing country increases, the net marginal effect of technology on exports decreases, especially in the case of exports by those countries in which technological levels are currently catching up. This finding implies that the strong IPR protection in the North acts as an obstacle to exporting from the South, in which countries are currently catching up in terms of their level of technology. In this sense, IPR protection is identified as a source of MIT.

The barriers against catch-up by the latecomer often take forms other than IPR disputes. Incumbent firms often charge dumping prices to crowd out new and late-entrant firms. The case of the industrial robot with a six-axis vertical multi articulation structure that was accused of antidumping by the Korean Trade Commission in April 2005 is a typical example.[44] Up to 2000, Korean firms, including Hyundai Heavy Industry, have occupied over half of the country's domestic market share, whereas world-class robot manufacturers, such as Najji, Kawasaki, Yaskawa, and Hwanak, accounted for 53.3% of the Korean market share in 2004. These incumbent firms sold their products to Hyundai Motors, Kia Motors, and GM Daewoo, and then staged a price war to drive out the Hyundai Heavy Industry by supplying their products at dumping prices from 2003. As a result, the market share of domestic robots sharply dropped to as low as 30%. Numerous similar cases have been observed, such as the dumping of prices by the incumbent firms upon receiving news of the entry of local producers into markets that they had formerly monopolized. The cases filed by Korean enterprises along with the Korean Trade Commission since 1988 also reveal the tendency of dumping by foreign firms.[45]

The IPR disputes and predatory pricing imposed by incumbent firms against latecomer firms tend to be particularly serious and frequent in the capital or intermediate goods industries, as shown in the aforementioned examples. Meanwhile, the recently proposed growth theory focuses on the role of the intermediate goods industry

---

[44]   These cases are also from Kim and Lee (2009).
[45]   See Table 2 and Appendix in Kim and Lee (2009).

in understanding economic growth and technological development (Rodríquez–Clare, 1996; Rodrik, 1996). This theory indicates a strong mutual dependence between the final and intermediate goods industries; therefore, the different degrees of development of the intermediate goods industry may give birth to multiple equilibria in the growth path, thereby causing either a vicious or benign cycle.

In the benign cycle, the higher the expertise and diversity induced by the development of the intermediate goods industry, the more productive the final goods industry becomes. In turn, this cycle yields higher returns, increases the demand for intermediate goods, and improves the expertise and diversity of the intermediate goods industry. A repetition of this cycle results in continual growth and high-technology equilibrium. By contrast, if the initial condition is not satisfied or if a structure in industry linkage is not established over some critical point, then a low-technology equilibrium or underdevelopment may be observed. Rodrik (1996) showed that if middle-income countries fail to harmonize the different decisions of enterprises and successfully develop their intermediate goods industry, then they may become stuck in the low-technology equilibrium. Given that the goods from high-technology sectors are often highly priced, high-technology equilibrium is not only Pareto-superior to low-technology equilibrium but is also more desirable in terms of social welfare by providing wages that are higher than those provided in low-technology states (Rodrik, 1996).

2.5 NEED TO TAKE A DETOUR AND TRY A NEW PATH OR LEAPFROGGING

The upward transition from middle- to high-income status is possible but rarely achieved. The transition path is very narrow, because innovation capabilities are not easy to develop and because the IPR protection by incumbent economies and firms makes this passage even narrower. Thus, the fundamental solution to avoid IPR disputes is not to follow the same technological trajectory of the incumbent but to create a new path, take a detour, or try leapfrogging.

Another and possibly more important reason to try a new path is the possible decrease of the so-called catch-up effect as the latecomers get close to the frontier. At the earlier stage of development, many immediate benefits can be obtained by learning from and copying the practices of forerunning economies, as suggested by Lin's theory of latent comparative advantages (Lin, 2012). However, these low-hanging fruits may be depleted, and some economies may need to reach high-hanging fruits with much effort or less marginal benefits. Eventually, an economy may need to grow its own fruits, and growing fruits that taste differently from those grown by others may be even better because in such a way, an economy does not have to compete directly with others.

The foregoing discussion leads to the "catch-up paradox" introduced in the preceding chapter. This paradox states that "you cannot catch up if you just keep catching-up," where the former "catch up" means closing the gap between you and your targets, while the latter "catch up" means imitating your targets. This idea makes sense because if the latecomer keeps following the same path taken by their forerunners, then the latecomer cannot easily catch up or over-take them. In other words, the inferior cannot beat the superior if the former fights using the same weapon or strategies. In the old fable, David was able to beat Goliath by using a different weapon instead of engaging in physical contact. Another analogy can be made by refer-ring to Xenon's paradox, which was introduced in the preceding chap-ter. This paradox explains how Achilles cannot overtake a turtle in a marathon by referring to the gradual exhaustion of the catch-up effect, which is observed as the latecomer gets closer to the target. Therefore, the latecomer must find an alternative path to free itself from the exhaustion of the catch-up effect.

The latecomer may also try taking a shortcut. However, this shortcut may become crowded when it becomes known to everybody, thereby jamming the latecomer in the road and preventing them from reaching the goal. This phenomenon is similar to the so-called adding-up problem, in which latecomer economies all try to export the same or similar products, thereby flooding the market and ending up with record-low prices. As an alternative, these economies may take detours that may be longer yet less crowded than the main path, thereby allowing them to move fast if they have innovation capabilities.

This discussion has suggested that one of the most fundamental questions in the economics of catch-up is whether a latecomer must traverse the same path, probably at a faster speed, taken by their forerunners or whether they must create a new path or take a detour. Traditional or early studies observe that latecomers attempt to catch up with advanced countries by assimilating and adapting to the more-or-less obsolete technology of the incumbents.[46] By contrast, Lee's studies suggested that latecomers do not simply follow the advanced countries' path of technological development; rather, they skip certain stages or create their own paths that differ from those taken by the forerunners.[47] This argument has been verified by the experiences of several sectors in Korea in Lee's studies. For instance, Korean television makers began to manufacture digital televisions instead of following the Japanese incumbent that manufactures high-definition televisions adopting analogue technologies.

With regard to whether a latecomer firm catches up with a forerunning firm in its market shares by using technologies that are similar to or different from those of the latter, another study used patent citation data to investigate the catch-up of Huawei in China with Ericsson in Sweden. The research found that Huawei relied on Ericsson as a knowledge source in its early days but subsequently reduced such reliance and increased its self-citation ratio to become more independent.[48] The investigation of mutual citations (direct dependence), common citations (indirect reliance), and self-citations strongly indicates that Huawei has caught up with or overtaken

---

[46] Examples of the traditional or early studies include Lall (2000), Kim (1980), and Hobday (1995).

[47] Lee and Lim (2001) discuss the path of creating and leapfrogging, while the case of Korean leapfrogging into digital TV ahead of Japan is discussed in Lee et al. (2015).

[48] The study of this leading IT company from China was done in Oh et al. (2016).

Ericsson by taking a different path. Moreover, unlike Ericsson, Huawei developed its technologies by relying on recent technologies, which resulted in a patent folio with short citation lags (which means that its technologies have a short cycle). Huawei also relied heavily on scientific knowledge (so-called non-patent literature), which is a public good that is free from IPR disputes with the incumbents. The citations to non-patent literature and the patent folio with short citation lags all imply that Huawei has extensively explored basic research and maintained up-to-date technologies to accomplish a technological catch-up, thereby avoiding another patent dispute with incumbent firms. In 2011, Huawei faced a big patent dispute with Cisco, a US high-tech firm, and since then has had to turn away from the US market to focus on the markets in emerging economies or Europe.

Overall, the examination of successful catch-ups (or overtaking cases) in East Asia suggests that exploring a technological path that differs from that taken by forerunners presents a possible and viable catch-up strategy for latecomers and, in this sense, a "necessary" condition for overtaking. However, this strategy is not a sufficient condition as it involves a higher amount of risk (than going along a straight yet probably jammed road) and may end up in failure or accidents along the road. Moreover, Huawei's case reconfirms the hypothesis that a catch-up in technological capabilities tends to precede a catch-up in market shares, which has been verified in the case of Samsung versus Sony on consumer electronics as investigated by another study.[49] Huawei (Samsung) initially overtook Ericsson (Sony) in terms of both the quantity and quality of its previous patents and only later in terms of annual sales. These results suggest that the latecomers' ability to overtake and catch up with the incumbents is not attributed merely to their cost advantage but also to their technological strength and independence.

---

[49]   See Joo and Lee (2010) for Samsung vs. Sony.

The next chapter discusses the issue of taking detours in building innovation capabilities. This discussion involves several dimensions, of which one refers to the reliance on petit patents (utility models) rather than on regular invention patents as a means to protect and simulate technological learning and innovation at the transition stage. The other dimension involves sectoral specialization, where the latecomers do not try to construct the same or similar industrial structure. Instead, they attempt to be different by seeking niche sectors with low entry barriers and by entering different sectors, such as short-cycle technology-based sectors and those that are firmly dominated by incumbent economies such as long-cycle technology-based sectors or segments.

3 The Three Detours and Capability-Building

3.1 INTRODUCTION

The preceding section proposed that the advanced economies and latecomer economies have different economic growth mechanisms and that a very "narrow passage" exists between these countries. The narrowness of this passage can be attributed to the presence of two failures (capability and size failures) and one barrier (IPR protection by the incumbent North). This chapter discusses how these two failures and one barrier can be addressed for latecomer economies to realize a transition from middle- to high-income status.

The first step is to correct capability failure by providing latecomers with learning opportunities in order for them to enhance their innovation capabilities. The next section proposes several ways in which latecomer firms can obtain learning opportunities and cultivate their innovation capabilities. However, from the Schumpeterian perspective, cultivating firm-level capabilities does not only involve the firms but also the sectors and NIS surrounding them. In other words, learning and capability-building by domestic firms must be complemented by three elements. The first element is the designing of working innovation system that comprises various actors that affect the innovation and production of domestic firms (e.g., suppliers, users and consumers, universities, public research laboratories, and government agencies). The second element is the presence of specific institutional settings (e.g., financial systems, education systems, norms, regulations, and standards). The third element is made up of the links and interactions among the actors that compose the system.

When there is a mismatch among the components of the NIS, capability-building becomes a more time-consuming and costly activity that may even result in failure. Therefore, firms must consider a diverse level of innovation capabilities, such as imitation, adaptation, or minor innovations (often represented by petit patents) versus creative or radical innovations (often represented by regular patents). Given that not all technologies and related sectors are the same in terms of their learning and catching-up possibilities, strategic thinking is required when setting priorities and sequencing over diverse technologies and sectors. The same can be said with regard to the degrees and modes of participation in GVCs.

Considering the above arguments, Sections 3, 4, and 5 of this chapter discuss the three detours that can help latecomers effectively and promptly build their innovation capabilities as well as catch up with their forerunners. The first detour involves promoting imitative innovations and diffusion in the form of petit patents and trademarks under loose IPR regimes instead of providing a higher level of IPR protection. The second detour involves specializing in short-cycle technology-based sectors/segments (with low entry barriers) instead of long-cycle ones (with high entry barriers) that serve as hallmarks of advanced economies. The third detour involves promoting domestic value-added (DVA) and reducing the reliance of economies on GVCs instead of merely trying to increase the level of their GVC participation.

These detours are necessary because technological catch-up (closing the technological gap) does not only involve learning and building capabilities but also finding niches and room for specialization along strategic priorities and sequences. Such a strategy is necessary because the latecomers are faced with several sources of failures and barriers when looking for entry points into the already-established international division of labor. The goals of effective specialization and seeking niches are consistent with those of technological diversification because repeated entries into new technological areas will result in diversification. In other words, no diversification can be achieved without a series of successful specializing in a few sectors.

A starting point for a latecomer firm to build innovation capabilities is to establish its own in-house R&D center. Independent R&D efforts are required because foreign firms become increasingly reluctant to grant technology licenses to the rising latecomer firms, especially when the latter attempts to enter the higher value-added or profitability markets that are dominated by advanced countries. Thus, investing in R&D is required not only for the further absorption of advanced technologies but also for the development of the latecomers' technological capabilities. Developing in-house R&D capabilities is crucial for a firm to engage in product differentiation, produce high-end goods, and afford the higher wage rates that prevail at the upper middle-income stage; meanwhile, the continuous production of low-end goods alone cannot sustain the price competitiveness of a firm, thereby placing this firm in MIT.

By establishing in-house R&D laboratories, firms may explore diverse channels of learning and access foreign knowledge beyond simple licensing. Accessing foreign knowledge and trying new modes of learning are crucial because isolated in-house R&D efforts are often insufficient in building indigenous R&D capabilities. A diverse set of alternative modes of learning is available, including co-development with foreign R&D specialist firms and/or public R&D institutes, mastering the existing literature, establishing overseas R&D outposts, and initiating international mergers and acquisitions (M&As). For example, since the early 1990s, a small number of Korean firms began to establish overseas R&D posts to obtain easy and fast access to foreign technologies that cannot be easily acquired through licensing.

These diverse channels of learning are explained in the following section.

3.2 SEVERAL WAYS TO CULTIVATE TECHNOLOGICAL CAPABILITIES[1]

Forming and Participating in a Public–Private R&D Consortium[2]

Forming and participating in a public–private R&D consortium can be an effective mode of learning for private firms with low R&D capabilities. In their early stage, these firms cannot take the lead in the consortium, in which public research agencies play the key R&D roles and teach and transfer their outcomes to the participating private firms. We can find many examples of this case in Korea, Taiwan, and other catching-up countries.

A noteworthy example is the government-led R&D consortia in the telecommunications equipment industry, specifically the accompanying local development of telephone switches. Such development resulted in the successful localization of telephone switches in the 1980s and 1990s in several latecomer countries, including China, Korea, India, and Brazil. Most developing countries used to face serious telephone service bottlenecks in the 1970s and 1980s; they had neither their own telecommunication manufacturing equipment industry nor their own R&D program. As a result, they imported expensive equipment and related technologies, and local technicians merely installed foreign switching systems into their domestic telephone networks. Given the rapid development of industrial and commercial bases along with population growth, a number of countries decided to build their manufacturing capabilities.

Starting with Brazil in the 1970s, followed by Korea and India in the mid-1980s, and trailed by China toward the late 1980s, all of these

---

[1] This section relies heavily on the author's chapter (Lee 2016a) in an edited volume of Foxley and Stallings (2016), as well as Chapter 7 of Lee (2013a: 7.4), which in turn relies on the findings of Lee, Mani, and Mu (2012), Mu and Lee (2005), Lee and Mathews (2012), and Mathews (2002b) for the cases of Taiwan.

[2] This section relies heavily on Lee, Mani, and Mu (2012) and Mu and Lee (2005) for the case of China, and Mathews (2002b) for the cases of Taiwan.

countries crafted a state-led system of innovation in the telecommunications equipment industry with a government research institute placed at the core. This research institute developed more or less "indigenous" digital telephone switches that were then licensed to public and private domestic enterprises. In these countries, a common pattern in the indigenous development of digital switches was the tripartite R&D consortium among government research institutes in charge of R&D functions, state-owned enterprises (SOEs) or the ministry in charge of financing and coordination, and private companies in charge of manufacturing at the initial or later stages. However, the subsequent waves of industry privatization and market liberalization in Brazil and India, as compared to the infant industry protection in Korea and China, differentiated the trajectory of the industries in these four countries. At one extreme, the indigenous manufacturers in China and Korea took over the roles of importers and MNCs. Their enhanced capabilities in wired telecommunication, which had accumulated over the previous decades, also led to the growth of indigenous capabilities in wireless telecommunication. At the other extreme, Brazil and India have increasingly become net importers of telecommunications equipment, and their industries are now dominated by affiliates of MNCs.

Similar cases from Taiwan include upgrading transition from producing calculators to laptops as studied by Professor Mathews.[3] Given that it was too big a jump to be borne by the SMEs, the public–private R&D consortium led by the Industrial Technology Research Institute developed the architecture for laptop computers from 1990 to 1991. This consortium proposed a common mechanical architecture for a prototype that could easily translate into a series of mass-produced standardized components. The consortium represented an industry watershed and, even after some failed attempts, this consortium successfully established new "fast follower" industries in Taiwan.

---

[3]   See Mathews (2002b) for the cases of Taiwan.

Co-Development Contracts with Foreign/R&D Specialist Agencies or Firms

The case of Hyundai Motors in Korea presents an excellent example of the co-development mode.[4] Originally focused on the construction industry, Hyundai entered the automobile industry in the early 1970s as an assembly maker for Ford, a car manufacturer in the United States. Such entry as an assembly maker is commonly observed in developing countries. However, Hyundai Motors and Korea's status as a stronghold of the automobile industry would not have been possible without the company's brave decision to cut its ties with Ford and sell its own brand of automobiles. For this, Hyundai then entered a joint venture (JV) with the Japanese car maker, Mitsubishi, where the latter provided engines and other key components while the former merely assembled these parts. In this JV, Hyundai acted as a licensed producer but not as an OEM producer because this firm used its own brand in the local and export markets. However, when Hyundai decided to develop its own engines, Mitsubishi (which held 20% of the equity) refused to teach the former how to design and produce these engines on its own. Most businesspeople from developing countries would have given up at that point, but Hyundai's founding chairman, Chung Ju-yung, was steadfast in his ambition and decided to spend an enormous amount of money on R&D focused on engine development. Fortunately, Hyundai gained access to the external knowledge of specialized R&D firms, such as Ricardo in England. This process of joint R&D was difficult was a long story; not only did Ricardo provide Hyundai with an engine design, but these two companies also co-developed a completely new design. In fact, these firms had to try more than 1,000 prototypes until they finally launched the project seven years later in 1984. Ricardo is currently working with the Chinese automaker, Geely, in a similar mode of cooperation.

---

[4]   For details on the history of Hyundai Motors, see Lee and Lim (2001).

Promoting Indigenous Firms by Learning from FDI Firms:
The Chinese Way[5]

After realizing the attractiveness of China's market size and bargaining power, the Chinese government has actively approached multi national suppliers to engage in technology transfer and JV negotiations by adopting the purposeful strategy of "trading the (domestic) market for (foreign) technology." Although not entirely successful, this strategy worked and contributed to technological catch-up in some cases, an excellent example of which would be the telecommunications equipment industry. China took advantage of its large market size to pressure its foreign partners to transfer their core technologies. Shanghai Bell and other JV establishments fostered the diffusion of technological know-how on digital telephone switches across the country. Thus, indigenous manufacturers emerged and began to compete directly with JVs in the mid-1990s, initially in rural markets and subsequently in urban markets. Although a similar diffusion of knowledge also occurred in other Southeast Asian countries, China was more successful in transforming diffusion into the promotion of indigenous companies. China achieved a stage-skipping catch-up, a variation of leapfrogging, in the telecommunications sector. Given its limited experience in developing and producing electromechanical switches, China skipped the development and production of analogue electronic switches and jumped directly to the production of digital automatic switches. Similar phenomena can be observed in other sectors. Chinese authorities regard JV as a channel through which they can learn a specific technology. Thus, even after the country's accession to the WTO, the Chinese government has made no commitment to lift its restrictions on the maximum percentages of foreign shares (which are usually 50% for the automobile sector) in JVs in key industries, including the automobile, telecommunications, and banking sectors. This continuing restriction on foreign shares sharply contrasts with the market opening phenomenon in China as exemplified

---

[5]   This section relies heavily on Mu and Lee (2005).

by its reduction of tariffs to approximately 10%, which is lower than the average tariffs in most developing countries.

Promotion of Academy-Run Enterprises in Forward Engineering

China has successfully reared a number of national champion firms in high-technology sectors by exploiting their own scientific knowledge base as exemplified by the cases of Lenovo, Founder, Tsinghua Tongfang, and Dongruan. These firms have all been established by and affiliated with academic institutions. These academy-run enterprises are widespread in China. Although their share in the national economy is not that big, these enterprises are considered important in key high-tech regions, such as Beijing and Shanghai. "Forward engineering" refers to the direct involvement of academic institutions in industrial business.[6] Meanwhile, in "reverse engineering," the latecomer firms acquire technological principles by conducting autopsies on final (typically imported) products. Reverse engineering is a *bottom-up* mode of technological development, while forward engineering is a *top-down* mode of development in which the creators (academic institutions) that already possess scientific knowledge further process nascent knowledge until such knowledge can be applied for commercial use. Forward engineering is an inherently Chinese characteristic that differentiates China from other East Asian economies. Taiwan and Korea have rarely exploited their academic institutions for technological development, with academia mainly supplying engineers to local firms. By contrast, Chinese universities and research institutes, such as those under the banner of the Chinese Academy of Sciences, have played an active role in commercializing new technologies based on the outcomes of their research projects.

Acquisition of Foreign Technologies and Brands by M&As[7]

Until the 1990s, the outward FDIs of China were highly regulated compared with those of other major FDI source countries. However,

---

[6]   Eun et al. (2006).

[7]   This part relies on Lee et al (2011), which discusses the Chinese model of catch-up.

the 16th Congress of the Chinese Communist Party in 2003 introduced a significant shift in its policy after the Premier announced
a new strategy for encouraging Chinese companies to "go global" by
investing overseas. This policy change reflected the desire of the
Chinese government to acquire foreign technologies and brands, as
can be seen from the many M&As that targeted foreign companies in
the manufacturing sector. This strategy can reduce the time for catch-
up given the amount of time and effort required for building original
brands and technologies. A well-known case is Lenovo's purchase of
the PC division of IBM in 2004 and TCL's acquisition of a European
company (Schneider) for electricity technology. The decision of BOE,
a Chinese cathode ray tube maker, to acquire the TFT-LCD division
(HYDIS) of Hynix in Korea was encouraged by technology rather than
brand. Similar cases of targeting foreign technologies include Geely's
acquisition of Volvo, D'rong's acquisition of a German passenger air-
plane maker (Fairchild–Dornier), and Shanghai Automobile's acquisition of a Korean automaker (SsangYong).

3.3   DETOUR ONE: FROM IMITATIVE TO INNOVATION

A large volume of literature on the relationship between IPR protection and economic growth tends to represent the former using the
degree of protection of patent rights. From the catch-up perspective,
this practice entails two problems. The first problem is whether or not
patents are the most appropriate measures of innovation for latecomer
developing economies, where the capability of firms is too weak to
generate innovations, and thus firms often tend to produce minor,
adaptive, or non-patentable innovations. The second problem is
whether or not the provision of stronger IPR protection (including
patent protection) can lead to more innovation, especially in developing economies where firms usually do not have pre-existing innovation capabilities, which is referred to as a capability failure in this
book. This section discusses the detour of providing a lower level of
IPR protection to encourage minor innovations in the form of petit
patents or trademarks during the transition stages. This is done

because a higher IPR protection cannot stimulate innovation under the condition of capability failure. The nature of this detour is that one must learn and build its capabilities first before receiving monetary incentives for correcting market failures.

The Detour of Promoting Petit Patents Instead of Regular Invention Patents

Given the two problems raised above, previous studies have generated divided findings on the direct impact of patent rights on output growth in developing countries, with some researchers finding significant effects while others do not. Most of these studies do not examine alternative means of protecting IPRs and their possibly different impacts on countries at different stages. The effectiveness of patents for appropriating returns to innovation in developing countries also warrants further research.

A well-known study based on a survey of US firms shows that these firms apply patents for various purposes other than as mechanisms for appropriating returns.[8] For example, the possession of patent rights plays an important role in litigation (to deter threats of infringement suits or countersuits) and in cross-licensing negotiations where firms can access the technologies of their rivals if they are able to reciprocate their own patent rights. However, this survey finds that smaller firms or inventors are less able to utilize patents for such purposes and hence are dissuaded from availing patent protection. Litigation costs are especially onerous for small firms with low levels of output over which they spread the overhead costs of legal protection (e.g., legal staff). Furthermore, small firms or inventors have few and perhaps less valuable technologies to offer in cross-licensing negotiations. Many developing economies do not engage intensively in producing patentable innovations. This is because patents are not very effective in appropriating returns from and stimulating innovation in developing countries. Further, in some cases, strong and broad patents

---

[8]   The survey was reported in Cohen et al. (2000).

may impede the development of indigenous innovation capabilities by creating entry barriers.

Thus, in developing countries, utility models (often called petit patents) may serve as useful alternative outlets for emerging innovation. Both patents and utility models are exclusive rights granted for an invention that allow the rights holder to prevent others from commercially using the protected invention without authorization for a limited period. However, utility models and patents protect different types of innovations for various durations.

Patents protect innovations of relatively high inventiveness, while utility models protect those of relatively low inventiveness. Patents are granted for inventions that are novel, non-obvious, and have industrial applicability. They are typically effective for 20 years beginning from the date of application, cover several products and processes, undergo substantive examination, and are costly to obtain (filing fees, attorney costs, and translation fees where applicable). By contrast, utility models offer second-tier protection for minor inventions exhibiting a practical or functional advantage over existing ones.[9] The processes or methods of production are typically excluded from these models, the protection of which typically lasts for six to 10 years. Applying for utility models is generally less expensive than applying for patents and does not require substantive examination (for novelty, non-obviousness, and industrial applicability). The inventiveness threshold of utility models is much lower than that of patents, and utility models are thus usually sought for small, marginal innovations that may not meet the patentability criteria.[10]

---

[9]   Examples of cases that are not patentable yet qualified for petit patents include an improved device that is capable of reducing the amount of water used to flush a toilet or a bottle cork remover that can operate faster than known devices. See Bently and Sherman (2001) and Beneito (2006) for additional information.

[10]   Utility models are granted to devices embodying a creative idea that is applicable to the shape, structure, or other technological aspects of a product. Examples include an improved device capable of reducing the amount of water used to flush a toilet or a bottle cork remover that can operate faster than known devices. These devices are not patentable yet inventive enough to receive protection from utility models.

Not all countries that provide patent rights, especially those with an Anglo-Saxon legal tradition such as the United States and the United Kingdom, also provide utility models. The developed countries that protect utility models include Germany and some European countries following the tradition of a continental legal system. This observation is not surprising because utility models have originated from Germany, a former latecomer economy that attempted to catch up with the United Kingdom. Given their origin, utility models have been sought as a device for catch-up, and Japan quickly adopted this system by trying to learn from and catch up with Germany. Thus, the countries being protected by utility models are mostly former or current developing economies, such as Korea, Taiwan, and China, that adopted the continental European-style legal systems India, following the British legal tradition, did not adopt the utility model system. Utility models were thus the dominant form of IPRs in these countries in certain years (e.g., 1970s and the 1980s in Korea and from 1990 to the early 2000s in China).[11]

Korea is among those developing countries that intensively exploit utility models.[12] In 1961, the Korean government revised its intellectual property laws and established its first autonomous IPR system, which protects both conventional and minor innovations. Given that the technological capabilities of Korean firms lagged during the 1960s and 1970s, they relied heavily on imported technologies and reverse engineering, and then adapted these technologies to satisfy local needs. This practice enabled these firms to learn from foreign technologies. Accordingly, Korean inventors actively filed for utility model protection for their incremental innovations; the number of utility model applications exceeded that of invention patents until the early 1990s. Consequentially, the ratio of utility models to patents reached nearly 2:3 in the 1970s and early 1980s. This ratio

---

[11]   Utility models and patents accounted for nearly two-thirds and 10% of the total IPRs granted in China from 1985 to 1998, respectively. Even though the share of utility models in the total number of IPRs in China has declined, these models still account for about half of these IPRs in the 2000s.

[12]   This discussion relies heavily on the findings of Lee et al. (2003) and Lee and Kim (2010).

began to decline after peaking at over 6 in 1984. Although patent and utility model applications continue to increase, their composition has shifted radically.

Since the mid-1980s, Korea has had its own valuable patentable assets to protect, while foreign companies have such assets that they want to protect within Korea. Major IPR reforms were legislated in the mid-1980s, and both the strength and scope of patent protection within Korea has increased since 1987. Substance patents for pharmaceutical and chemical materials and products were introduced along with protection for computer software and materials. The term of patent protection was also extended from 12 years to 15 years. By 1995, the number of patent applications exceeded that of utility model applications. These trends correspond to the transformation of Korea from a nation doing imitations to one doing innovations.

The above case of Korea is consistent with the view that different forms of IPRs have varying effects on different stages of economic development. More importantly, it shows that petit patents can serve as a transition variable for latecomers to increase their innovation capabilities during the intermediate stage and to generate higher-level patentable innovations at the later stage. This process creates a "detour" in the sense that the latecomer economies do not directly replicate the practices of advanced economies but take a different road before heading toward the same direction. Therefore, patent protection matters to industrial activities only after these countries reach a threshold level of indigenous innovative capacity as well as an extensive science and technology infrastructure.

Some researchers argue that utility models helped eventually to initiate a patenting and innovation culture in East Asia, and a World Bank study also reports that utility models allowed domestic producers in Brazil to adapt foreign innovations to their local needs and conditions.[13] Thailand also witnessed a surge in its petit patent applications after introducing this system in 1999. Formal econometric

---

[13]   See Kumar (2002) and World Bank (2002).

evidence is also available at both the country and global levels.[14] A study of Japan reveals that, on balance, the adoption and promotion of utility models positively affected the increase in Japan's total factor productivity. A study using world data shows that patent protection contributes to innovation and economic growth in developed countries but not in developing ones, while utility model protection allows developing economies to build up their indigenous innovative capacities. In our firm-level analysis of Korean firms, we find that when firms are technologically lagging, utility models (or minor inventions) contribute to the growth of firms and to their capacity to produce (future) patentable inventions. After firms become technologically advanced, their performance is driven less by utility model innovations and more by patentable innovations. These results indicate that specific types of IPRs are more appropriate for countries at different stages of their economic development.

The Detour of Promoting Trademarks Instead of Regular Invention Patents

The preceding discussion shows that a latecomer economy may try to enhance its innovation capabilities (measured by patents) by promoting minor forms of IPRs, such as petit patents in early stage. However, one may wonder whether an alternative path of technological development exists, such as those that involve trademarks. Trademarks have been recently recognized as proxy measures of innovation that complement or substitute patents. While both patents and utility models deal with technological or scientific invention or improvement, trademarks are more of a market-based than a technology-based IPR. Registering trademarks is a brand strategy, as the name itself indicates the value of a product. A trademark encourages firms to make high-quality products and adhere to a consistent level of quality. Thus, a product that is made using tacit knowledge can be

---

14   The Japanese study can be found in Maskus and McDaniel (1999), while global and Korean evidence can be found in the widely cited work of Kim et al. (2012).

protected and distinguished from those of competitors in the market and can establish its market power by registering a trademark.

Using Korean data, our work suggests the possible existence of a trademark-based path of technological development.[15] We find that trademarks have become the dominant form of IPRs in some sectors, such as food, apparel, and pharmaceuticals. Trademark registrations has also outnumbered patent registrations from the initial stage of development. By contrast, other sectors, such as electronics and automobiles, considered patents as their dominant form of IPRs during the 1990s and into the 2000s. In this case, we must explain the differences in the number of registered trademarks and patents across all sectors.

Although trademarks may represent innovations, they can be filed even without formal R&D activities that target technological advances. Thus, one may hypothesize that those sectors relying more on trademarks than patents may be lagging in terms of technological advances and are thus more oriented toward domestic than international markets. Patents also tend to reflect codifiable or explicit knowledge more than does tacit knowledge. Therefore, trademark-dominant sectors correspond to those sectors that employ tacit rather than codifiable knowledge.

When examining the dynamic patterns of patent- and trademark-dominant groups across several periods, we find two stylized facts that require explanation. First, at the beginning of Korea's industrial development, trademarks were the main form of IPRs in almost all sectors, as typical manufacturing firms registered trademarks more often than did other IPRs until the 1980s. This finding is consistent with the fact that until the late 1980s, the in-house R&Ds of firms were very low or just starting, and thus these firms had no technological innovations for which to file patents. Second, the division of these groups appeared only after a certain level of technological development was achieved in the mid-1990s. Even after this period, the firms in the trademark group continued to register trademarks more

---

[15]   What follows is based on our joint work with Dr. R. Kang as shown in Kang et al. (2017).

than patents. However, this trend does not necessarily mean that the firms in this group do not engage in any R&D, but it may reflect the fact that R&D outcomes may not be patentable as they involve tacit knowledge that reflects the knowledge base of the sectors. We can therefore suppose that the registrations of trademarks and patents are related to different sectoral knowledge bases and the different levels of technological capabilities of firms from various sectors.

One interesting case is the pharmaceutical industry, which relies more on explicit (codifiable) knowledge rather than tacit knowledge yet belongs to the trademark group as shown in the Korean IPR data. The case of the pharmaceutical industry can be explained in terms of the slow or lagging development of its technological capabilities and its domestic market orientation, which differs from that of the IT sector given its strong and rapid technological advancements and export orientation. Given that the Korean pharmaceutical industry has grown through producing license-in or generic products until recently, this industry employs trademarks as its main IPR. In general, when firms have no capability to produce complex or scientific products, a trademark provides the only means to protect the products of these companies in the market. Filing more trademarks also implies that these firms are oriented toward domestic markets more than international ones.

The preceding discussion supports the trademark-driven path of latecomer firms' technological development. Such an idea is verified by some econometric analyses, which reveal that the bifurcation of sectors into trademark- and patent-dominant groups is explained by different sectoral knowledge bases (e.g., tacitness of knowledge) and by the different levels of technological capabilities of firms from different sectors.[16] The analyses also confirm that trademark-dominant groups use more tacit knowledge, are oriented toward the domestic market, and show a slow progress in their technological capabilities. These results imply that those firms facing slow

---

[16] What follows is based on our joint work with Dr. R. Kang, as shown in Kang et al. (2017).

technological progress in mostly tacit-knowledge-based sectors tend to rely on trademarks for their growth, as well as on the domestic market, rather than on export markets. These results suggest that latecomer firms from different sectors have an alternative path of economic development besides the patent-driven path that has already been discussed in the earlier part of this section.

3.4 DETOUR TWO: FROM SHORT-CYCLE TO LONG-CYCLE TECHNOLOGIES

The previous section shows that different sectors may pursue a unique road for building technological capabilities. The fact that all sectors differ from one another in terms of their innovation patterns and market structure is one of the key ideas in Schumpeterian economics, as exemplified by the concept of sectoral innovation systems. This concept implies that the patterns and possibility of technological catch-up by latecomers may also differ across sectors. This observation introduces the sectoral choice or specialization of latecomers as another important question in our search for the transition path from poor to rich nations. Sector choices are important because not all sectors are the same in terms of their entry possibility, and latecomers who are "late entrants" in the already-established international division of labor must seek suitable entry points.[17] Therefore, catch-up must be considered as a matter of learning and building capabilities as well as of finding niches and sectoral specialization for latecomers. Therefore, as firms build more or new capabilities over time, they may enter new and different sectors.

Given that many developing countries initially face labor (natural resource) abundance, they are advised to specialize in labor (resource)-intensive sectors in early stage of development; thus, capital–labor ratio is a key variable in sectoral specialization.[18] In economies that are far behind the frontiers of technological know-how and skills, that have an

[17]   Baldwin (2016: 272) briefly explained the issue of finding entry points to GVCs but did not provide a systemic answer.
[18]   See Kuznets and Murphy (1966).

abundant supply of labor, and that have a scarce amount of capital, market forces and traditions generally support labor-intensive sectors and do not require high levels of technological or business sophistication to be effective. However, successful economic development beyond the low-income level requires the development of the competences of firms and the institutions that support them.

Historical experience shows that as these capabilities continue to develop, the next stages of economic development occur as resources continue to flow into those sectors with high capital intensity and labor productivity. These sectors may require a certain amount of technological know-how, skills, and managerial sophistication. Therefore, choosing from a list of capital-intensive sectors becomes difficult. Capital–labor ratio no longer works as a criterion because of the existence of many capital-intensive sectors. Historical experience also shows that latecomers first choose those sectors in which technologies are relatively constant and mature, thereby allowing a high degree of technology transfer at a low cost.[19] For developing countries that have built up a reasonably strong capability for training labor and that have at least a cadre of reasonably sophisticated business leaders, the competitive capability of their sectors is within reach and has low entry barriers despite requiring a considerable amount of learning time and effort. Paying lower wages can also help build the competitive capability of certain countries. The fact that the technologies in these countries are usually mature or fail to change rapidly indicates that upon achieving competitive competence, the problems in keeping up with technological advances can be managed. Entering these industries can help those countries behind the frontiers to climb the economic ladder.

Higher value-added sectors then become the next targets for middle-income countries that have built up relatively high levels of capabilities. Korea and Taiwan reached this stage by the mid-1980s. However, indigenous firms directly compete with firms in countries

---

[19]   See Viner (1958) and Lin (2012a, 2012b).

that are at the technological frontiers and that have a much greater amount of experience in the field. The lower wage rates alone do not generate a competitive advantage in these sectors, and continuing competitiveness is strongly tied to the ability of firms to keep up with others even as their technologies change rapidly. Thus, finding a niche in many high value-added sectors/segments presents a challenge for catching-up economies at the upper-middle-income stage.

Choice with the Product Space Concept

Some studies propose solutions to the challenge of sector choice based on the product space concept. A group of scholars involving Hausman and Hidalgo introduced the product space concept to measure the sophistication of the trade structure of a country.[20] They divided the specialization pattern of a country into core versus peripheries based on the sophistication of its products. They proposed that a country can achieve gradual sophistication (and diversification) in its trade structure by moving into neighboring spaces or capturing low-hanging fruits. Therefore, the export structure of a country must be diversified into highly sophisticated products to achieve sustained export performance and economic growth. However, such an idea has some limitations from the perspective of developing countries.

These scholars considered the proximity among product spaces as an important variable in determining the feasibility of diversification. However, their criterion did not disclose much information about the "directions" of diversification among numerous neighboring spaces. In other words, they focused on the "distance" rather than on the "directions" of diversification. The distance-based argument of diversification fails to determine which sectors in latecomer economies must be diversified first. Furthermore, their empirical findings were based on trade data, which do not contain any information regarding the value-added of traded products or how these

---

[20]   See Hausman et al. (2007) and Hidalgo et al. (2007).

products are made. Therefore, technological (or value-added) content cannot be assessed based on such data. Although a developing country exports high-tech goods as reflected in its trade data, the most important value-added components of these goods are often produced in third-world countries, as noted by the emerging literature on GVCs.[21]

These scholars also used income level as a weighing factor to calculate the degree of sophistication of a product; in other words, those countries that produce the goods that are currently being exported by high-income countries are considered highly sophisticated. This method makes such measure somewhat tautological, that is, a country can become rich by producing goods that are currently being produced by wealthier countries. Specifically, this strategy informs latecomer countries that they must try to produce those products that are being produced by the incumbents, but do not inform them how they can compete with incumbents in the same or similar sectors. In other words, this method does not consider the ability of a country to compete in the international market. We propose that while trying to avoid direct collision with incumbent countries, latecomer countries must find a niche for themselves to survive and compete effectively in the different market.

In sum, these scholars did not propose an effective way for middle-income countries to reach the core structure. They merely argued that "countries can reach the core only by traversing empirically infrequent" (meaning long) distances or by making a long jump, which is very difficult to achieve. In addition, the researchers did not discuss how these countries could traverse the long distance to the core space, a problem that resembles leapfrogging in our terminology. In our framework, realizing a diversified entry into new sectors through leapfrogging is a critical part of the overall catch-up strategy that will be discussed in Chapter 5.

---

[21] For example, only $4 out of the $299 retail price of an Apple iPod goes to China (Linden et al., 2007). See Baldwin (2016) for an example of the GVC literature.

Choice with the Concept of the Sectoral Innovation System

Let us now turn to Schumpeterian economics to address the issue of sectoral choices and specialization, particularly for upper-middle-income countries. The Schumpeterian analysis of technological catch-up has long established a relationship between the diverse elements of the knowledge regimes of sectors and the possibility of catch-up. In general, the various elements of knowledge regimes can be grouped into two categories. The first category involves those elements related to the accessibility of a foreign knowledge base (degree of embodied technology transfer and modularity), which are highly important at the early or entry stage of technological catch-up. The second category comprises elements related to the speed of learning (tacitness of knowledge and cycle time of technologies), which are highly important at the later stage of technological catch-up. We propose that catch-up possibilities are positively linked to the degree of embodied technology transfer and modularity, and that a higher degree of knowledge tacitness tends to interfere negatively with learning possibility. The impact of the cycle time of technologies becomes dubious depending on the absorption capacity of the latecomers. Quantitative and qualitative studies that compare the technological capability of advanced and catch-up economies have used patent data to prove how the catching-up countries at the upper-middle-income stage tend to achieve high levels of technological catch-up in sectors with a short-cycle time of technologies and in those sectors that are based on not tacit but explicit knowledge.[22] We discuss these elements of knowledge and their impacts on catch-up possibility in the following paragraphs.

First, we discuss the two elements that are related to the entry possibilities or early stages of catch-up. The concept of embodied technology transfer is important for firms in developing countries with low technological capability during the early stage of

---

[22] Econometric studies include Park and Lee (2006) and Jung and Lee (2010), while case studies include Lee and Lim (2001), Lee et al. (2005), and Mu and Lee (2005).

development. After these firms import capital goods such as machinery, they become capable of acquiring the advanced technologies embodied in capital goods. Therefore, the higher the degree of embodied technology transfer in imported machinery, the easier it is for productivity to catch up. Several studies have confirmed a positive relationship between the degree of embodied technology transfer and productivity catch-up.[23] Similarly, sectors or technologies with a higher degree of modularity can easily and rapidly achieve technological catch-up by helping latecomers enter the market through outsourcing the required components. The modularity of a sector may reach high levels if the units or modules that comprise the sectors are designed independently; thus, the components become highly standardized such that they may be supplied by independent component suppliers to final assemblers or manufacturers.[24] Previous studies identify the modularization of components as the main factor that underlies the rapid growth of PC industries. In the automobile industry, each automobile component is not separated from the main body of a specific type of car. Therefore, establishing a global market for each component becomes a difficult task. By contrast, PC parts and peripherals are sold as independent commodities in different markets.

---

[23]   At a cross-country macro level, Lee (1995) and Mazumdar (2001) presented some evidence to support the claim that imported machinery leads to the higher growth of production in developing countries. By using industry-level machinery import data from input–output tables, Jung and Lee (2010) measured the degree of embodied technology transfer as the share of imported machineries and equipment in the total imports of a sector, and then confirmed positive linkages between these variables.

[24]   According to Genba et al. (2005), the modularity of a product is defined as the inverse of the independent development percentage (IDP), where IDP (e.g., PC) = (total number of patents on a PC component filed by the PC manufacturer)/(total number of patents on a PC component). For PC industries, the above formula can be computed for a specific component, such as the CPU. If fewer patents are filed by a PC assembler such as Dell or Sony and if more patents are filed by a specialized supplier of CPU, then a low IDP ratio can be obtained. This finding implies that PC manufacturing has a high modularity. IDP ratios have been calculated for other PC components, such as memory and disk drives. Decreasing IDP trends indicate a high modularity in the PC industry. A similar calculation has been done for the automobile industry to confirm its recently increasing modularity. See Baldwin and Clark (1997) and Gao and Liu (2004) for additional information.

An example of an industry with a high level of embodied technology transfer is the automobile industry, which is now increasingly modularized than before. According to the classification of Pavitt (1984), the automobile industry is a scale-intensive industry that is less science-based than the electronics industry. Automobile production involves the assembly of various components and parts where integration is crucial. Therefore, entering the automobile industry as an assembler is not difficult as long as one finds suppliers of various parts and components. In this way, numerous latecomer countries, such as Malaysia, Korea, and China, were able to enter this industry.

Well-cited examples include Chinese automobile companies that are late entrants with no prior experience in the automobile industry.[25] Two indigenous firms from China entered this industry since 2001, namely, Chery from Anhui province and Geely from Zhejiang Province. Chery started as a manufacturer of automotive parts in Anhui Province, while Geely used to be a motorcycle company. These companies differ from SOEs in such a way that they are responsible for developing cars and sell their own brands, although they rely on various ways to obtain outside help, such as joint development, R&D outsourcing, and reverse engineering. For instance, in 1997, Chery bought the used assembly line of SEAT, a Volkswagen subsidiary in Spain, and an engine factory of Ford based in England. With the imported assembly line, Chery needed to recruit engineers to run its facilities. Therefore, they recruited engineers from China and overseas countries, such as Korea.

The "modularization" element of technological regimes is important because a higher degree of modularity allows latecomer firms to circumvent the difficulty in accessing knowledge by outsourcing specific components to external producers. This case is exemplified by Chinese mobile phone and automobile companies, which have relied on outsourcing to develop their products with the help of diverse component suppliers. The indigenous automobile

---

[25]   The following discussion on the automobile and mobile phone sectors in China relies on Lee et al. (2009).

manufacturers in China have adopted a module-based production system by purchasing key components from external manufacturers. Chery primarily sourced its engines and other parts from Mitsubishi, and then outsourced the critical task of integrating key components to other companies, such as Delphi. Chery also outsourced both the production and development of its key components to other firms. Module-based production and development allowed Chery to launch several car models within a very short period and enabled the firm to compete in the market.[26] Chinese mobile phone companies share a similar story. Given their high modularity, Chinese mobile phone makers relied on core technology parts (e.g., main platform and core software) from foreign suppliers and combined them with their own peripheral technologies during their entry days in the early 2000s.[27]

While the above examples from China suggest a case of quick success upon easy entry in sectors with a high modularity and degree of embodied technologies, not all firms can achieve long-term success, thereby suggesting that the importation of capital goods must be combined with local absorption capacity and other aspects of knowledge, such as tacitness, which make the catch-up process difficult or time consuming at the later stages of development.[28] The catch-up by

[26] Chery also tapped AVL in Austria to develop engines (e.g., ACTECO engine) and delegated the task of developing the main body of cars to European and Japanese design companies, such as Pininfarina (M14), Fumia Design (S16), Giugiaro, and Sivax (B14 series). The first three companies are based in Italy. The advancement of modern CAD/CAM/CAE and virtual design technologies facilitated the prevalence of reverse engineering for latecomer companies (Gao and Liu, 2004). Reverse engineering helped small companies to simplify their design process and reduce the costs for developing new products (Luo, 2005).

[27] According to Lee et al. (2009), in 2001, the Chinese company TCL purchased modules of the main body from Wavecom, a French wireless communication solution company. The purchased modules included integrated radio frequency, intermediated frequency, and base band, all of which compose the basic hardware architecture of mobile phones. TCL added internally developed peripheral parts afterward. This system allowed TCL to control part of the phone's appearance and benefit from low production costs. However, designing mobile phones required a considerable amount of time. Before 2003, approximately half of the indigenous mobile phone manufacturers in China adopted a module-based mode of production (Zhu et al., 2006).

[28] In African countries, imported capital goods have not been highly appropriated by local firms, thereby highlighting the importance of absorption capacity as well as the

Chinese automobile makers has not been that fast similar to the early case of Hyundai, whose rise was also plagued by many serious hurdles. Led by Hyundai, Korean-made cars entered the US market after a record-breaking amount of sales in imported car markets in the mid-1980s. However, the early success of Hyundai was short lived. Given its serious quality problems and unstable A/S services for a large number of units sold within a short period, Hyundai earned a poor reputation and American consumers soon turned away from products sold by the company. Thus, the market shares of Hyundai plummeted to less than 1% in the mid-1990s. Hyundai only started to recover after the late 1990s owing to the improved quality of its products backed by its in-house R&D capacity to develop its own engines and transmission. In the mid-1990s, Hyundai was able to develop its own engines after seven or eight years of effort.

Such slowed down of catch-up process can be attributed to the fact that a large part of automobile technologies involves tacit knowledge, which cannot be codified and cannot be learned quickly. Tacit knowledge can only be observed through application, whereas its learning can be acquired through practice. Therefore, the transfer of knowledge among people, firms, or countries is slow, costly, and uncertain.[29] As more tacit knowledge becomes involved in the learning of a target, latecomer countries cannot easily catch up with their advanced counterparts, and those companies that heavily rely on tacit knowledge tend to choose secrecy rather than patenting. By contrast, if knowledge is more explicit or less tacit, then such knowledge can be easily converted into information using formulas, diagrams, numbers, or words. A knowledge with high explicitness can be codified and learned easily. Therefore, the appropriability of such knowledge is expected to decrease as the degree of its codification increases. Some studies have verified that those sectors that involve the extensive use

concept of leveraging proposed in Mathews (1996). See Lee and Lim (2001) for the case of Hyundai.

[29]   The related literature includes Saviotti (1998), Grant (1996), Spender (1996), and González–Álvarez and Nieto–Antolín (2007).

of tacit knowledge, such as machineries and tools, achieve slow technological catch-up in terms of productivity.[30]

Detour of Specializing in Short-Cycle Technologies

The cycle time of technologies is another determinant of the late entry and speed of technological catch-up. Previous studies determine the cycle time of technologies based on how fast technologies change or become obsolete over time; specifically, cycle time can be calculated as the time difference between the application year of the citing patent and that of the cited patents.[31] Therefore, this variable reflects one important attribute of knowledge that becomes obsolete over time. In this regard, some knowledge becomes obsolete quickly, while others take a longer period to become obsolete. The speed of obsolescence is expected to affect the chances of catch-up. If knowledge has a long life expectancy, then mastering the knowledge and technology in that field requires more time. However, if knowledge is short lived, then catch-up countries are not required to master old technologies.

In another book, this author has shown that qualified latecomers can achieve great advantages by targeting and specializing in sectors/segments associated with a short-cycle time; in such areas, the dominance of incumbents is often disrupted, whereas the continuous emergence of new technologies can generate new opportunities.[32] Thus, specializing in short-cycle technology-based sectors/segments represents both low entry and quick growth,

[30]   While Kogut and Zander (2003), González–Alvarez and Nieto–Antolín (2007), and Hurmelinna et al. (2007) employed survey data to measure the tacitness/explicitness of knowledge, Jung and Lee (2010) used the number of patents per unit of R&D expenditure of sectors. This decision was based on the fact that explicit knowledge can be easily patented because such knowledge can be easily described, and because those companies that mostly use explicit knowledge adopt the patenting system as their defense mechanism. By conducting a regression analysis, Jung and Lee (2010) confirmed that those sectors with a high degree of catch-up show a high degree of explicitness in terms of their knowledge and technology.

[31]   See Jaffe and Trajtenberg (2002).

[32]   This argument was introduced in Park and Lee (2006) and later described in Lee (2013a) in a broader context.

which in turn are associated with few collisions with the technologies of advanced countries (less IPR disputes), less royalty payments, first- or fast-mover advantages, or product differentiation; for example, information technologies have a shorter cycle than pharmaceuticals in the sense that the new innovations in information technology tend to rely less on the existing stock of knowledge.[33]

The advantage of specializing in short-cycle technologies is consistent with the leapfrogging concept, in which the emerging generations of technologies allow catching-up countries to have a head start. In the competition within a new techno-economic paradigm, both incumbents and latecomers start from the same starting line, and incumbents often stick to their existing technologies from which they derive their supremacy. Leapfrogging is similar to the "long jumps" mentioned by Hidalgo, who argued that economies should shift to product spaces that are located far away from their current position to achieve a structural transformation.[34]

The technological development of Korea over the last three decades reflects the increasing specialization of the country in short-cycle, less tacit, and high modularity technologies during its catch-up.[35] Korea began to specialize in labor-intensive (low value-added) industries, such as apparel or shoe industries, in the 1960s. The economy then moved to the shorter- or medium-cycle sectors of low-end consumer electronics and automobile assembly in the 1970s and 1980s, to the shorter-cycle telecommunications equipment (telephone switches) sector in the late 1980s, and to memory chips, cellphones, and digital televisions in the 1990s. In sum, Korean industries kept moving to shorter-cycle technologies to achieve technological diversification.

---

[33] For this reason, not all emerging technologies are considered short cycle because even the new products in the pharmaceuticals sector tend to rely heavily on the existing or stock knowledge depending on the nature of such innovations (i.e., disruptive or competence enhancing). Therefore, information technology is prone to disruptive innovations than to long-cycle sectors.

[34] See Hidalgo et al. (2007).   [35] See Lee (2013a: Chapter 7) for more details.

We can discuss the actual trends in the cycle time of technologies as calculated from the US patents held by selected economies, such as Korea, Taiwan, and China. For example, a value of eight as the average cycle time indicates that the average cycle time of patents is eight years (i.e., the patents held by Korea and Taiwan tend to cite eight-year-old patents on average) and that the related technologies are considered outdated or useless after eight years. Since the mid-1980s, Korea and Taiwan have shifted to technologies with increasingly short cycles. Therefore, the average cycle time of those patents held by Korea and Taiwan was shortened from eight to six or seven years by the late 1990s. This duration is two to three years shorter than the average cycle time of patents held by European G5 countries, which patents have cycle times of 9 to 10 years since the late 1980s because of their strong performance in high value-added long-cycle sectors, such as pharmaceuticals and machine tools. Consequently, the patent portfolios of Korea and Taiwan completely differ from those of advanced countries. We consider the mid-1980s as an important turning point during which Korea and Taiwan achieved a sustained catch-up beyond the middle-income stage. Both economies reached the upper middle-income level during this period, and the GDP per capita of Korea reached 25% of that of the US. Since then, Korea and Taiwan continued to increase their R&D expenditures, and their R&D/GDP ratio surpassed the 1% level. Along with upgrading their technological capabilities, these economies shifted to short-cycle technology-based sectors, such as information technology products.

From Short- to Long-Cycle Technologies: Specialization to Diversification

After achieving technological catch-up, the specialization of Korea and Taiwan needs to reach maturity or to turn to long-cycle technologies. Figure 3–1 shows the trend of the normalized values of the average cycle time of technologies calculated from the patents registered in the USA. It is shown that after average cycle times reached their bottom in the early 2000s, their technologies turned toward long cycles, such as biological or science-based technologies. China is following the similar path with about 10 years lag. Such strategy can be considered a "detour" because latecomer countries do not directly and immediately replicate the path and industries of advanced economies that specialize in long-cycle technologies, such as Germany which tend to boast much longer cycle time of technologies. Instead, those countries that successfully catch up initially moved toward sectors with short-cycle technologies and then moved toward sectors with long-cycle technologies after reaching maturity. If you specialize long-cycle technologies as in Brazil in the figure, the economy would find difficult to achieve commercial success given their high entry barriers and more competition with the advanced economies.

In other words, in contrast to Hausman et al. (2007) who suggested that a developing country should become similar to a rich country, we propose that the transition strategy of a developing country must involve entering sectors that are based on short-cycle technologies instead of those that are based on long-cycle technologies and are dominated by rich countries. However, as economies reach technological maturity and develop a high level of capabilities (as Korea did in the early 2000s), they become driven to adopt long-cycle technologies, such as bio medical or pharmaceutical industries, which is what Samsung has been trying to achieve recently.

Therefore, the prospects of a country to move beyond the middle-income stage can be judged by whether this country is experiencing a "technological turning point" to enter sectors based on short-cycle technologies along the curve of the cycle time of technologies. Figure 3–1 shows that China has passed such a turning point from the mid- to the late 1990s or approximately 10 to 15 years later than Korea. The top 30 technologies in the US patents registered by China are similar to those of Korea and Taiwan from 1980 to 1995. China holds more patents for semiconductors, information storage, telecommunications, electrical lighting, electrical heating, X-rays, and computer hardware and software. The weighted average cycle time of Chinese technologies from 2000 to 2005 was 8.07 years, which was closer to the Korean/Taiwanese average of 7.69 years from 1980 to 1995 than to the

Period Average Cycle Time of Technologies in Selected Economies.
(normalized values)

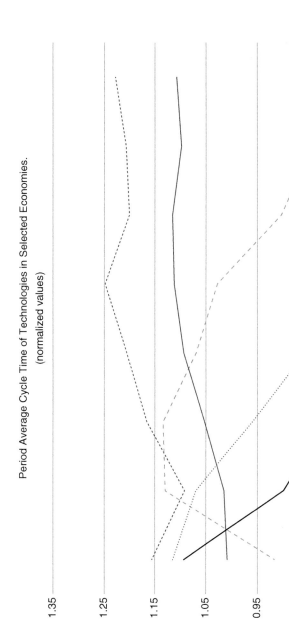
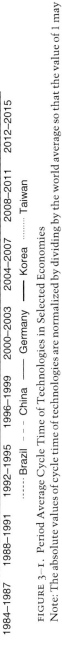

FIGURE 3–1. Period Average Cycle Time of Technologies in Selected Economies

Note: The absolute values of cycle time of technologies are normalized by dividing by the world average so that the value of 1 may be the average of the cycle time.

Source: Calculations following the method of Lee (2013a), using raw data downloaded from the USPTO Patent Grant Red Book (Full Text, 1976–2016, http://patents.reedtech.com/pgrbft.php) after data mining and cleaning.

Brazilian/Argentinean average of 9.26 years in the same period (note that Brazil and Argentina are more engaged in long-cycle technologies than in short-cycle ones).[36]

Overall, in contrast to the comparative advantages in trade (trade-based specialization) as initially determined by endowment conditions, we suggest that the dynamic comparative advantages in technology (technological specialization) are determined not by natural resource endowments but by the R&D and design capabilities that are accumulated by humans over time. This technology-based specialization complements trade-based specialization along the latent comparative advantages at the low- or lower-level middle-income stage as suggested by Lin. The latter focuses on low- or lower-level middle-income countries (e.g., China in the early 1980s) that are choosing between the right latent comparative advantage sectors and the wrong comparative advantage sectors, while the former focuses on upper-level middle-income countries (e.g., China today) that are choosing between short- (low originality) and long (high originality)-cycle technologies. In a sense, short-cycle technologies provide latecomers with a niche and ensure a certain rate of profitability as revealed in the firm-level analysis of the author as published in his early book. By contrast, directly replicating the activities of forerunning economies and focusing on highly original and long-cycle technologies may lead to a continuous reliance on advanced countries, thereby decreasing the chances for a country to consolidate indigenous knowledge bases. Latin American economies serve as examples of such specialization with very long average cycle times (longer than 10 years) in their US patent portfolios.

Increasing the specialization in short-cycle technologies results in technological diversification. As shown in their cycle time curves, Korea and Taiwan gradually shortened their cycle times since the mid-1980s. However, this gradual shortening does not indicate that these economies have specialized in a few sectors; rather, they continued to enter progressively newer sectors with shorter cycle times, which is

---

[36]   See Table 8–4 in Lee (2013a) for a list of the top 10 patent technologies. That book also contains data for the average cycle time in different countries.

essentially a process of industrial diversification into new or related fields at times of paradigm shifts or low entry barriers.

Technological diversification can be measured by the number of technological fields in which countries have registered patents from out of the 417 three-digit fields in the US patent classification system. High-income countries have registered patents in about 40% of the 417 classes in the US patent system.[37] Korea and Taiwan demonstrated an impressive catching-up performance compared with other middle-income countries; that is, they began from the same ground and eventually surpassed the average level of high-income countries by the early 1990s. This achievement is very important because many scholars consider the diversification of export structure as a necessary condition for sustained export performance and economic growth as well as an important challenge being faced by developing countries.

Given that diversification and specialization in short-cycle sectors occur simultaneously, one cannot determine which of these two is "driving" the other. However, we consider the cycle times of technologies as a policy guide variable that indicates to which direction an economy must diversify. Developing countries must diversify themselves by moving into short-cycle technology-based sectors. Our criterion is dynamic because we do not suggest that catching-up economies must target a specific or fixed list of short-cycle technologies. Instead, these economies must keep moving into shorter-cycle technologies to achieve technological diversification. Therefore, the catching-up prospect of countries can be determined by whether they experience a turning point at which they switch to short cycles along the curve of the cycle time of technologies.

Different Growth Mechanisms and Transition Path in Between

The concepts of detour and turning points are closely related to the issue of the different growth mechanisms adopted by poor and rich

---

[37]   See Figure 9.1 in Lee (2013a), drawn by the author based on NBER patent data.

nations as mentioned in the previous chapter. As previously noted, the transition of developed economies from one growth mechanism to another is a sensitive issue. To achieve such transition, these economies resort to capability-building or increase their R&D expenditure with a view to increase their R&D to GDP ratio or number of patents filed. However, this case may only represent half of the story. The issue of specialization must also be considered in the transition. Sound transition requires both capability-building and smart specialization into a niche where latecomers can find their own room (position) for survival in the international division of labor.

Thus, the results of the country-panel growth equation in Lee's book show that for four Asian economies, economic growth (per capita income growth) has a negative and significant correlation with the cycle time of technologies, and the opposite holds for typical middle-income countries.[38] This fact holds the secret for a successful transition. Fast-growing Asian economies, such as Korea and Taiwan, caught up with high-income countries by specializing in short-cycle sectors since the mid-1980s. These countries treat short-cycle sectors as their niches as shown by their high economic growth records and by the fact that having more patents in short-cycle technologies is significantly related to the profit rate of Korean firms as shown in the firm-level analysis results of Lee. By contrast, a wrong transition strategy would be to specialize in long-cycle sectors, which can be regarded as an attempt to directly replicate the knowledge base of high-income countries by specializing in high-quality and highly original technologies. Several advanced Latin American countries, such as Brazil and Argentina, have tried traversing this path because of their advanced level of scientific research. However, our analysis indicates that specializing in highly original technologies is not significantly related to economic growth. Therefore, countries on this trajectory must continue to rely on patents held by advanced economies. Countries on the high road also failed to catch up in the 1980s and 1990s.

---

[38]   Lee (2013a; Chapter 3).

Short cycles provide poor countries with opportunities to catch up with those economies when they command a certain degree of technological capability. However, frequent changes in technologies may create an additional barrier against catching up because these changes interfere with learning and lead to the truncation of the learning process. Thus, traversing the path of short-cycle technologies may not always be smooth and easy. Selecting the road of short-cycle technologies requires a certain threshold level of technological capability at the firm- and national-level institutions and policies. Such level of capabilities is only available to some upper middle-income countries. Inheriting mature industries from countries with high income levels may help build such capabilities, and this finding complements Lin's idea of latent comparative advantage. However, refusing to take risks may keep a country in MIT, while taking risks does not guarantee success. The transitional path is a necessary yet insufficient condition for eventual upgrading.

3.5 DETOUR THREE: MORE, LESS, AND MORE GVC AGAIN

The need to take a detour to realize an upward transition and a successful economic catching-up can also be discussed in relation to the dynamic patterns of an economy's participation in GVCs. Value chain refers to a series of value-creating activities that transform raw or intermediate materials into finished products. Supply chains have become global in scope, and more intermediate goods are being traded across borders. Thus, the GVC concept has become highly relevant in understanding emerging economic relations by helping establish a framework for understanding how international supply chains link economic activities within specific industries at the global, regional, national, and local levels.[39]

In his latest book, Baldwin proposed that joining a GVC will help in the industrialization of latecomer economies instead of building entire value chains in a latecomer economy. In other words,

---

[39]   See Gereffi (2014), UNCTAD (2013), and Baldwin (2011; 2016).

industrialization has become a radically less complex and faster process because the supply chain industry is less lumpy and less interconnected domestically. He attributed this idea to the fact that off-shored production brings elements (such as economy of scale) that took Korea and Taiwan several decades to develop domestically. His main point is that building an entire value chain in a latecomer economy (such as what was done by Korea) is very difficult and risky, and such activity will not provide enough economy of scale that is required to achieve cost competitiveness in each value chain due to the limited market size (as in the case of Proton in Malaysia). He observed that unlike the failed "build strategy" in Malaysia, a successful case is the "join strategy" of the automobile sector in Thailand where the Thai factories established by the Japanese firms (Toyota) only focused on the assembly and promotion of Thai component suppliers under the local contents requirements clause.[40] According to Baldwin, one of the key points for such success was the firms' focus on a particular market segment (e.g., light pickup trucks and vans) instead of trying to produce a whole range of models in order to achieve a sufficient scale economy at minimum cost for international competitiveness.

The contrast between variety and scale is not new; such difference has been initially discussed in new trade theory proposed by Krugman (1991: Geography and Trade), who pointed out the gains from trade in terms of the scale economy associated with specializing within a sector across different countries. However, a more important issue is whether a narrow specialization in a specific value segment is powerful enough to free a country from MIT. In fact, Thailand has not escaped MIT if the World Bank criterion of 20%–40% of the level of US is applied. Thailand's GDP per capita reached 20% of that of the US in the early 1990s but still has not surpassed the 30% level by 2015; recently, Thailand's GDP has been fluctuating between 27% and 28%. The same can be said for Mexico, which has a very high level of

---

[40]   See Baldwin (2016: 250–254).

participation in GVCs. The country's GDP per capita was 35% of that of the US in the early 1990s or around the time of NAFTA, but continued to decline steadily since then. Specifically, Mexico's GDP per capita stood at below 33% in 2015.

Baldwin's idea of the gains from GVCs has two problems. First, this idea focuses on the gains from cost savings rather than on rents associated with product differentiation or innovations. Second, this idea shows that latecomer firms forever remain as dependent suppliers to leading firms from high-income countries rather than become independent suppliers to multiple clients, thereby enjoying a better bargaining power in price negotiation or a bigger share in global profits. Regardless of the presence or absence of bargaining power, latecomer supplier firms under foreign-dominated GVCs are always subjected to the MNCs' shopping for lower costs either from low wages or from the devaluation of currencies. The mutual competition among latecomer firms and economies that trade the same or similar goods and services presents another problem, called the adding-up problem. The GVC clusters in emerging economies may present another enclave without much spillover or linkage to create domestic value-added in wider segments of the national economy and society of the relevant country; Baldwin himself recognized the possible limitation of GVC participation in the subsection in his book on the "expansion and sustainable question," to which he does not have an acceptable answer.

Taiwan is one of the few emerging economies (with a certain size) that used to have a high degree of GVC participation but moved beyond the middle-income status to join the ranks of high-income economies. Taiwan's income per capita has already reached more than 70% of that of the US. How did Taiwan move beyond the middle-income status? Taiwan's unique case can be understood by referring to its innovation capabilities, shown the fact that its number of registered US patents exceeded 10,000 in early 2010 and outnumbered that of the UK and France. Thus, Taiwan ranks fourth in the world after Japan, Germany, and Korea in terms of the number of registered US patents. For comparison, Thailand or Mexico has less than 200

US patents in the 2010s. Although Baldwin mentioned Foxconn as an example of a company that grows within GVCs, this firm continues to prosper not on its scale-based cost advantages but on its innovation capabilities. Furthermore, Foxconn acts as an independent supplier to multiple global firms, including Apple (which is in direct competition with Samsung), and has even acquired Panasonic, a former symbol of Japan's economic prowess. But, Thailand and Mexico have failed to generate such firms as Foxconn.

Taiwan has fewer OBM firms than Korea, but many of its firms reached the ODM status and achieved success in creating more domestic value-added by taking more segments in GVCs and in obtaining a certain degree of independence from the foreign flagship firms in the existing GVCs.[41] Taiwan has also generated a large number of locally owned or controlled firms that used to be FDI firms or subsidiaries of MNCs.[42] Both Korea and Taiwan have created a large number of global big businesses relative to the size of their economies; by the early 2010s, Taiwan had eight companies included in Fortune 500, Korea had 13 such companies, and Thailand, Mexico, and Turkey only had either one or zero companies.

Merely joining GVCs does not guarantee an entry into higher value-added segments and a transition to high-income status because an economy may be stuck in performing low value-added activities without value upgrading. However, we note that latecomers "must" join GVCs at their early stage of development to facilitate their learning and capability-building. While joining GVCs is necessary for learning, the joining economies are still at risk of being stuck in low value-added activities without moving toward the higher tiers in the value chain, consequently placing them in MIT. In other words, determining who captures and how to capture the "bigger share" of the value in GVCs is very important, and a battle for this position may occur among the key involved parties. Their experiences indicate that

---

[41]   See Yeung (2016) for this strategic coupling with the MNCs.
[42]   This observation on Taiwan was made by Amsden and Chu (2003). The comments on global big businesses are taken from Lee et al. (2013).

Taiwan, Korea, and China have been able to create more domestic value-added after learning through their participation in GVCs.

The degree of participation in GVCs can be measured by the FVA (the share of foreign value-added in gross exports), which indicates what percentage of a country's gross exports consists of inputs that are produced and imported from other countries. In other words, a higher (lower) value of FVA indicates further (or less) integration with the global economy through GVCs. This index can represent the degree of an economy's participation in GVCs as shown in Figure 3–2.[43]

Figure 3–2 shows the FVA estimation results for Korea and China. Since the 1960s and 1970s the FVA in Korea continued to increase since the country's participation in GVCs through OEM-based exports starting from labor-intensive goods until reaching its peak in the early 1980s. Since then the FVA in Korea started to decline until the mid-1990s and rose again after the country joined the OECD. Specifically, Korea's FVA peaked over 36% in 1980 and dropped to 28% in 1993, the year Korea became an OECD member. Actually, Korea experienced a rapid catch-up between the mid-1980s and the mid-1990s, but was facing the possibility of falling into MIT from the early to the mid-1980s because of its rising wage rates and low value-added export structure. This pattern of more GVC, less GVS and then more GVC again suggest that Korea escaped from MIT by increasing the share of local value-added in its exports since the mid-1980s. Although not shown here, the trend of FVA in Taiwan is similar to that in Korea, and its FVA decreased in the 1980s and increased again since the 1990s.[44] Figure 3–2 also shows the case of China since 1995. China's FVA peaked at 37% in the early 2000s and declined to 31% in the late 2000s. This trend implies that as a successful catching-up

---

[43]   The figures and related discussion rely on Lee et al. (2017). The index is estimated following the method of Hummels, Ishil, and Yi (2001).

[44]   According to Lee et al. (2017), the FVA of Taiwan hit the bottom in the late 1980s at 32%. Taiwan hitting the bottom one year before Korea makes sense because Taiwan had an early start in the 1950s (while Korea entered a civil war) and had constantly been leading Korea in every aspect, including its GDP per capita, until the mid-2000s.

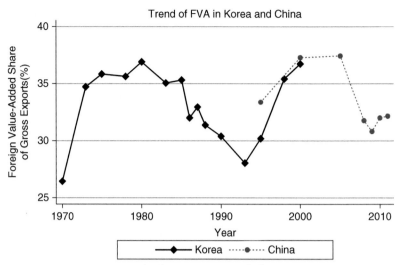

FIGURE 3–2. Trends of FVA in Korea and China
Source: Author's estimation (Korea), OECD TiVA (China)

economy, China is replicating the pattern of Korea and Taiwan with some lags (approximately 15 to 20 years).

These successful catching-up economies experienced a decade-long decline in their FVA, which decreased by over 5% point or from approximately 35% to 30% or lower. Accordingly, we check if a similar pattern has occurred in other Southeast Asian or Latin American economies and find no such case.[45] After the launch of NAFTA, Mexico showed the highest degree of integration with GVCs but experienced no period of decline in its FVA to create local value chains. By comparison, Brazil and Argentina showed extremely low levels of GVC participation, which could reflect their orientation to agriculture (Argentina) or mineral exports (Brazil). Chile demonstrated short-term ups and downs but did not show any trend of declining FVA over a considerably long period. This pattern suggests

---

[45] A possible exception might be Malaysia, which experienced a decline in its FAV from more than 45% in 2000 to less than 40% in 2009. Such phenomenon may explain why Malaysia is currently showing some signs of overcoming MIT after having reached over 47% of the GDP per capita of the US in 2015.

that the degree of FVA depends not only on the degree of international integration but also on the industrial structure, such that a country with a heavy dependence on the primary sectors will have a low degree of FVA.

With regard to the determinants of the degree of FVA in gross exports, Korea and Taiwan experienced an increase in their local value-added (or a decrease in their FVA as shown in Figure 3–2) from the mid-1980s to the mid-1990s or after they improved their NIS by rapidly increasing their degree of local creation and diffusion of knowledge, which can measured by the national-level self-citation of a country or the share of country-owned patents in the total citations made by all patents owned by a country.[46] The knowledge creation and diffusion of Korea and Taiwan reached 5% (similar to the average of middle-income countries) in the mid-1980s and increased to more than 10% (the average of high-income countries) by the late 1990s. Knowledge localization is a key NIS variable that is related to the source of knowledge acquisition. This variable reflects the dependence of the created knowledge on domestic knowledge bases. In other words, knowledge localization measures how much knowledge is created domestically in terms of citing the patents owned by assignees of the same nationality. The correspondence between knowledge localization and decreasing FVA (or increasing local value-added) implies that increasing local value-added has been supported or made possible by the increasing degree of local knowledge creation and diffusion by indigenous actors. By contrast, the knowledge creation and diffusion of other middle-income countries, such as Brazil and Argentina, remained below 5% throughout the entire period.

An econometric study verifies a linkage between local knowledge creation and FVA by performing simple regressions to explain the degree of FVA as a function of knowledge localization, per capita income, economy size (measured by population), and industry

---

[46] This idea goes back to the arguments of Jaffe et al. (1993) and Lee (2013a: 49; Figure 3.1). For international comparison, this measure requires a proper normalization. However, the national-level self-citations are sufficient in most cases.

structure (measured by the share of manufacturing in GDP).[47] The authors confirm that the degree of the local creation and diffusion of knowledge is negatively (positively) related to FVA (domestic value-added). Although such relationship may be limited to correlations, these correlations imply a linkage between the innovation system variables (knowledge localization) and the GVC variable of FVA. In his previous book, this author proved that a higher degree of knowledge localization is positively related to faster economic growth (per capita income). The intermediate links between knowledge localization and economic growth is now shown to be the creation of domestic value-added by reducing the dependence of economies on foreign value-added.

The following question can be raised: how can we increase the degree of knowledge creation to promote the creation of local value-added instead of foreign value-added? We try to answer this question by looking at the experiences of Korea and Taiwan, which are widely known to have increased their R&D/GDP ratio rapidly over their catch-up period compared with Latin American countries. We also take note of the fact that the increasing degree of knowledge localization since the mid-1980s coincided with a period of increasing specialization in short-cycle technologies. As noted in the previous section, a link between short-cycle technologies and knowledge localization exists because the use of such technologies suggests a reduced reliance on existing or old knowledge stock. Thus, specializing in short-cycle technologies can increase the chances for an economy to rapidly increase its degree of knowledge localization. This finding implies that delving further into short-cycle technology-based sectors will facilitate an increase in the local creation of knowledge and thus local value-added. An increasing specialization in short-cycle sectors can also be considered as a feature of inter-sectoral diversification and upgrading into new sectors and new value segments. In this sense,

---

[47]　See Lee et al. (2017), whose regressions use FVA data from OECD sources and knowledge localization data from the dataset of Lee (2013a) available at www.keunlee.com.

knowledge localization (national self-citation) reflects both intra- and inter-sectoral upgrading, which explains the changes in FVA.

We examine the role of GVCs in the transition from low- and middle-income to high-income status using the more–less–more again hypothesis, which posits that participation in GVCs is desirable at the initial stage of growth to allow economies to learn from the outside, and that the upgrading and transition at the middle-income stage requires some effort or stages of seeking separation and independence from foreign-dominated GVCs. At the final stage, latecomer firms and economies may have to seek for an opening to integrate themselves back into GVCs after building up their own local value chains. However, gaining independence is a difficult and risky process. The key to overcoming these difficulties is to command a certain level of in-house capabilities in both marketing and technological innovation. Avoiding the road toward independence may be a short-term option, but such option cannot be sustained in the long run because the leading MNCs in the existing GVCs are always looking for locations with cheap wages and contract firms as shown by the cases of firms in the Brazilian footwear sector.

In a sense, this study aims to see both the perils and potentials of GVCs. These perils emerge because GVCs may simply mean a global profit maximization that is led by MNCs and driven by the waves of global financialization, which squeezes the profits from the lower tier of GVCs. Such attempt is not aimed toward the creation of more local value-added or employment opportunities. Some potentials may also emerge because GVCs may offer initial learning channels. However, an eventual separation or independence from these chains must also be considered; otherwise, an economy may lose in its competition against other sites and firms in other lower-wage economies. As such, these economies must aim for a transition from their participation in GVCs to the creation of local value chains and innovation systems. According to the experiences of Korea's, Brazil's, and India's plush toy, footwear, and information technology sectors to be discussed in the next chapter (4.4), respectively, such a transition becomes possible if economies have the "decision and will" to achieve eventual independence based on the indigenous ownership of their firms.

3.6   SUMMARY AND CONCLUDING REMARKS

This book begins by acknowledging the differences in the economic growth mechanisms employed by advanced economies and latecomer economies at middle- or lower-income stages and by highlighting a very "narrow passage" between these countries. In this case, how to achieve a transition from low- and middle-income to high-income status warrants a thorough examination. Taking detours is necessary to achieve such transition because of the two failures (capability and size failures) and one barrier (IPR protection in the North). Therefore, this chapter has explained how capability failure can be corrected by promoting the learning and capability-building by firms in emerging countries. This chapter then explained the nature of the narrow passage in terms of three detours. The first detour is promoting imitative innovations in the form of petit patents and trademarks instead of trying to promote a high level of IPR protection, including patent rights. The second detour is specializing in short-cycle technology-based sectors instead of trying to directly enter long-cycle technology-based sectors/segments that are the hallmarks of advanced economies. The third detour is promoting domestic value-added and reducing a country's reliance on GVCs.

While the consolidation of technological capabilities has long been suggested as a vital requirement for economic catch-up, this chapter shows that such consolidation must be carefully designed and implemented with the equally vital strategic idea of the three detours. Otherwise, the process of capability building becomes derailed and delayed. For the first detour, capability-building becomes less effective if a latecomer economy provides a very high level of IPR protection and only recognizes regular patents instead of petit patents. The selection of technologies becomes derailed if a latecomer attempts to enter those sectors/segments with long-cycle times or high entry barriers. Latecomer economies may also participate in GVCs because they must be open to learn from the outside at the initial stage, but the final goal of learning is for these economies to stand alone with their own learning and innovation mechanisms; it is like a child who learns to walk is to eventually walks alone. Thus, independence is the end point of learning. Likewise, participating in GVCs must be accompanied by an effort to build a local knowledge base and to increase domestic value-added at the intermediate stage.

Before moving to the next chapter, the issues of technological specialization and selection criteria need to be summarized in view of the NIS framework given that Section 4, which discusses technological specialization, touches upon the elements of technological regimes other than the highly emphasized element of the cycle time of technologies. This element warrants further research because the cycle time of technologies is probably the only element that is associated with low entry barriers and high growth prospects, while the other elements, such as the degree of embodied technological transfer, tacit or explicit knowledge, and modularity, are mostly about the niche or the entry barrier aspect. Therefore, one can say that while the elements of embodied technological transfer and modularity are involved in the earlier stage of technological catch-up and entry, the cycle time and tacitness of technologies are involved in the later stage of catch-up because they affect not only the entry possibility of an economy but also its speed of learning and catch-up. For instance, the more tacit the knowledge is, the more time it takes for an economy to learn and master such knowledge.

The degree of knowledge localization and technological diversification of successful catching-up economies has rapidly increased over time as they increasingly specialized in short-cycle technologies. These three variables seem to answer the question regarding the mechanism of technological catch-up given that Section 4, which discusses the GVC-related detour, also verifies the contributing role of knowledge localization (local creation and diffusion of knowledge) in consolidating a basis for replacing the foreign value-added from

GVCs with local value-added.[48] In sum, while both technological diversification and knowledge localization are end-state variables, the cycle time of technologies is the effective transition variable that guides us to the end-state. As explained before, the cycle time of technologies indicates which direction an economy must diversify. This variable also promotes a faster localization of knowledge creation because a short-cycle time means a reduced reliance on existing or old technologies that are dominated by incumbent countries. Another way of positioning these three variables is by saying that each of them represents the questions of "who" must conduct, "how" to achieve, and "what" is a technological catch-up. For the "what" question, technological catch-up economies are becoming similar to advanced economies in terms of their degree of technological diversification. Meanwhile, for the "how" and "who" questions, technological catch-up tends to be led by locally owned companies that are gradually specializing in diverse short-cycle technologies.

---

[48]   According to Lee (2013a), knowledge localization has a very high degree of correlation with technological diversification. By contrast, cycle time does not show high correlation with either of these two variables. While advanced countries tend to show a high degree of knowledge localization and technological diversification, they have more patents in long-cycle technologies. The exact opposite is observed for the successful catching-up economies.

4   Detour of Promoting Big Businesses and SMEs during Transition

4.1   INTRODUCTION

The preceding chapter discussed the three detour strategies and other mechanisms for expanding capabilities in technological innovation to realize upward transition from middle to high income. Technological capabilities are needed to overcome the difficulties associated with capabilities failure and IPR barriers. Another source of failure is "size failure," wherein latecomers have an insufficient number of world-class big businesses (BBs). This chapter discusses the roles of BBs and SMEs.

As discussed in Chapter 2, world-class BBs have a significant causal effect on economic growth compared with SMEs. The presence or absence of BBs is one of the important reasons for being stuck in MIT or not. Many emerging economies (except the successful cases of Korea, Taiwan, and China) have fewer BBs than predicted by their size. Thus, they failed to get out of MIT. The optimal scenario would be to have some number of world-class BBs to trigger economic growth and lead innovation, aside from having a sizeable number of SMEs to diffuse economic growth by creating jobs.

The mechanism by which BBs achieve growth beyond MIT is to locate their headquarters in their home countries to conduct R&D and marketing, which are more high value-added activities than assembly-based manufacturing. This mechanism is important because typical upper-middle-income economies such as Thailand face the problem of rising wage rates, which become too high for traditional low-end manufacturing. The next question is how to promote or develop BBs that can afford high-end segments, such as capital goods and R&D. A clue to the answer can be obtained by examining the past experience of catch-up episodes around the world wherein BBs tend to take the form of business groups (BGs).

Granovetter (1995) defined BGs as a collection of firms bound together either formally or informally and characterized by an intermediate level of binding; this means that the firms are neither bound merely by short-term strategic alliances nor legally consolidated into a single entity. In Korea, family-controlled, diversified firms, or chaebols, serve as the leading engine of economic growth. These firms tend to be a form of BG. In other words, the term chaebol refers to the whole BG as a unit consisting of members or affiliated companies, whereas chaebol firms, chaebol affiliates, or group firms refer to individual firms that belong to a chaebol BG. These affiliate firms are legal persons who are often listed on the stock market and are mostly interlocked by circular shareholdings. By contrast, a BG is not a legal person unless it refers to a holding company of the group.

In addition to the example of early development in Japan, the presence of BGs tends to be heavy in successful latecomer economies, starting from Japan and followed by Korea, Taiwan, China, and India.[1] Korean chaebols and Japanese keiretsu are regarded as symbols of economic growth, and they remain important players even in the era of globalization and market liberalization as long as they command higher technological capabilities.

Following Williamson's analysis in his book, *Market and Hierarchies* (1975), conglomerates or BGs are naturally considered a form that firms take to save on transaction costs in an environment with a high degree of market failure. Thus, it is not surprising that BGs are highly prevalent in developing countries, which have high transaction costs due to less-developed market institutions, or "institutional voids."[2]

---

[1]   Choo et al. (2009) confirmed the importance of chaebols in the 2000s and onward. The role of BGs in China is discussed in Lee and Woo (2002), Peng (2000), Keister (1998), and Lee and Jin (2009); in India, this role is examined in Khanna and Palepu (2000) and Ghemawat and Khanna (1998).

[2]   The transaction-cost view on BGs was first discussed in Leff (1978) and then in Goto (1982). The concept of "institutional voids" was described in Khanna and Palepu (2000) and Khanna (2000).

However, interesting policy or strategic issues cannot be considered if we regard the BG as a simple evolutionary response to the institutional environment of the economy. Thus, we will instead examine BGs from a new perspective, namely, the economic catch-up perspective. We view the BG as an organizational device for economic catch-up. We suggest that BGs do not only emerge in response to market failure but may also serve as a vehicle for economic catch-up. In this light, we call attention to the phenomenon wherein BGs facilitate affiliate firms to enter new markets by providing cross-subsidies (via internal capital markets) during their initial phase of business. These firms tend to settle down with low variation and levels of profitability, but they pursue sales growth and associated expansion.

Thus, Sections 2 and 3 discuss the roles of BGs in the economic catch-up of emerging countries. Section 4 explores SMEs, while the last section provides a summary of our view on latecomer firms, which include BBs and SMEs.

4.2   UNDERSTANDING BGS

Berle and Means (1932) discussed the rise of managerial capitalism many years ago. A survey article by La Porta, Lopes-de-Silanies, and Schleifer (1999) observed that the classic separation of ownership and control is an exception; they also found that family-controlled firms that take the form of BGs are globally common. One of the issues BGs confront is their dynamic performance and efficiency. In terms of chaebols, most studies that used 1990s data reported a lower productive efficiency or profitability of chaebol firms than standalone firms; by contrast, studies that used recent data had different results (i.e., better performance of chaebol firms).[3] Using pre- and post crisis data,

---

[3]   For example, Choi and Cowing (1999) and Joh (2003) confirmed the lower financial efficiency of chaebol firms by comparing individual group-affiliated firms and non-group firms. Lee et al. (2008) estimated the group-affiliation premium in terms of profitability over the 1980s and 1990s and found that the premium decreased from positive values to negative values. Using early- to mid-1990s data, Ferris et al. (2003) concluded that chaebol-affiliated firms suffer a value loss relative to non-affiliated firms. One exception would be Chang and Choi (1988), who revealed a higher profitability of chaebols relative to non-chaebol firms using early 1980s data.

an earlier study of mine also revealed that chaebol firms performed relatively well in the 1980s and poorly in the 1990s, and then exhibited a stunning turnaround after the restructuring following the 1997 crisis.[4] In summary, chaebol firms served as a device for catch-up in the 1970s and 1980s, but they were criticized as one of the causes of the financial crises that swept Asia in the late 1990s. During the 2000s, chaebols that survived the crisis have been reborn as global players.

Thus, the following questions surfaced. Why are BGs prevalent in many countries? Why do BGs tend to fall into trouble? How can they maintain their performance as global players despite market opening and liberalization?

The first question is not new; BGs arise in settings with market failures or high transaction costs, such as emerging economies. The existence of BGs in emerging and/or transition economies, such as Korea, India, Taiwan, Latin America, China, and Russia, confirm their association with market failure or "institutional voids" in the context of emerging economies.[5] The argument in the extant literature is that BGs emerge to fill institutional voids because many of the institutions that support business activities are absent in many parts of the world.

The Institutional voids refer to market failures in diverse markets as follows. First, companies in emerging markets face higher costs in building credible brands than their counterparts in advanced economies, given the lack of information about products and transaction-related claims-processing institutions in product markets. Hence, a reputable conglomerate can use its group name to enter a new business and spread the costs of maintaining brand names. Second, investors in capital markets refrain from investing money in unfamiliar ventures when they have no access to

---

4   See Choo et al. (2009), for which I am a corresponding author.

5   BGs are discussed in the context of Hong Kong (Au, Peng, and Wang, 2000), Latin America (Khanna and Palepu, 2000; Guillen, 2000; Strachan, 1976), and Russia (Freinkman, 1995).

information. Established diversified groups have superior access to capital markets in these contexts. Third, BGs in the labor market can create value by developing promising managers and spreading the fixed costs of professional development over the businesses in the group, given the lack of well-trained businesspeople and educational facilities. Running an internal labor market within a group can provide additional room for flexibility when the labor market is rigid. Finally, as governments in emerging economies intervene extensively in business operations, diversified groups can create value by acting as intermediaries when their affiliate companies are required to deal with regulatory bureaucracy. The larger the group, the easier it is to carry the costs of maintaining government relations.

Answers to the second question (why BGs tend to fall into trouble) can be obtained by referring to the concept of controlling minority structure (CMS) firms proposed by Bebchuk, Kraakman, and Triantis (2000). This approach helps to explain why BGs tend to fall into serious agency costs, which lead to unjustifiable investment drives and the moral hazard problem. A shareholder in CMS firms exercises control while retaining a small fraction of equity claims on a company's cash flow. This radical separation of control and cash flow rights is the cause of the agency costs and can occur in three principal ways: through cross-ownership ties, dual-class share structure, and stock pyramids. These methods are employed by BGs in many countries, including chaebols in Korea.

Chaebols used to be tightly owned by founding families, but their shares became increasingly small as many of them opted for public listings to raise additional funds. The data compiled by the Korea Fair Trade Commission show that shares held by owner-families in the top thirty BGs in Korea declined steadily from 15.1% in 1987 to 8.5% in 1997 and to less than 5% in 2000.[6] Similarly, shares held by the affiliated firms increased from 30% to 40% during this period. Thus, CMS emerged in the ownership of chaebols with the

[6]   These data were obtained from Chang (2003, p. 164) and Jwa (2002, Table 3.5).

increasing separation of real ownership (cash flow rights) and control rights. This structure was utilized as a device for the owner-controller to maintain control over group-affiliated firms while simultaneously financing their growth.

However, under the CMS structure, the separation of real ownership and control rights provides the owner-controller with an incentive to seek private benefits by pursuing unjustifiable growth, and by subsidizing and maintaining loss-incurring affiliates. The separation of cash flow rights and control might deepen in the long term, unless government regulations or reforms are implemented to reduce private benefits that accrue to the owner-controller. This opportunistic behavior was regarded as one of the seeds of the 1997 financial crisis. Several previous studies pursue this line of thought.[7] Some studies found that chaebol-affiliated firms tend to invest excessively in low Tobin's-Q sectors and too little in high Tobin's-Q sectors. Thus, they overinvest in low-performing industries, and such over-investment tends to be positively associated with the gap between cash flow rights (owner's share) and control rights in BGs.

However, this agency cost thesis cannot be easily reconciled with the post crisis turnaround of the surviving chaebols under the same and persistent family-controlled structure. In other words, chaebols now perform quite differently under the same ownership and governance structure. Two previous studies of mine verify that they stopped overinvesting in low-return businesses, reduced cross-subsidies over the low-performing affiliates, borrowed less than before, and thus carried a similar level of tax burden as the stand-alone firms.[8] Explaining the post crisis performance of the BGs that survived the crisis is an important and challenging question for agency cost and market failure views on BGs.

---

[7] See Ferris et al. (2003), Joh (2003), and Kim (2002) on the investment and financial efficiency of chaebol-affiliated firms.

[8] See Choo, Lee, Ryu, and Yoon (2009) and Lee et al. (2010) on the changed behavior and performance of chaebols after the crisis.

The performance turnaround of BGs in the 2000s was problematic for the market failure view because this view predicted the decline of BGs as the markets substantially matured in the 1990s and 2000s. However, this view fails to provide an explanation for the re-emergence of premium BGs in the 2000s. This turnaround is also a concern for the agency costs view, which centers on the concept of CMS firms, because chaebol firms remain family-owned with a considerable gap between cash flow and control rights.

The observation on Korea shows that many chaebols continued to prosper after surviving the crisis. How can we explain the recent peak performance of the biggest groups, which also tend to be the most diversified, such as the Samsung Group, the LG Group, and the Hyundai Motor Group? Given that postcrisis reforms in Korea focused on corporate governance issues,[9] one might conjecture that such reforms caused performance changes for the better. However, numerous reports claim that corporate governance in Korea did not improve considerably and has kept the same family-controlled structure. In contrast, my hypothesis is that the enhanced technological capabilities of chaebol firms can be identified as possible causes of the postcrisis turnaround.[10]

Understanding changes and recent improvement in the performance of BGs requires an improved theory. Given the insufficiency of market failure and the agency cost views of firms, we may consider a different approach to BGs by borrowing insights from the resource-based theory of the firm originally proposed by Penrose (1959). Her theory significantly influenced later works in the study of the firm, which evolved into several variations such as capability-based theory, knowledge-based theory, and evolutionary theory of the firm.[11] In her book, Penrose (1959, ix) defined the firm as "a collection of resources

---

[9]   See Haggard et al. (2003) for details on postcrisis reform.
[10] See Choo et al. (2009).
[11] An edited volume of *The Legacy of Edith Penrose* (Pitelis, 2002) was published in commemoration of the fortieth anniversary of the Penrose book. This is discussed in Hoopes et al. (2003).

bound together in an administrative framework, the boundary of which is determined by the area of 'administrative coordination' and 'authoritative communication.'" One of the key ideas of this theory is that because the firm is a bundle of resources (or capabilities), its growth depends on what kind and how much of the diverse resources it commands and can utilize for its growth.

By relying on this resource-based firm theory, we recognize that a certain intrinsic advantage of BGs exists that is not subject to the law of long-term decline with market maturing or agency cost considerations. First, BGs have a resource-sharing advantage. The importance of this feature is that it does not need to disappear even with the development of free-market institutions. A notable study regarding this point is that by Sea-Jin Chang, who used 1990s data to reveal that chaebol firms tend to be associated with superior financial performance (or profitability) because of group-level sharing of technology skills, advertising, and internal transactions.[12] Specifically, he found that the performance of chaebol firms is positively related not only to their own firm-level resources but also to group-level resources. For instance, chaebols such as Samsung, LG, and Hyundai substantially upgraded their global brand power, and the group brand is shared by the affiliates that pay royalties to the core companies. For Samsung, Samsung Electronics collects royalties from other Samsung affiliates. Resource-sharing among affiliates is not necessarily a violation of free-market principles as long as it is done at market prices. The point is that such internal market transactions can occur more frequently and willingly only when the firms are linked through circular shareholding and common ownership.

Our view is that certain resources or inputs are "lumpy," or indivisible, and can be installed only in certain sizes. R&D units and brand values may be considered examples of such inputs. Once built up, R&D and brand power are also a kind of inseparable (indivisible) input, and the existence of such input gives BGs

---

[12]   See his work in Chang and Hong (2000).

a distinctive advantage vis-à-vis stand-alone firms. The presence of this lumpy input may increase production capacity only in substantial, lumpy increments. The dynamic process of such expansion is viewed as the development path of Penrose's resource-based firm. Furthermore, these intangible assets are not usually available in the market for purchase, and thus we have to develop such assets for ourselves. This finding indicates that BGs have certain advantages because affiliate firms can share the costs of acquiring or building such intangible assets. Moreover, such assets are more likely to be used fully in the context of BGs than in the case of a stand-alone firm. By performing regression analysis based on the Korean firm data, we showed that such an advantage exists regardless of market failures.[13]

In the preceding sections, we studied three theoretical views on BGs, namely, market failure view, agency cost view, and resource-based views. Each of the three has its own strengths and weaknesses. The first and classic view, such as market imperfections or institutional voids, adequately explains the origin of BGs but cannot fully explicate the continuing growth process and dynamics of these groups. The second view, namely, agency costs, illuminates the poor performance of BGs in terms of excessive investment and appropriation of private benefits by controllers. However, this view does not sufficiently clarify performance improvement, e.g., such change in post crisis Korea under similar governance and ownership structures. The third view convincingly expounds not only on building initial capabilities but also explains longer-term dynamic changes, as seen from the long-term evolution of BGs in Korea. Nevertheless, that view cannot justify why some BGs failed in the 1990s. Hence, an emerging conclusion may be that we require all three views to have a balanced understanding of BGs in terms of both their potential and peril.

---

[13]   See Cheong et al. (2010); this author is the corresponding author.

4.3   GROWING BBS AND ATTAINING ECONOMIC CATCH-UP

The preceding section discussed the three theoretical views on BGs (market failure, agency cost view, and resource-based views) and concluded that we need all of these for a balanced understanding of BGs in terms of their potentials and perils. We now examine the roles of BGs as an organizational device for long-term economic catch-up by latecomers. We regard BGs mainly as facilitating devices in terms of three aspects: first, for promoting BBs; second, for facilitating late entry; and third, for building capabilities through resource-sharing. Each of these three aspects is related to each of the three theories discussed thus far, namely, market failure, agency cost, and resource-based theory of firms.

The first advantage of BGs has to do with the fact that they are an effective response to market failure in developing countries. Note that this chapter began with a remark that the presence or absence of world-class BBs is an indicator of transcending the MIT or being stuck within it. Hence, the challenge is how to grow BBs in the context of developing economies. Of course, one of the difficulties in growing BBs in developing countries is the initially higher degree of failures in capital, production, and labor markets. In other words, the size and nature of market forces constitute a barrier for the natural emergence of BBs. Thus, unless the government intervenes to create BBs in the form of SOEs or with sizeable amounts of subsidies, the only other possible way may be to scale up the growth of family-owned businesses in the form of BGs.

The preceding section indicated that the condition of market failure in developing countries tends to lead to the emergence of many firms taking the form of BGs. Capital market failure is a particularly serious disadvantage for the latecomer economies. These economies face capital scarcity unless they have enough domestic savings—even from the early stage of industrialization—as did Taiwan and Korea. When Korea started industrialization in the early 1960s, its growth potential was obviously seriously constrained by the extremely low savings available for investment. Given the limited size of the financial resources available, a reasonable solution was to pool the capital into several big hands in the business. In other words, the government wanted to promote a few BBs to expedite economic growth. Since then, rapid economic growth achieved in Korea has often been associated with the growth of big BGs or chaebols, whose Chinese characters are similar to the zaibatsu, the prewar ancestor of the keiretsu in Japan.

Scholars of Japanese BGs took an active position to use keiretsu and chaebols as the organizational basis for the rising strength of their economies; this form of industrial organization increases the difficulty for foreign firms to penetrate the Japanese or Korean markets.[14] We call this view a catch-up device view of the BGs, which contradicts the market failure view. In China, which is another catching-up economy, the government promoted the development of big BGs.[15]

Another means to grow BBs is to create them in the form of state-owned enterprises (SOEs) and subsequently privatize them once they become more competitive in international standards. Many leading firms in Korea used to be SOEs, such as SK-Telecom (a top telephone service firm), POSCO (a global steel firm), Korean Air (a global air-carrier), and Doosan Heavy Industry (a turbine producer). Numerous leading firms in China, such as Geely Auto and Haier, also used to be SOEs or still carry equity shares owned by the state.

The second reason for the advantage of BGs in capturing growth opportunities is that they may serve as devices for late entry into existing or new markets, which are already dominated by firms from the advanced economies. We conceptualize "latecomer firms" from emerging economies as resource-poor late entrants, following Mathews (2002). In particular, the point of entry in the global division of labor and production network of such firms is late in the sense that

---

[14] See Gerlach (1989) and Steers et al. (1989)

[15] See Chi (1996), Lee and Woo (2002), and Seo et al. (2010).

when latecomers begin their manufacturing activities, the value chains of production are already established and occupied by firms in advanced countries. Arguably, latecomers that lack technologies and managerial resources (because of the lower level of development in their home countries) have no choice but to inherit certain low-end or low-profitability segments from the firms in advanced economies in the form of OEM or FDI firms to gain access to world markets via MNCs or subcontracting-led exports. If latecomer firms try to enter higher ends or more profitable segments or sectors, they have to surmount high entry barriers and fierce competition with the incumbents; thus they incur substantial losses during the initial settlement period. Entry as a BG is significantly helpful in this situation because initial losses can be "socialized" among brother and sister affiliates in the same BG. In this sense, BGs are an alternative to industrial policy.

The group-level initiative to launch a new business by covering its losses during the initial period is a well-known phenomenon in Korea. A famous example is Samsung's memory chip business. This business is now Samsung's biggest cash cow, but the transition involved considerable losses—seven years' worth—during the initial period. This kind of collective catch-up strategy is especially effective when the technology involved shows a rapid learning curve. The strategy ensures that efficiency improves quickly with the accumulation of production experience. Finance literature also reports the so-called "socialism" in the internal capital markets of BGs to ensure that investment flows into loss-making or underperforming affiliates or to the division inside the group or conglomerates (Shin and Park, 1999). The literature tends to interpret this observation as inefficient behavior. An alternative interpretation of this finding is that this is a market entry strategy used to undertake a group-level endeavor, which makes sense in a dynamic context.

This reasoning originated from the studies on Japanese BGs, which find that the keiretsu ties go beyond the main bank-based network, and that a redistribution effect reduces the variability of the keiretsu firms.[16] In other words, weak companies, such as those in their starting period, benefit from group affiliation (they recover or grow faster). By contrast, strong ones do not (they are subsequently outperformed by independent firms). Similar behavior was also confirmed in the Korean context in my own studies, which confirm less variation of productive or financial efficiency of chaebol firms compared to non-chaebol firms.[17] This finding suggests the interesting "double-edged sword" nature of the CMS structure of BGs. Poor performance by the CMS structure, as predicted by finance theory, would lead to an unjustifiable expansion of firms into loss-making businesses. Conversely, if the structure fares well (as in the 1970s and 1980s Korea), rapid growth and diversification into new sectors will occur. In this way, the Korean industry achieved both intrasectoral and intersectoral diversification and upgrading.

During the 1990s, the chaebols were criticized for "excessive investments" and thus becoming a seed for the 1997 crisis. My own study finds that although those investments can be regarded as overinvestment in the static standard, they are responsible for growth and profitability in the 2000s.[18] In other words, those over investments were not simply wasteful; some were useful for learning and building capabilities for longer-term rebounds. This point leads us to the final or third advantage of BGs in facilitating firm growth, which is the insight gained from the resource-based theory of the firms.

Motivated by a somewhat static bias of the traditional resource-based view, strategy scholars such as Teece began to explicitly acknowledge the importance of the dynamic process, including the acquisition, development, and maintenance of differential bundles of resources and capabilities over time.[19] This literature focused on a dynamic capabilities perspective, which is concerned with the mechanisms by which firms accumulate and dissipate new skills and capabilities. This perspective builds on the same principles as

---

[16] See Lincoln, Gerlach, and Ahmadjian (1996).
[17] See Choo, Lee, Ryu, and Yoon (2009) and Lee et al. (2010).
[18] See Lee et al. (2010).   [19]   See Teece et al. (1997) and Teece (2007).

resource heterogeneity but focuses more on the dynamics of capability development than stock capabilities at any given point in time. According to Teece, dynamic capabilities refer to a firm's ability to integrate, build, and reconfigure internal and external competences to address rapidly changing environments.[20] These ideas on the development of firm capability over time should be highly relevant in understanding the growth of firms in developing countries. Some studies applied this insight to a particular form of firms in developing countries, that is, BGs.[21] They consider the diversification of BGs from developing economies as a means of using their own unique capability or resources, termed as "project execution capability." This capability denotes the skills required to establish or expand operating and other corporate facilities.

The acquisition of such capability by firms in developing countries is related to the unique origins of firms. In the case of Asia, the generalist who established itself as a chaebol in Korea emerged from the rent-seeking and business opportunities surrounding American foreign aid allocation in the 1950s (Amsden, 1989: 38–40). In the absence of proprietary technology for use in related industries and in the presence of potentially high profit rates in "pre-modernized" start-up industries, their initial pattern of diversification tended to be opportunistic and technologically unrelated. Latecomer firms learned and accumulated "project execution capability" through diversification. Moreover, this idea of project execution is consistent with the eventual accumulation of sector-specific expertise, especially when the projects tend to fall more within the same areas. In other words, a need exists for dynamic perspectives on firm growth.

Firms from developing countries often did not have deep sector-specific knowledge. Hence, they often ended up diversifying into entirely unrelated areas only to follow market demands. Synergies

[20]   Helfat and Peteraf (2003) also introduce the concept of capability life cycle, which articulates general patterns and paths in the evolution of organizational capabilities over time.

[21]   For instance, Kock and Guillen (2001), Guillen (2000), and Amsden and Hikino (1994).

Table 4-1. *Evolution of the Core Capabilities of BGs*

	Stage 1	Stage 2	Stage 3	Stage 4
Capability	Few/Networking	Project Execution	Integration: Vertical/Horizontal	Technological Innovation Product Development
Behavior	Rent-Seeking	Diversification Related/Unrelated	Replication: Geographical Diversification	Specialization
Specificity	Random	Less Sector-Specific	Sector-Specific/ Across Several Sectors	Technology Specific (e.g., Nanotechnology)
Periods in Samsung	1960s, 1970s	1970–1980s	Mid-1970s, 1980s, 1990s	1990s, 2000s

Source: Lee and He, 2009
Notes: Overlaps between stages are unavoidable because the beginning of each period is clear, whereas the endings are not.

among affiliates were formed through this process of running businesses in numerous areas, which led to vertical integration. Furthermore, novel entries could appear in new geographical areas but in the same sectors. In this case, project execution capability itself would differ in various sectors and would be stronger in those sectors that firms entered most frequently.

In other words, we can consider a dynamic path of capability development by BGs similar to that shown in Table 4–1.[22] BGs in the early stage are less capable and pursue rent-seeking behavior. In such a context, what determines market competition should be more about how to build, maintain, and utilize their connections and network with the government, which is in charge of key resource allocation.[23] In the second stage, these BGs diversify into whatever related or unrelated sectors they consider promising or profitable because of market demand or government industrial policy, thereby accumulating project execution capability, which is not highly sector-specific. Given the diverse sectors in the third stage, BGs can expect integration benefits associated with horizontal integration among less-related sectors or VI (vertical integration), which is more sector-specific. Such an integration would be a significant advantage in an environment with input market deficiencies and could help companies maintain better quality, efficient coordination, and punctuality than the levels possible through outsourcing.[24]

Finally, BGs could develop technological innovation capability, which is very specific to certain technological areas or knowledge and which can be represented by patents or new products. The VI stage that precedes the innovation stage is reasonable because increased interaction between buyers and sellers can enhance technology development.[25] The advantages of BG style organizations in innovation include the fact that they may share costs for building and provide efficient utilization of lumpy intangible (not available in market) competences, including R&D capabilities. BG style has also

---

[22] See my own study, Lee and He (2009). [23] This point is from Kim et al. (2004).
[24] Observed in Chang (2003: 120). [25] See Chang (2003: 121).

been shown to facilitate innovation by allowing for a higher level of within-group (or within-network) spillovers of knowledge than the level prevailing at the arms'-length, market-like relationship among independent firms.[26]

One possible difficulty with this framework is the process of distinguishing between Stages 2 and 3 given that related diversification can also be seen as VI or horizontal integration. The often-heard story of LG's diversification appears to suggest that Korean BGs pursued some degree of VI from their early days. However, chaebols initially practiced unrelated diversification and staged VI at later stages because benefits from the former are often linked with artificial rents and become exhausted, along with industry vacuum depletion and market liberalization.[27] For example, Samsung hardly pursued any VI until the 1970s, when it entered the electronics business. This entry itself was an unrelated diversification, as Samsung's main business areas used to be textile and apparel, and food and beverage. Samsung entered the electronics industry because the government declared a plan in June 1968 to promote the electronics industry as a leading export industry. Korean BGs were not highly motivated to develop such high-level capabilities (integration) until they faced greater competition among domestic and foreign rival firms. Only after this entry into electronics did Samsung realize the needs and benefits of VI as a way to outperform rivals from domestic and overseas markets. Thus, we prefer to reserve the term "integration" to refer to more explicit and intentional pursuits of synergies among affiliates, rather than emerging passively as a consequence of entries into profitable business areas.

A typical example of this dynamic process of capability-building is Samsung, the largest BG in Korea.[28] The Samsung Group experienced an indifferent start in retail trading in 1938, which was revived

---

[26] See Lee et al. (2015), which verified such impact of more knowledge spillover within group-affiliated firms.

[27] See Kim et al. (2004) for this argument.

[28] The story about Samsung is from my own study, Lee and He (2009).

in 1953 with the establishment of an affiliate in a typical import-substitution and capital-intensive industry, i.e., sugar refining. Although Samsung began its business mainly in labor-intensive industries, it rapidly branched out into capital-intensive production and services. One important fact about the Samsung Group is its project-executing mechanism, which has led to the creation of synergies between different lines of businesses that extensively employ its affiliates. The outstanding performance of Samsung Group in the global market is explained by the VI among its affiliates and the continuous deepening of its integration.

VI in electronics consists of the Samsung Electronics Corporation (SEC) at the top, Samsung Electro-Mechanics and Samsung SDI (Display, Digital, Interface) at the middle, and finally Samsung Corning at the bottom. As it is in charge of the final assembly process, SEC is closely linked with Samsung SDI, a manufacturer of television tubes. In turn, Samsung SDI relies on Samsung Corning, which produces glass bulbs for the tubes. Sixty-one percent of Samsung Corning's total revenue comes from Samsung SDI, which in turn supplies 52% of its products to SEC. Finally, Samsung Electro-Mechanics, a producer of electronic parts, sells 69% of its products to SEC.[29]

Samsung's entry into China took advantage of VI and a long-established network of resource-sharing. To produce monitors in China, SEC established a joint venture called the Tianjin-Samsung Electronics Display Co., Ltd. (TSED) in 1996. Three years after its initial creation, TSED became the largest supplier of monitors with total sales of 450,000 units and a 20% market share in the self-branded market in China.[30] In November 2000, total TSED sales reached 1 million units, which represented 30.5% of market share. TSED was followed by Philips with a 26% market share. TSED maintained a stable position with 1.4 million unit sales and a market share of 25.8% and 29.6% in 2001 and 2002, respectively, which reached 34%

[29]   The information source is Chang (2003: 120–121).
[30]   These figures are from Table 2 of Lee and He (2009).

in 2006. Thus, Samsung's entry into China is an excellent case of resource-sharing and coordination among affiliates for executing a late-entry project into a new market. This VI network among affiliates was first developed in Korea and then replicated in many parts of the world, including China.

In summary, there is a growing body of literature on BGs in numerous economies around the world. However, interesting policy or strategic issues are not involved if we view BGs simply as an evolutionary response to the institutional environment of the economy. This chapter argues that BGs may not be simply a passive response to the environment but can serve as an organizational device for economic transition. We observe that the main strength of BGs during catching up is to facilitate entry into new markets or lines of business formerly monopolized by forerunning companies. BGs can expedite market entry by mobilizing financial resources into new affiliates and helping them during the initial period of business by providing markets, capital, technology, and brand names. The other advantages of BGs entail sharing the costs to build, promoting the efficient utilization of lumpy intangible assets such as R&D units and enabling innovation through a high level of knowledge spillovers among group affiliates.

4.4 HOW TO GROW GLOBALLY SUCCESSFUL SMES

In the preceding section, we argued for the need of world-class BBs in the latecomer's journey beyond the middle-income stage. This section discusses the case of SMEs. Most SMEs in emerging economies tend to be dependent suppliers that are dependent on BBs, but dynamic high-income economies tend to have many independent SMEs operating in domestic and global markets. Developing global SMEs out of the typical environment of emerging economies is quite difficult. This section discusses this issue.

The global competitiveness of SMEs generally differs from that of large enterprises because of the severe resource shortage faced by the former. Thus, many of them tend to start by joining the GVC as an

OEM supplier to big or foreign MNCs; in this context, OEM is a form of subcontracting, wherein a complete and finished product is produced in accordance with the specifications of the buyer, as explained by Hobday (1994). A few OEM firms evolve into ODM (own design manufacturing) firms that perform the majority of the product design process while allowing the firms of their customers to perform the marketing functions. A typical upgrading path for latecomer firms is from OEM to ODM and then to OBM. OBM firms work comprehensively on their own brands by designing and manufacturing new products, conducting R&D on their products and production processes, and conducting sales and distribution.

In the OEM mode, latecomer firms do not take risks but remain dependent on MNC vendors or large client firms. This mode of participation at the GVC leads to stable growth in the medium term; however, the future of firms that follow such a strategy is often uncertain because new latecomer firms that offer lower wages and costs continue to emerge from somewhere in the GVC or from the next tier of emerging countries (Lee and Mathews, 2012). Warnings about the possibility of upgrading within the GVC differ among GVC advocates such as Baldwin (2016), who proposes that joining a GVC works better for latecomer industrialization than does attempting to build entire value chains. This is because offshore production brings elements (such as economy of scale) that took Korea and Taiwan decades to develop domestically.

By taking the perspective of a detour, we argue that more GVC is not always beneficial. But attempting to be independent, with less GVC, and acquiring domestic value added is required at the interim stage of attempting a catch-up. This warning is justified given the many stories of failure to upgrade in the GVC. For instance, in their studies of firms in Latin America, Giuliani and her colleagues reached the vital conclusion that process or product upgrading has been occurring to a certain extent but that functional and intersectoral upgrading are rare.[31] Therefore, the key task is to determine the "right and dynamic" mode and ways of

[31]   See Giuliani et al. (2005).

engagement with GVC, with the long-term goal of building and upgrading own "local chains for value and knowledge creation," thereby leveraging a bigger piece of the pie from the global profit.

GVC participation as a detour strategy becomes necessary because the upgrade transition from one mode to the next is neither automatic nor easy. This condition is especially true for the transition to OBM because this step involves several risks, including counterattacks from flagship firms in existing GVC or incumbents; this finding was noted in my own studies in the case of Korean SMEs trying OBM and in another investigation of the case of the footwear and furniture sectors in Brazil.[32] Thus, this stage can be prolonged by a slowdown, which may even lead to a decline in sales or market shares and, eventually, to a possible crisis for firms that attempt this functional upgrade. For instance, in the case of consumer goods, former vendor companies (brand owners) often stop giving OEM orders to destroy a company that has begun to sell their competing brands. In the case of capital goods, incumbent companies suddenly charge predatory prices in the market once they realize that latecomer firms have become successful in developing their products, which poses a threat of competition against the products of the incumbent. In certain cases, the incumbent reacts by filing lawsuits against the latecomers and claiming that the latter copied their products. In other cases, small supplier firms face difficulties with client firms over selling prices and delivery time, which sometimes lead to a sudden halt in purchasing orders from the client firm. The aversion of former buyer firms to their suppliers for converting to OBM was documented in earlier studies on Latin America.[33]

This possibility of interference by incumbent leading firms in the GVC implies that functional upgrading to OBM often requires a fight for independence against leading firms in the GVC. To some extent, this recognition contradicts several studies in the GVC

---

[32]   See Lee et al. (2015) for the case of the Korean SMEs and Navas-Alemán (2011) for the Brazilian firms.

[33]   See Giuliani, Pietrobelli, and Rabellotti (2005) and Navas-Alemán (2011).

literature that tended to concentrate on collaborations between the flagship firms in the North and firms in the South.[34] Latecomer firms from the South have the option of choosing "no fight and no associated risk," but they could choose to stay dependent on a single or a few MNC vendor firms or a single client firm. This strategy of dependent, or path-following, catch-up is not entirely detrimental because it may lead to stable growth for a while. However, in the long term, the strategy is often uncertain as new late entrant firms emerge from the next tier in catching-up countries and offer lower wages and costs. The limitations of these dependent catch-up strategies are shown in the case of other countries reported in previous studies.[35]

This discussion leads us to formulate the hypothesis that increased integration into the GVC is desirable at the initial stage to learn from foreign sources of knowledge, and that functional and sectoral upgrade at later stages requires the effort of seeking a separation and independence from existing foreign-dominated GVC. But then, latecomer firms and economies might seek more opening or integration after building their own local value chains.

My earlier studies illustrated that the first phase of participating in the GVC is to obtain operational knowledge or skills in the "learning by doing" mode of participating in the arrangement of OEM or FDI.[36] The intermediate stage of separation is to build capabilities in design, R&D, and marketing.[37] The last phase of re-increasing GVC participation tends to emerge when the firms often become internationalized in production, face rising domestic wages, and relocate their factories to lower-wage sites as exemplified in the next subsection by stories of Korean firms, including SMEs and BBs. The following section illustrates the points of this hypothesis by looking at the cases of firms in Korea.

---

[34]   For instance, Ernst and Kim (2002) and Sturgeon and Lester (2004).
[35]   For instance, Van Dijk and Bell (2007) and Rasiah (2006).
[36]   See Lee (2005) and Chapter 7 of Lee (2013a).
[37]   The explanation of this occurrence relies heavily on the works of authors, such as that of Lee et al. (2015), that discuss learning at different stages in detail.

In the early phase (entry stage in the international division of labor), the typical mode of business is OEM, wherein latecomer firms have their own equipment and facility. However, these firms perform an assembly or processing style of production following the order and designs of foreign MNC vendors in charge of branding and marketing. The sustainability of the OEM strategy is questioned. Thus, we called it the "OEM trap."

For example, more than 500 OEM plush toymakers operated in the mid-1980s in Korea. Currently, the number is almost zero because most of them either went bankrupt because of increased domestic wages and the entry of other cheaper wage-based OEM sites (such as Indonesia in the 1980s and China in the 1990s) or moved their factories to countries with lower wages.[38] Thus, by the 2000s, Korea had approximately 10 ODMs and only one OBM toymaker (Aurora World). The CEO (Mr. Roh) of this company explained that he made a fortune in the 1980s via OEM, but he saw its long-term limitations and the constant squeezing of the profit margin and erosion of price competitiveness with the rising wages in Korea. This case of a possibility of the OEM trap at the firm level could lead to a country-level MIT. These circumstances forced Mr. Roh to risk an attempt to become an OBM. The limitation of the OEM-based catch-up strategies are discussed in the case of other countries, similar to the instances of the pulp and paper industry in Indonesia and the electronics industry in Malaysia.[39] These authors found that latecomer firms achieved some form of catch-up in terms of sales and capital accumulation, but without technological innovation.

However, moving beyond the OEM to the ODM or OBM mode is challenging and involves risks.[40] The first challenge is to sell one's

---

[38]   The story of this company is also from Lee et al. (2015).

[39]   For the Indonesian case, see Van Dijk and Bell (2007), and for the electronics industry in Malaysia, see Rasiah (2006).

[40]   Lee et al. (2015) illustrate the cases of risky but successful transition toward OBM, such as those of Aurora World, Shimro Musical Instruments, and HJC Helmets, which produce toys, musical strings, and helmets as their main competitive items, respectively. These firms eventually caught up with leading brands in the global market,

product independently. Thus, these firms are compelled to adopt the sales-on-credit strategy because customers are not willing to purchase products of unknown brands. To avoid confrontation with the incumbents, firms often ventured into emerging markets and subsequently entered developed countries. The emergence of new and less-costly marketing channels served as a window of opportunity for several latecomers. When Aurora World began to sell its own brand in 1991, incumbent vendors cancelled and stopped their OEM/ODM orders to prevent the company from rising as a new brand owner. The sales of the company declined from 1991 when the firm took the road to being an OBM and stagnated for five years. We call this period the "OBM river," which must be crossed to establish oneself as an OBM company. A similar turbulence in sales was observed in other firm cases discussed in the same study. An interesting note is that the shape of the sales of this company is similar to the hypothesized in-out-in shape (rising, declining, and rising again). The share of the FVA in their production or exports rose again because these firms become internationalized. For example, Aurora World is an SME, but it relocated all its factories to Southeast Asia or China. Only its R&D and headquarter functions remained in Korea.

We find a similar story from the footwear sector in Brazil, which was discussed in several studies.[41] This sector used to be extremely strong and expanded through the increasing integration into the GVCs controlled by large international buyers. However, it gradually declined in the 2000s because of increasing competition from China and the limitations associated with the subordination of local shoe companies to a large GVC. We then noted two groups of firms in the sector. The first group of producers maintained their integration into the GVCs and continued to specialize in the low-price and low-end segments based on cost-lowering and intensive use of subcontractors or informal employment. This group fell into a gradual and eventual

such as Ty for Aurora World, Suzuki for Shimro Musical Instruments, and Shoei or Bieffs for HJC Helmets.

41   See Lee et al. (2017), Szapiro et al. (2015), and Vargas and Alievi (2003).

decline. The second group looked for a position in premium and higher-end markets through strategies that involve not only productive improvement, design investment, and efforts to open up new market niches and new commercialization channels but also the development of their own brand. Ultimately, this second group of firms achieved better integration in the export marketplace through direct trading of shoes with their own brands and designs. Several leading firms are identified within this group, including Grendene, Alpargatas, and Arezzo.[42] Their commonality is the investment in formal R&D activities. This R&D effort resulted in numerous patents and their own technological capabilities and was the basis for their leaving foreign-firm-dominated GVC and gaining independence from the major international shoe dealers in the United States and Europe.

Stages of SME Growth

An emerging conclusion from the studies on global SMEs is that SMEs can transition to OBM, but this process involves tremendous risk and challenges, which should be carefully managed. This transition becomes possible only when the firm makes a structural break by adopting its own path-creation strategy, but it is impossible if the firm stays on the path of subcontracting or collaboration. [43] The new path (or product) created by these SMEs is not entirely new, but is often based on new combinations of existing paths (or products). Some elaboration follows on the path-creation of several successful global SMEs from Korea. For example, Shimro Musical Instruments combined two opposite production methods for manufacturing string instruments. These methods are European-style customization and Japanese-style mass production. Cuckoo's new product combined gas-pressure technology with the old electric rice-cooker technology. HJC Helmets developed new synthetic plastics by mixing two kinds of materials. The resulting hybrid plastics provided an exceptional balance between hardness and shock absorption.

---

[42] See Lee et al. (2017).

[43] This subsection relies heavily on Lee et al.'s (2015) examination of the Korean SMEs.

We can conceive five stages of SME growth and upgrade. The five stages include entry, gradual catch-up, path-creation (or crisis), rapid catch-up, and post-catch-up. The first stage is entry. An SME starts a business by engaging in low value-added activities or by acting as an OEM supplier to one or several vendors. The founders usually have experience working as salespeople or as after-sales service staff in foreign firms or in firms selling imported products.[44] At this stage, an important advantage of the small supplier firms is the low cost of wages. The second stage is gradual catch-up based on increased learning and productivity. New cost advantages become apparent and available as SMEs undergo the process of "learning by doing" (production). These SMEs retain foreign orders because of their low cost, and they gradually increase their market share by increasing productivity. This initiative can be regarded as an effort to catch up by following a preset path or simply as path-following. Successful consumer goods firms then move toward ODM by being able to design a few of the products they previously manufactured. Capital goods firms may similarly transition toward medium value-added segments, particularly by the production of more sophisticated parts and supplies.

The third stage, path-creation, begins when the SMEs attempt something new, such as developing their own products and selling them under their own brand. This effort toward independent marketing is difficult and involves several risks. Those risks include counter attacks from incumbents, such as sudden disconnection in the supplier relationship, litigation over IPRs, initiation of a price war, and dumping. The third stage can be prolonged by a slowdown, which may lead to declining sales and possibly even to a crisis. The performance of SMEs is generally subject to more turbulence compared with large enterprises with diversified business structures and cross-subsidization among affiliates. If firms fail completely, then the process is classified as an aborted attempt to catch up. The situation wherein latecomers choose not to take risks and decide to stay

---

[44]   The founders of both Aurora World and Jusung used to work for a foreign firm as a local salesperson and a maintenance engineer, respectively.

dependent on one or more MNC vendor firms is also possible. However, the limitations of this catch-up strategy of path-following are well documented, and these latecomers may eventually face decline because of the rise of next-tier entrants.

The fourth stage is rapid catch-up. If a latecomer firm successfully overcomes various risks associated with its transition to OBM and succeeds in launching new products, then its sales will start to increase along a steep curve. This movement signals the beginning of the stage of rapid catch-up in sales and market shares. At this stage, the SME consolidates its global system of production, marketing, and R&D. Therefore, the firm ends up acquiring marketing channels and production factories overseas. Once the firms establish their global networks, they can enjoy faster growth in market share and greater profitability as a result of the greater flexibility from the management of its GVC. Notably, the latecomer SME becomes a small MNC.

The final stage is post-catch-up. At this stage, the main concern of the newly established OBM firm is to sustain and defend its current position against possible challengers.

Finally, we can compare the pattern of upgrade and business scope of the SMEs with those of BBs. As pointed out by Tidd et al. (2005: 196), the particular difference between SMEs and large firms is that the former tend to specialize. This contrast between diversification (large firms) and specialization (small firms) translates into different upgrade patterns. Large businesses diversify and make successive entries into new or high value-added industries, whereas SMEs upgrade into high value-added segments in the same industry. By pursuing diversification and resource-sharing, large latecomer firms (or BGs) build synergic bases across affiliates. These firms also adopt a scientific R&D-based approach in the acquisition of proprietary knowledge facilitated by their vast financial resources. Thus, large BGs tend to be involved in both types of inter- and intra-industry upgrading. By contrast, SMEs tend to be less involved in inter-industry upgrading but more involved in intra-industry upgrading efforts within a specialized field of business.

4.5   GROWTH DETOUR OF LATECOMER FIRMS

Researchers such as Mathews, Hobday, and Bell define "latecomer firms" from emerging economies as "resource-poor late entrants."[45] We can observe that one of the most fundamental differences between firms in the advanced and developing economies is the fact that diverse resources are available for the former within the firm or from other firms. By contrast, in emerging economies, these critical resources are not readily available either from within the firm itself or from other neighboring firms. Thus, the main tasks of the firms for catching up include utilizing existing resources, acquiring critically lacking resources, and improving their availability over the course of the firm's life. Profits are sought not to be distributed back to shareholders but to be reinvested for further expansion of firm resources. Alternatively, accounting profitability might be low owing to the additional "growth costs" borne by the firms from developing countries, as confirmed by empirical analysis of Korean vs. American firms, wherein the former represents catching-up (latecomer) firms. Growth costs would include the resources spent to increase brand power and the capabilities of workers, managers, and R&D teams. These costs are borne by all firms, including those from advanced economies, but firms from developing countries will incur higher costs they are faced with more imperfections in markets and other constraints in business environments or investment climates.[46]

The difficulty of building up the initial capabilities of firms in developing countries involves the unique origins of the firms themselves. By starting with simple labor (natural resource)-intensive sectors, latecomer firms in developing countries face severe entry and growth barriers in many of the new, capital-intensive industries. Given the absence of proprietary technology to exploit related industries, and in the presence of potentially high profit rates in "pre-modernized" start-up industries, their pattern of diversification

---

[45]   See Mathews (2002a), Hobday (1995), and Bell and Figueiredo (2012).
[46]   See Tybout (2000), World Bank (2005), and Lee (2013a: Chapter 5).

tends to be opportunistic and technologically unrelated.[47] The latecomer firms in developing countries learn and accumulate knowledge through diversification, which can be called project execution capability. They often pursue diversification not because of internally available strong competences, but to acquire and build new competences by entering new business areas.

This discussion can be summarized by comparing the catching-up firms with the firms in advanced economies depicted in a neoclassical framework (see Table 4–2).

Table 4–2 provides an effective summary of the important differences in the firms of emerging and advanced economies. Given their stark disparities, we can also regard a detour in terms of the evolution of firms in emerging economies, which implies that the latecomer firms should be understood "as they are" and not necessarily as an inferior form of business that should be replaced post haste. Rather, they should undergo their own long-term process of evolution. Specifically, we should not say that latecomer firms should become, as soon as possible, "more specialized rather than diversified," be run by professional managers instead of family-managers, be stand-alone firms rather than BGs, or seek higher profitability and firm values than sales growth. The specific forms of organizations they take must be understood in consideration of the initial, external, and internal conditions they face. Such conditions include a higher degree of market failures in the external environment, and the lack of key resources and competences as the internal conditions associated with their short history. These circumstances have made them grow as a BG and forced or enabled them to diversify in unrelated businesses, often while being run by families.

Notably, this chapter focused on the role of BGs as an organizational device for catching up and upward transition. Such organizational forms allow the sharing of limited resources during the initial entry and growth stages, while subsidizing losses during the entry

---

[47] See Amsden and Hikino (1994).

Table 4–2. *Comparing Catching-Up and Advanced/Mature Firms*

	Advanced firms in developed economies	Catching-up firms in emerging economies
Initial conditions	All resources (competences) available	Many resources lacking
Objective	Profit maximization	Sales growth (or market shares)
Means	Optimization	Acquiring resources and building capabilities
Behavior	Low leverage and low investment; high profitability; high firm value	High leverage and high investment; low profitability; low firm value
Theory	Neo-classical economics: A homogenous, representative firm	Resource-based theory of the firms and evolutionary economics; firms are heterogenous
Examples	American firms	Korean BGs in the 1980s and 1990s
Ownership	Dispersed	Family-controlled (with circular shareholding)
Organization	Stand-alone firms	BGs
Business scope	Specialized	Diversified

Source: Synthesis based on Mathews (2002a), Lee and Temesgen (2009), and Lee (2013a: Chapter 5)

stages. In other words, BGs worked, particularly in several East Asian economies, as an entry device and by solving resource constraints at the firm level. In the innovation stage, they were advantageous in sharing the costs to build and in the efficient utilization of lumpy, intangible (not available in market) assets, such as R&D units. Furthermore, BGs facilitated innovation by allowing a higher level of within-group spillovers of knowledge.

Hence, the core competences of BGs have evolved from simple project execution capabilities at the earliest stage to vertical or horizontal integration at the middle stage and finally to innovation capabilities at the mature stage. The SMEs have also evolved from being the OEM form doing only production to the ODM or OBM form, which performs both marketing and production. Fast decision making in family-controlled firms can usually be identified as an additional source of advantage in sectors such as IT, where technological and product market cycles tend to be short and thus regarded as niche for latecomer firms (Chapter 3).

Given that many economies in Latin America also tend to have BGs, one may wonder why the growth-enhancing effect of BGs did not play out in that region. One possible clue to understand the difference between East Asia and Latin America may entail the different origins and nature of BGs in the two continents. As noted by Guillen (2000), BGs emerged in East Asia in the somewhat asymmetric environment of the protected domestic market, combined with outward-looking and export-oriented regime. By contrast, those in Latin America emerged in another kind of asymmetric environment featuring liberalized domestic markets combined with inward-looking and import-substituting businesses and policy biases. Thus, the East Asian BGs reaped the double benefits of learning by exporting and discipline by world markets (pressure for upgrading their efficiency to meet the market demand). By contrast, Latin American BGs are increasingly oriented toward rent-seeking in domestic markets. This orientation is often aligned with foreign MNCs, which are not necessarily engaged in manufacturing but more involved in resource sectors.

Finally, the use of BGs as a device for catch-up has a number of issues. This caveat has to do with the simple possibility that the more successful the BGs, the more politically powerful they are. If they grow to have strong vested interests, then the BGs would try to manipulate the economic policy of the government, such as market liberalization.[48]

---

[48] A theoretical argument for such distortion was made in Khanna (2000) and Kali (1999), and the example story in Korea is available in Lee, Lee, and Lee (2002).

In Korea, concentration of economic power emerged as a policy issue in the 1990s, and the existence of big players like chaebols distorted the course of financial liberalization in the mid-1990s. A proper sequence entails that "inward" financial liberalization should first allow foreign banks and financial institutions to enter Korea and compete against local financial institutions, but the reverse happened in Korea. That is, "outward" financial liberalization allowed chaebols and chaebol-owned banks and other non-bank financial companies to go abroad to borrow at interests lower than the local rates. This policy choice is perceived by the government as a kind of "give-and-take" between itself and chaebols. Eventually, that choice sowed the seeds for the 1997 financial crisis because of over borrowing in the mid-1990s.

In summary, we conclude that BGs are useful as a form of business organization during the catch-up stage, but long-term costs and benefits should be carefully managed to minimize accompanying risks and political costs. However, these costs and risks are real only after firms succeed in developing into major BBs.

5 Flying on a Balloon Out of the Windows of Opportunity

5.1 INTRODUCTION

This chapter discusses the role of leapfrogging as the final stage of catching up or the overtaking of the incumbent by latecomers. In our context, leapfrogging refers to latecomers adopting the newly emerging techno-economic paradigm while bypassing investment into an old one, thereby attempting to be a leader in the new paradigm era. Leapfrogging simply describes a latecomer doing something earlier than or different from the incumbents. We need leapfrogging beyond detours because detours mostly involve building capabilities, which may not be sufficient to attain the radical reversal of market shares and leadership changes from incumbents to late entrants from emerging economies. This often requires firm-level efforts and exogenous moments of disruption called "windows of opportunity," which in a broad sense refer to arrivals of new techno-economic paradigms and in a narrow sense to disruptive innovations.[1] Without such efforts and windows of opportunity, the chance for hegemony change is often low because incumbents prevail under the existing paradigm.

Such leapfrogging is similar to the "long jumps" that latecomer economies must perform to shift themselves to product spaces located far from their current position or to core spaces dominated by high-income economies.[2] The rise of a national economy is often associated with its success in a certain number of leading sectors. Thus, achieving leapfrogging in some sectors is critical for a nation to rise beyond

---

[1]   Perez and Soete (1988) discussed the role of the rise of new techno-economic paradigms in generating leapfrogging by latecomers who take advantage of new paradigms, thereby surpassing old incumbents.

[2]   This point is mentioned in Hidalgo et al. (2007).

middle-income status to become a high-income economy. This final stage of catch-up tends to involve hegemony competition with incumbents in high-income economies.

In our catch-up dynamics, leapfrogging is similar to flying on a balloon when the ladder to catch-up is kicked away. As we cannot fly a balloon every day and instead have to wait for good weather to do so, economic leapfrogging is more likely to succeed when exogenous windows of opportunity emerge. In relation to the internal dimension, preparation for flying includes having strengthened capabilities, often in big businesses, as discussed in the preceding chapter. Without such preparation, an economy may fall through "windows" rather than fly into the sky.

In discussing leapfrogging, this chapter utilizes "catch-up cycles" developed by Lee and Malerba (2017), which pertain to successive changes in industrial leadership. Catch-up refers to a substantial closing of the market share gap between firms in a leading country and those in a latecomer or follower country. Many industries have witnessed several changes in industrial leadership and the successive catch-up by late entrants. The incumbent often fails to maintain its superiority in production or market shares, and a latecomer catches up with the incumbent. The latecomer who gains leadership then loses to another latecomer. In addition to the lead article by Lee and Malerba (2017), attempts to explain these phenomena were made in sectoral studies collected in a special issue on catch-up cycles published in *Research Policy*. The studies include cases of various sectors, such as cell phones, the memory chip segment of semiconductors, cameras, steel, mid-sized jets, and wine.

The framework of catch-up cycles originated from the belief that the product life cycle theory of Vernon (1966) cannot explain the phenomenon because the theory merely focuses on the location change of factories from advanced to developing countries, and leadership is assumed to remain with firms from advanced countries. The catch-up cycle concept is based on Schumpeterian notions of innovation systems applied at the sector level and the evolution of these systems over time.[3] Several discontinuities may occur during such an evolution. These discontinuities are called windows of opportunity, which refer to the role of the rise of new techno-economic paradigms in generating leapfrogging. These windows of opportunity can be extended to additional dimensions corresponding to the building blocks of a sectoral system, such as changes in demand conditions or in regulation and policies by the government.

With the notion of windows of opportunity, the catch-up cycle framework also uses the concept of "responses" by firms and systems at sectoral or national levels. A few firms from emerging countries and the sectoral system supporting them may respond to the opening of windows and then rise to global leadership. Current leaders from a certain country may fall behind due to a lack of effectiveness in firm and sectoral system response, such as in "incumbent trap" behavior, which leads to misalignments with the new window. The gist of our theory is that diverse combinations of windows of opportunity and the responses of firms and sectoral systems of latecomers and incumbents determine the pattern of successive catch-ups that are most likely to emerge in a sector. We can obtain diverse patterns, such as a standard cycle, an aborted catch-up, or a sustained leadership by incumbents. The standard cycle of a country's leadership consists of four stages, namely, entry, gradual catch-up, forging ahead, and falling behind, as discussed by Lee and Malerba (2017).

This chapter focuses mainly on the observation that leapfrogging is commonly involved in most cases of leadership change or of substantial increase in market shares by latecomers. Thus, although leapfrogging may not be a "sufficient condition" for latecomers to rise to the leadership, it is a "necessary condition" for latecomers to successfully rise to the position of hegemony within the sector, meaning that most leadership-change cases tend to involve the leapfrogging strategy adopted by latecomers. We also hypothesize that typical cases of leadership change involve certain variants of incumbent trap

---

[3] For the concept of the national systems of innovation, see Freeman (1987), Lundvall (1992), and Nelson (1993), and for the SSI, see Malerba (2002, 2004) and Malerba (2004).

behavior, which occurs when incumbents continue using existing technologies rather than switching to new ones or new business models. Without such behavior, hegemony change is not very likely to happen.

This chapter is organized as follows. Section 2 explains the theoretical framework called the catch-up cycle. Section 3 provides a brief summary of stories about changes in leadership in six sectors, with reference to diverse windows of opportunity. Section 4 discusses the preconditions for such leadership changes, such as the capability-building process. Section 5 discusses the role of leapfrogging and incumbent trap behavior in leadership changes. Section 6 discusses sectoral or national responses to the opening of windows and the interaction between the firm and sector-level responses. Section 7 discusses the case of China, which is emerging as the leading country in almost all sectors and is thus leading the next catch-up cycle, as well as the case of leapfrogging by IT service firms in India. Section 8 provides a summary and considers policy implications.

5.2   CATCH-UP CYCLE FRAMEWORK[4]

The product life cycle theory of Vernon (1966) is mostly concerned with factory location changes at the product level. Alternately, the catch-up cycle framework considers diverse factors at the firm, industry, and even national institution levels and the interactions among them. Thus, this framework relies on the Schumpeterian concept of the sectoral innovation system, in which a sector is defined as a set of activities that share common knowledge and that are unified by certain linked product groups for a given or emerging demand. We match each component of the SSI (sectoral systems of innovation) to diverse windows of opportunity to explain the successive changes in industrial leadership.

Several window types can be opened for late entrants. One is the rise of a new techno-economic paradigm that tends to threaten the

---

[4]   This section relies heavily on the author's work, such as Lee and Ki (2017) and Lee and Malerba (2017).

advantage of existing first movers or incumbents involved in investment in the existing capital vantage. When a new paradigm arrives, latecomers and incumbents stand at the same starting line with the new technology. However, incumbents may fall behind by grasping onto old technology, the use of which has placed them in a dominant position. The propensity for incumbents to remain with the old paradigm for a prolonged time can be considered rational as they have considerable investment in it.[5] In this study, instead of dealing with the techno-economic paradigm shift, we deal with a mini-paradigm, a new generation of technologies.

The second window of opportunity type is derived from the secondary components of SSI, namely demand conditions or market regimes; that is, a business cycle and/or abrupt change in market demand, including the rise of new consumers. Mathews (2005) indicated that business cycles create opportunities for challengers to rouse the industry as downturns play a cleansing role. Thus, during downturns, weak players are forced into bankruptcy, and resources are released at low prices to be acquired by challenger firms aiming to enter the industry. These demand changes can be exogenous or intrinsic to the sector but exogenous to firms (e.g., the short-term cyclical behavior of prices of IT sector memory chips and panels).[6]

The third window of opportunity can be opened by the government. This opportunity usually generates an asymmetric environment for incumbents and entrants through a range of regulations and supportive actions for entrants. Latecomers can utilize such asymmetries to offset initial cost differences associated with late entry.

---

[5] Innovation replaces the existing profits of incumbents. By contrast, a late-entrant firm has few profits to replace. Thus, compared with incumbents, entrants have strengthened incentives to adopt or undertake an innovation (Lee and Ki, 2017). Although similar reasoning was discussed in Brezis et al. (1993), the authors tended not to refer to the phenomenon as a replacement effect but as collective irrationality.

[6] Therefore, determining which of the two business cycles (i.e., long-term Kondratieff cycle or short-term investment cycle) matters more than the other is not easy. Business cycle length also differs in every sector. In Mathews (2005), the business cycle length in the LCD panel industry was short (i.e., less than a decade), whereas that in the steel industry was considerably long.

Although the three types of windows of opportunity are assumed to be events that are exogenous to latecomer firms, the firms should recognize and take advantage of these open windows to realize their potential. Firm strategies interact with the windows of opportunity and the technological and market environments affecting their performance. Although our model is not deterministic, it emphasizes the role of actors, particularly firms and governments.

Latecomers have several strategy options available to them for possible entry or catch-up, such as path-following, stage-skipping, and path-creating, in which "path" is the trajectory of technologies and "stage" pertains to phases in trajectories.[7] These three strategies are explained in Figure 5–1, which shows different trends over time of the productivities (vertical axis) of different generations of technologies, with the horizontal axis representing time. The idea of generations of technologies is consistent with the theory of technology life cycle (Abernathy and Utterback, 1978). However, we focus on the implications of generation changes instead of innovation types (i.e., product vs. process innovation) for latecomer entries. Let us suppose that the current time is period 91 in Figure 5–1, and that leading incumbent firms have adopted up-to-date, second-generation technology, thereby enjoying the highest productivity. Now there are three previously mentioned strategies available to latecomer firms intending to make a late entry.

The first option is to adopt the first-generation or oldest technology with the lowest price; the path-following strategy states that latecomers should move along the old technological trajectories of incumbents. An advantage of this strategy is that established firms have reduced concern about the transfer or leakage of proprietary technologies. This is because latecomers target and want to purchase the oldest technologies, as they are readily available at low prices, particularly during business downturns. However, late-entrant firms cannot compete successfully with the

---

[7] What follows relies on Lee and Ki (2017) as well as Lee and Lim (2001), for which the current author is the corresponding author.

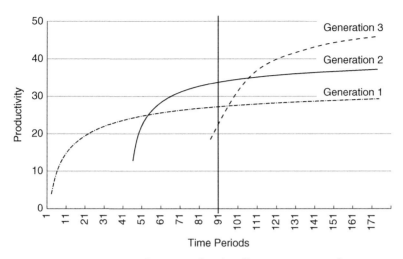

FIGURE 5–1. Leapfrogging and Path-Following Strategies of Latecomer Firms
Source: Lee and Ki (2017), adapted from Lee et al. (2016)
Notes: Path-following strategy = To adopt the oldest (Generation 1) technology
Stage-skipping strategy (leapfrogging I) = To adopt the latest (Generation 2) technology
Path-creation (leapfrogging II) strategy = To adopt emerging (Generation 3) technology.

incumbent in the same market given their low productivity level. Thus, these firms must attempt to enter the market from a different segment (i.e., low-end segment), typically during the mature stage of a product life cycle, while utilizing other advantages such as low labor costs. For instance, the late entry and gradual catch-up by Korean steel company POSCO used a path-following strategy supported by the government to survive as a late entrant while utilizing business downturns in the global steel industry to purchase facilities and equipment at low prices.[8]

The second option is the stage-skipping strategy, in which latecomer firms follow the same path as incumbents but skip previous-generation technologies (Generation 1 in Figure 5.1) to adopt the most

---

[8]   For details, see Lee and Ki (2017).

up-to-date ones (Generation 2 in Figure 5–1), which are of the same generation as those of incumbents.[9] Thus, fierce competition may occur between incumbents and late entrants as the latter take advantage of their capability to adopt up-to-date technology.[10] In addition to the issue of how to raise financial resources to purchases such technologies, late entrants also face the challenge of how to gain access to market for products made from such technology, as well as of whether or not any established firm is willing to transfer such technology to them. The IPR-based protection of technologies by the incumbent may also be a barrier to catch-up.

Thus, a small window is likely to open during downturns of business cycles in that some firms under performance pressure may be willing to sell technologies for smaller, rather than no, compensation. Once the matter of technology transfer or acquisition is resolved for the benefit of a late entrant, the firm may emerge as a powerful rival because it enjoys the same productivity level as the incumbent but also probably avails itself of reduced labor costs or other factor conditions. The rapid progress of POSCO in Korea, with its expansion in capacity through a second mill, is an example of a firm opting for a stage-skipping strategy: it adopted up-to-date technologies, an action that was facilitated by a downturn.[11]

The third choice is the path-creating strategy, which is aggressive and involves risk-taking. This strategy refers to the case of a latecomer exploring its own path of technological development by utilizing a new techno-economic paradigm or a new generation of technologies. Figure 5.1 shows that in this strategy, the late entrant chooses emerging or third-generation technology ahead of incumbent or leading firms that have adopted second-generation technology. This strategy is consistent with the idea that leapfrogging can happen

---

[9]   The productivity curve in the figure is drawn with a strong and simple assumption. In reality, the productivity of entrant firms adopting a stage-skipping strategy may not be as high as that of incumbents with up-to-date technology because an entrant can imitate only part of the experiences of the incumbent.

[10]   On the advantages of latecomers, see Gerschenkron (1962).

[11]   See Lee and Ki (2017) for details.

during generation or paradigm shifts in technology. An apparent advantage of this leapfrogging strategy is that the latecomer chooses technologies with high long-term potential or productivity, as shown in Figure 5–1. However, a risk is that the emerging or new technology is neither stable nor reliable and has low productivity or high costs in its early stages, as shown by the low productivity level in Figure 5–1.[12] Thus, this emerging technology resembles an inferior one with low productivity at its early stages. Despite the high potential of this emerging technology, a firm that adopts it must endure high costs. Thus, losses may be incurred during initial stages in the market.

The preceding idea is consistent with the theory of S-curves, which posits that the inferiority of a new technology at its first appearance discourages incumbents from introducing the new generation of that technology.[13] Thus, a new technology can cause the incumbent to fall into a "trap" of sticking to existing technologies rather than adopting new generation of technology. This situation of the "incumbent trap" can be a window of opportunity for latecomers to be ahead of the incumbent in adopting new generation of technology. This may happen because the latecomers are free from the replacement effect of new technology.[14] Incumbent firms tend to ignore, by rational calculation or mistake, emerging technologies with potential and remain complacent with high productivity from current technologies. This choice may be rational in the short term, but incumbent firms may lose to entrant firms that risk the adoption of emerging technologies. These firms will eventually attain higher productivity than incumbents, thereby winning the market from them.

Not every firm—but probably late entrants or inferior firms with lower productivity levels than the leading firm—has reasons to shift rapidly and lightly to new technologies. Latecomers have a greater incentive than incumbents to take the risk of adopting new

---

[12] Two kinds of risk with leapfrogging strategy are discussed in Lee et al. (2005).
[13] On the S-curve, see Foster (1986) and Utterback (1994).
[14] A number of related studies exist; on the incumbent trap, see Chandy and Tellis (2000), and on the replacement effect, see Arrow (1962).

technologies. However, even risk-taking by latecomers usually requires initial support from the government or venture capital. Without subsidies or incentives, few latecomer firms would take the risk of adopting emerging technologies because they tend to face small or weak demand during the initial entry stage. Thus, the firms would experience difficulties in achieving the initial production volume required for scale economy.

In the above discussion on the catch-up strategies of latecomers, technologies are treated as exogenous, and firms—especially latecomers—are treated as though they face the binary choice of either adopting new technologies or not. However, latecomers usually assimilate the adopted technologies and improve them substantially. This approach is often called follow-on innovation, incremental innovation, or reinvention.[15] Reinvention occurs at the implementation stage for numerous innovations and for many adopters, and it leads to an increased adoption rate of an innovation. We can therefore conceive of two path creation types. This depends on whether a new path is created by the in-house, endogenous innovation activities of latecomers or by the earlier adoption of exogenous or supplier-driven innovation of incumbents, followed by further improvement of the adopted technologies. The former may be common in product innovation or IT sectors such as semiconductors, whereas the latter may be relevant in process innovation-prone sectors such as the steel industry and can thus be called the adoption and follow-on innovation mode.

Although the path-following strategy based on initial factor-cost advantages serves as the gradual catch-up of late entrant market shares, a sharp rise in such shares is likely to occur only when a shift in technologies or demand conditions (particularly downturns) occurs. These shifts are utilized in latecomer by path-creation or stage-skipping. Decisive investment upon the opening of new windows irreversibly changes industry leadership; this forging ahead by latecomers pushes the old incumbent to fall behind. Windows are

---

[15]   This observation was suggested by Martin Bell, who mentioned Rogers (2003).

always deemed to open because generations of technologies and business cycles frequently change. Therefore, leadership change and catch-up by latecomers are predicted to occur repeatedly. This observation also means that the sudden decline and then falling behind of the current leader is always possible. Leadership decline can be predicted by the rise of latecomers and the "falling into a trap" behavior of the incumbent. Leaders tend to be complacent and entrenched in their current success and thus pay less attention to the emerging technology or market paradigm, which includes new consumer brands.

5.3 LEADERSHIP CHANGES AND WINDOWS OF OPPORTUNITY

Record of Leadership Changes

This section provides a summary of the leadership changes in six sectors of manufacturing: cell phones, memory chips, cameras, steel, regional jet aircrafts, and wine. It relies on the highly detailed stories included in the previously mentioned special issue of *Research Policy*.[16] Table 5–1 summarizes events in these sectors in terms of leadership changes or the rise of latecomers and incidents of leapfrogging and incumbent traps.

First, Giachetti and Marchi (2017) found that leadership change in the **cell-phone** sector occurred twice, with an interval of fourteen years. The first change was in 1998 when Nokia and its digital cell phones dethroned Motorola, which invented analogue cell phones. The second leadership change occurred in 2012, during the transition from regular cell phones to smartphones, when Samsung, together with Apple, dethroned Nokia in market shares.

The **memory chip** segment in the semiconductor sector also experienced leadership change twice, namely, from the United States to Japan in 1982 and from Japan to South Korea in 1993. Since

---

[16] The special issue in *Research Policy* includes six articles: Giachetti and Marchi (2017) on cell phones, Shin (2017) on memory chips, Kang and Song (2017) on cameras, Lee and Ki (2017) on steel, Vertesy (2017) on mid-sized jets, and Morrison and Rabellotti (2017) on wine.

Table 5-1. *Types of Catch-Up Strategies and Incumbent Traps in Leadership Changes*

Events/Time	Cell Phones	Memory	Camera	Jets	Steel	Wines
Event (I)	1998	1982	Mid-1960s	1995	1980	Mid-1990s
	US (Motorola) → Finland (Nokia): Path-creation I. Lock-in.	US → Japan: Stage-skipping. Weak investment during downturn.	Germany → Japan (SLR): Path-creation II. Lock-in.	Netherlands → Canada (Fokker → Bombardier): Path-creation I. Slow response to new demand.	US → Japan: Path-creation II. Lock-in.	Rise of new world producers (e.g., US, Australia): Path-creation I. Slow response to new demand.
Event (II)	2012	1993	1980s	2005	1998	Mid-2000s
	Finland (Nokia) → South Korea (Samsung): Path-creation II. Lock-in.	Japan → South Korea: Stage-skipping. Weak investment during downturn.	No change (DSLR).	Canada to Brazil (Embraer): Path-creation I. Slow response to new demand.	Japan (Nippon Steel) → South Korea (POSCO): Stage-skipping. No mistakes.	Return of old world producers (e.g., Italy).

	Event (III)	As of today	Mid 2010s*			
		No change, South Korea leader.	Change likely with rise of new entrants mirrorless camera: Path-creation I. Some lock-in.			
No. of Years (From Event I to II or III)	14	11	50 or so	10	18	10
No. of Events	2	3	3	2	2	2

DSLR = digital single-lens reflex

SLR = single-lens reflex

Total number of events = 14. Event with leadership change = 11 (including two substantial rises). Event without leadership change = 2. Return of the Old World = 1.

Leapfrogging cases (skipping and the two types of path creation, I and II) = all 11 cases of leadership change.

Cases of incumbent traps (lock-ins, weak investments, slow responses to demands) = 10 out of 11 cases.

then, the leadership of South Korean companies has continued, according to Shin (2017). The two leadership change events occurred only eleven years apart, and no signs have been observed regarding any potential leadership change in the near future. Thus, we classify this sector as the case of two occurrences of leadership change and one occurrence of persistent leadership.

The **camera** industry has seen three major technological shifts, as studied by Kang and Song (2017). The first and third technological shifts allowed changes in industrial leadership, whereas the second technological shift allowed the incumbents to maintain their market shares. The first leadership change was from Germany to Japan in the mid-1950s, when German companies manufacturing rangefinder cameras (RFs) were replaced by Japanese firms on a new technological path involving the development of single-lens reflex cameras (SLRs). The second-generation shift was from analogue to digital SLR cameras (DSLRs) in the 1980s. However, this shift did not remove the leadership of Canon and Nikon, which were the established firms. In mid-2010, the invention of compact system cameras (CSC), which are often called mirrorless cameras, led to new or late entrants such as Sony, Olympus, and Samsung, which claimed bigger market shares in some segments or in Asian countries than old incumbents did.

The **steel** industry has experienced two leadership changes (Lee and Ki, 2017). The first change was from the United States to Japan in the late 1970s and early 1980s, and the second was from Nippon Steel in Japan to POSCO in South Korea during the late 1990s. We consider these leading firms in comparing the two countries.

The **regional jets** industry witnessed two instances of leadership change in the past three decades, as explained by Vértesy (2017). The first instance involved British Aerospace (BAe) and Fokker, which were the European incumbents in the sector because of their product lines covering seventy- to 120-seat ranges. They lost their leadership position to Bombardier of Canada in 1995, which created a niche for the fifty-seat market. The second leadership change occurred in 2005 with the rise of the Brazilian Embraer.

The case of the **wine** sector, as studied by Morrison and Rabellotti (2017), can be discussed in terms of "new world" producers (mainly France and Italy) vs. "old world" producers (primarily the United States, Australia, South Africa, and other late entrants such as Chile). European countries dominated the international wine market until the end of the 1980s, with France in the lead, followed by Italy. Two new global leaders have emerged since the early 1990s, namely, the United States and Australia. The mid-1990s can be identified as the period when new world producers substantially grew because their global export market shares increased to a larger amount than that of old world producers. The second period is from early 2000 to the present, which can be characterized by the return of old world producers, particularly Italy, resulting in the coexistence of new and old world producers.

Windows of Opportunity for Leadership Changes

In these stories of leadership changes, diverse windows of opportunity play important roles in introducing successive changes in industrial leadership, such as changes in knowledge and technology, demand and business cycles, and institutions and public policy. This section provides a brief discussion on various windows of opportunity, which are important in the six sectors.

Our main interest is the window of opportunity for the forging-ahead stage of latecomers resulting in either radical changes in leadership or the coexistence of old and new leaders. This clarification is important because such a window of opportunity may play a role in various stages of catch-up cycles. For example, some external conditions play positive or negative roles for entry or gradual catch-up stages. However, we use the term "initial conditions" for early stages and reserve "windows of opportunity" for the forging ahead of latecomers or the substantial rise of new leaders.

Regarding the second window (i.e., the demand window), we observe that expanding demand is not always a favorable window of opportunity for latecomers. The exceptions are the existence of a specific reason or evidence of a strong demand that is more favorable for latecomers than incumbents, or a situation causing the incumbent to fall into complacency or trap-like behavior. We are rather interested in verifying the hypothesis that downturns can be a window of opportunity for latecomers because they can purchase capital equipment and acquire human capital at a lower cost compared to upturns. This case is similar to the forging ahead of South Korean steel firms during the downturn in the early and mid-1980s.

Regarding the third window, the types of "institutional" changes should be distinguished. The emergence of regulatory regimes or public strategy/policy clearly paved the way for decisively providing a window of opportunity contributing to forging ahead and leadership change. Such a case was evident, for example, in the first instance of leadership change in the cell phone industry, which occurred because of the EU-exclusive GSM standard. Another example of the institutional window is the "scope clause" in the aircraft industry.[17]

In contrast to these two cases, there are the cases that we do not consider as an institutional window of opportunity but rather as the "facilitating role" of the government, which influences the effectiveness of responses to windows that had been opened by other factors. In these cases, the opening of other windows of opportunity occurred first, and public policy subsequently assisted firms in exploiting windows that had already emerged. An example includes the second leadership change in the mid-sized jet industry in Brazil where demand changes preceded and the government support followed. The other example is related to public support for memory-related R&D in South Korea, which followed the emergence of new technology as a preceding window of opportunity.

Finally, in many cases, such as the wine industry, innovations occur in response to a demand window. These innovations are

---

[17]   A scope clause is an agreement between a large airline company and the union of pilots regarding paying those employed by large airlines higher wages than those paid by regional airlines, who are subcontracted to fly commuter routes but who cannot fly aircrafts larger than those with fifty seats.

therefore demand-driven and are not considered technological windows. An inevitable issue is distinguishing the windows' relative degree of effect because some windows can play a significant or marginal role in different cases.

The role of various windows of opportunity in leadership changes in the six sectors is subsequently discussed using stories from the special issue of *Research Policy.*

In the **cell phone** sector, technological change was the most significant window of opportunity in both leadership change incidents. The emergence of digital technology was the window of opportunity in the transition from Motorola to Nokia, and the change from regular phones to smartphones was the significant window of opportunity in the transition from Nokia to Samsung. Unlike previous mobile operating systems, such as the Symbian of Nokia, the Android OS of Google was custom-built to support the touch interface that gained popularity among consumers. The first mobile phone vendor that incorporated the Android OS was Samsung.

In the rise of Nokia to leadership, the demand window was important, too, given that the number of individual rather than business phone users increased. There was a significant role by the institutional window, too, associated with the exclusive support of the EU for digital GSM standards by Nokia, which is in contrast to the policy stance in the United States allowing multiple standards to compete in markets. In the transition from Nokia to Samsung, the role of the demand or institutional window was unclear during the forging-ahead stage in 2000, whereas the entry and gradual catch-up of Samsung in the 2G era in the 1990s were facilitated by regulatory intervention by the Korean government. This intervention established the code division multiple access (CDMA) as the exclusive standard in the Korean market.[18]

The **memory chip** segment of the semiconductor industry was characterized by rapid technological progress, with continual

---

[18]   See Lee and Lim (2001).

generational changes of products every three to four years. Thus, late entrants should pursue "not fixed but moving" targets. Late entrants can forge ahead by simultaneously developing two generations (i.e., current and next) of technologies and by taking advantage of the cyclical and predictable nature of technological change.[19] Frequent generational changes in production technologies can be regarded as a window of opportunity for latecomers because they may largely increase investments during such changes, and thus be at a productivity level similar to or higher than that of incumbents. By contrast, the demand window was marginal as the demand for memory chips grew for all players, not just for late entrants. The institutional window can be considered as having some role as Japanese firm investments were stimulated by the Very Large Scale Integration (VLSI) Project coordinated by the government.

A significant institutional window opened in the forging-ahead stage of South Korean firms. However, this window was inverted because it was opened in the United States and not in South Korea at the conclusion of the Semiconductor Trade Agreement (STA) in 1986. STA effectively established a floor price for dynamic random-access memories (DRAMs) in the US market. The selling price of 256 K DRAMs stopped decreasing and instead increased slightly for almost three years after STA was introduced, which helped late entrants in South Korean firms.[20] The entry of South Korean firms, such as Samsung, into the memory chip sector was not supported by the government and was instead a decision of a private firm; the government was unsure of the prospects of Samsung.[21]

In the **camera** sector, the leadership shift from Germany to Japan benefitted significantly from the technological window associated with the emergence of SLRs, which replaced RFs. The SLR was originally a German invention, but Japan adopted and improved the device. Another significant factor was the demand surge associated with

[19] This statement is the key point of Shin (2017).
[20] See Langlois and Steinmueller (1999).
[21] See Lee and Lim (2001) and Shin (2017).

World War II and the Korean War, which focused on Japanese products, given the proximity of Japan to South Korea. The institutional window was present in the form of sector promotion by the government, which included private–public joint R&D.[22] However, this promotion may be considered facilitating rather than significant. Although a technological shift from SLR to DSLR occurred in the 1980s, the shift was a "competence-enhancing" discontinuity because DSLR technology was developed primarily from existing SLR technology, except for the image sensor. Thus, a continuation of the leadership of established firms is evident. This leadership was challenged only in the mid-2000s with the rise of a "competence-destroying" innovation, namely, the so-called mirror-less cameras. In this leadership shift, the technology window was accompanied by a demand window represented by the rise of new "ordinary" users in emerging Asia.

In the **regional jets** sector, technological changes did not play a role as a window, although demand-driven innovations were present (Vértesy, 2017). First, the demand shift from the seventy- to 120-seat range of European firms to the fifty seats of the Canadian Bombardier was significant, together with the reduction in oil prices, market liberalization, and the expansion of regional services. These services improved through the introduction of scope clauses, in contrast to the shrinking demand for large regional jets. In the second leadership shift, the Brazilian Embraer benefitted from a window of new demand and the regulatory windows of opportunity. This time, oil prices hiked and the air transport market became highly competitive with the arrival of low-cost carriers. The seventy- to 120-seat market increased at the expense of the fifty-seat regional jet market and the 150-seat "large civil jet" market. Although scope-clause limitations were relaxed from fifty to seventy or more seats, fluctuations in the world economy caused regional and mainline carriers to become increasingly inclined to adjusting the sizes of aircrafts to market demand. Embraer was the first to

---

[22]   See Alexander (2002:26) and Donze (2014).

undertake the seventy- to–120-seat niche by developing a new product line. This scope-clause change can also be regarded as an inverted window because it happened in a foreign country (the United States). The role of scope-clause change as a window is also consistent with the idea that business cycle downturns serve as a window for latecomers because the clause change is affected by the oil price hike and the succeeding recession (Vértesy, 2017).

In the **steel** sector, the leadership shift from the United States to Japan involved the technological and institutional windows but not the demand window. Japanese firms immediately adopted the Austrian innovation of the basic oxygen furnace method (BOF) that they further improved through follow-on innovation (Yonekura, 1994). The Japanese government was also involved because it arranged the collective licensing of BOF for significantly reduced royalty fees (Nakamura and Ohashi, 2012). The Korean state-owned firm, POSCO, outperformed its "teacher" firm, Nippon Steel, in Japan in the late 1990s. The demand window in this case was significant because POSCO purchased state-of-the-art technologies at considerably lower costs as a result of the global recession in the 1980s (D'Costa, 1999). The institutional window was also present for POSCO because the government participated in indicative planning for the growth of steel-consuming sectors, such as shipbuilding and automobile sectors.

Wine is another sector in which the technological window did not play a significant role (Morrison and Rabellotti, 2017). For the substantial increase in new world producers in the 1990s, the demand window led to the emergence of new, inexperienced consumers from the United Kingdom, the United States, and Scandinavian countries. For the return of old world producers in the 2000s, the demand window indicated a strong demand for additional sophisticated and varied wines in new and traditional markets, as well as the recent upsurge of the Asian market. Although several technological innovations were developed, they can be regarded as a response to these changing demand and consumer preferences. With respect to the second change or return of the old leaders, several producers in the old world responded to increasing competition from new world countries by upgrading quality and adopting new tastes for wines.

Summary

We consider six sectors, with each sector having two or three instances of leadership change, leadership persistence, or the return of old leaders that results in the coexistence of new and old leaders. We consider fourteen events in our analysis. First, cases of leadership changes include eleven events (Table 5–1), two of which contributed to the substantial rise of late entrants, namely, in the wine and camera sectors in the mid-1990s, and mid-2010s, respectively. Second, the persistence of leadership involves two cases, namely, those in the memory chip and camera sectors, since 1993 and in the 1980s, respectively. One case refers to the return of incumbents in the wine sector since the mid-2000s and the eventual coexistence of old and new firms.

5.4 INITIAL CONDITIONS AND CAPABILITIES FOR LEADERSHIP CHANGES

This section discusses the role of capability-building at the initial or preparation stage as a precondition for leapfrogging. Such capability-building is referred to as "correcting failures" and "overcoming barriers" in preceding sections. Capability-building is often used interchangeably with "initial conditions," "inherited advantages," or previously accumulated "stocks" of capabilities and resources that were already present before the windows of opportunity emerged. These aspects are the important elements of the sectoral or national innovation system shaping and constraining firm responses. System-level responses and any misalignments can also be discussed under the forging-ahead stage. Thus, this section details the initial conditions for leadership change. The next section discusses leapfrogging and other catch-up strategies of latecomers and the responses of incumbents, such as lock-in or the incumbent trap, as well as sectoral system-level responses or macro-level factors of leadership changes.

In the **cell phone** sector, one of the favorable initial conditions for Nokia was the locational specificity of Finland, which spends a large amount of money on connecting sparsely populated areas using fixed wires. Thus, the installation of wireless phone services was highly promoted, and strong incentives were provided for establishing cellular services (Giachetti and Marchi, 2017). In Finland, the critical and initial condition for entry into the GSM market in the late 1980s and early 1990s coincided with the collapse of eastbound exports to the Soviet Union, whereby resources could be relocated from existing mainstream markets to "wireless fringe" markets (Palmberg and Martikainen, 2005). In terms of required technological capabilities, Nokia was an entirely new entrant and also an "incubating entrant." Nokia possessed latent competencies in GSM-related technologies because of its many years of experience in technologies related to digital signal processing, the software logic of which was highly similar to that specified in the GSM standard (Palmberg and Martikainen, 2005). Accordingly, Nokia had already been an actor in the early 1980s.

For Samsung's introduction of the CDMA-standard cell phone, crucial initial conditions included the exclusive standard policy of the government. However, while the firm had no previous experience in manufacturing analogue or GSM cell phones, Samsung and other South Korean firms chose to develop a CDMA cell phone by collaborating with Qualcomm, a foreign technology start-up (Lee and Lim, 2001). Thus, a tripartite joint R&D consortium consisting of public, private, and foreign entities was the main channel of initial learning and building technological capabilities, along with their pre-existing capabilities in manufacturing various consumer electronic products.

In **memory chips**, the main channel for accessing foreign technology was licensing. For example, Samsung purchased a 64 K bit DRAM design technology from Microelectronic Technology, a small US-based venture and technology manufacturing company from Japan-based Sharp (Lee and Lim, 2001). Thus, for the gradual catch-up stage, the strategy of Samsung can be considered a path-following catch-up. The sector-level initial condition was that before Samsung entered the memory chip sector, several South Korean firms were already engaged in wafer processing and absorbing production technology as FDI firms or OEMs, with facilities provided by foreigners. These early-starting firms were acquired by big conglomerates, such as Samsung, when they decided to enter the memory chip business. Another favorable sectoral system-level initial condition for Japanese and South Korean firms in memory chip production was their tendency to be conglomerates (i.e., a BGs) instead of stand-alone firms. As conglomerates, they have a massive capacity for aggressive and timely investment backed by resource-sharing among affiliates, which is an important factor for success in cycle-sensitive sectors such as memory chips (Shin, 2017; Kim and Lee, 2003). For example, the entire Samsung Group had to accommodate accumulating losses from its first seven years of operation in the memory chip sector by mobilizing funds from its affiliates.

The initial, sector-level condition for Japanese entry and gradual catch-up in the **camera** industry occurred during World War II (Kang and Song, 2017). To cope with the surging demand for optical military equipment, Germany sent optical engineers to Japan, enabling the latter to absorb advanced knowledge in the fields of optics and imaging. For example, Nikon acquired most of its early technologies for optical products with the help of German firms before the war. This technological aid was further accelerated during World War II when Nikon began producing optical instruments for military use (Alexander, 2002). Thus, the main channel of learning for Japanese producers, particularly Canon and Nikon, was the knowledge and technology transfer and information leakage from Germans. Naturally, the Japanese initially imitated German camera designs and technologies to develop a "Japanese Leica" through reverse engineering (Donze, 2014). Thus, the Japanese strategy during the gradual catch-up stage can be considered a path-following catch-up.

In the **regional jet** sector, particularly for Bombardier, the strong sectoral innovation system in the aerospace industry was among its favorable initial conditions (Vértesy, 2017). Canada had accumulated a strong knowledge base over the preceding half century. Its aerospace firms, which have been sponsored by the National Research Council since the 1950s, are the largest R&D spenders, which has resulted in the local development of gas turbines and the high capability of firms located in Montreal and Toronto clusters to offer wind tunnel tests (Niosi, 2000).

The initial condition in Brazil for the rise of Embraer was similar to that of Bombardier in Canada, because Brazil also has a long history in small aircraft production and aeronautical research. After the mass production of sport planes and military trainers under a license that ended after World War II, the Brazilian government continued financing aeronautical research and training. In the 1950s and 1960s, the Institute for Training Aeronautical Engineers and the Aeronautics Technical Center, a technological research organization, became the backbone of the Brazilian aerospace innovation system (Vertesy, 2011). A research team from the center designed a twenty-seat turboprop, which filled a market niche in the US commuter market. In 1969, the team finally established a new SOE called Embraer. Linkages with the Brazilian Air Force and the government were strategically employed to finance development, access technology, protect the nascent market, and facilitate export market access, which is the use of diplomacy to hasten the certification of new models (Ramamurti, 1987; Silva, 2005). These developments allowed accumulated capabilities to adopt and modify technologies developed elsewhere.

In the **steel** sector, Japan has a long history of absorbing foreign technology that dates back to the prewar period before their forging ahead in the 1970s. The South Korean entry into the integrated steel mill sector was extremely late (i.e., the early 1970s) and was in the form of an SOE, which was part of the government-level initiative to promote the industry. The favorable condition was the global recession in steel that occurred after the first oil shock, which enabled POSCO to purchase a license for factory facilities and equipment at a low cost, mostly from Japanese steel firms. Thus, POSCO pursued a path-following catch-up strategy during its gradual catch-up period in the 1970s to the mid-1980s (Lee and Ki, 2017).

In the **wine** sector, one of the favorable initial conditions was the change in UK regulation in the 1970s that allowed supermarkets to retail wine and thus established a new market (Anderson and Nelgen, 2011b). This was immediately exploited by Australia, given its close historical ties with the United Kingdom. Supermarkets in the United Kingdom thus required large volumes of consistent, low-priced but branded premium wines. New world wine producers were also different from incumbents in terms of their organization. They were mostly large corporations that commanded the branding and volume capabilities of producing wines of a consistent quality, as well as directed strong investments to modernize and improve viticulture and enology techniques (Cusmano et al., 2010).

A quick **summary** follows. Despite their apparent diversity, the three main categories of sector-level initial conditions are geographical locations, historical legacy, and firm organization (i.e., conglomerates or BGs facilitating entry on the basis of internal capital markets and cross-subsidy). Regarding the method of learning and accessing advanced foreign knowledge, the main channel is primarily technology transfer, mostly through licensing (particularly for non-information and communications technology (ICT) and secondarily by public–private or domestic–foreign joint R&D (mostly in ICT sectors). The importance of licensing is that late entrants can adopt external technologies rather than innovate on their own. However, all cases involved a long history of learning efforts and the accumulation of capabilities, particularly in the case of jets in Canada and Brazil. Thus, late entrants in many cases tend to adopt the path-following strategy for the early or gradual catch-up stage, which involves following technological trajectories that are the same as or similar to those of incumbents.

5.5 THE ROLE OF LEAPFROGGING AND INCUMBENT TRAPS

Latecomer Response to the Opening of Windows

Although the three windows of opportunity types are assumed to be exogenous to latecomer firms, as discussed in preceding paragraphs, firms should recognize and take advantage of the opening of a window to realize their potential. The capabilities and strategies of firms and the sectoral system interact with windows of opportunity to generate diverse outcomes. Regarding the responses and strategies of the latecomers, Section 2 discussed strategies, such as path-following, stage-skipping, and path-creating, which were divided into either a path-creation along the endogenous innovation mode (path-creation I in Table 5–1) or an adoption and follow-on innovation mode (path-creation II in Table 5–1).

Table 5–1 also provides information for each sector on the type of catch-up trajectory and strategy employed. Every leadership incidence tends to involve variants of leapfrogging, including either stage-skipping or path-creation I or II.

First, in **mobile phones**, the progress of Nokia can be classified as path-creation along the endogenous mode because the company opted for a new path for digital cell phones that is different from that for analogue by Motorola. Samsung forging ahead in the 2000s over Nokia can be classified as path-creation along the adoption and follow-on innovation mode. Samsung adopted the Android OS of Google for its smartphones, which differed from Nokia feature phones and its Symbian OS-based smartphones. However, Samsung also adopted path-creating leapfrogging at its early stage of growth as it, together with Qualcomm, invented the first mobile phone in the world that was based on the CDMA standard, unlike the TDMA–GSM standard followed by Nokia (Lee and Lim, 2001).

Both incidents of leadership change in the **memory chip** sector involved a stage-skipping type of leapfrogging or dynamic catch-up because Japan and South Korea tended to target next-generation chips in their dynamic catch-up process to be ahead of incumbents (Shin, 2017).

The rise to the leadership by Japanese firms in the **camera** sector in the 1950s became possible because they created a new technological path (SLR) different from the German incumbents. This event is regarded as path creation along the adoption and follow-on innovation mode because Japanese firms adopted and improved the SLR that was first invented by a German firm.

Both incidents of leadership change in the **regional jets** sector can also be classified as path creation along the adoption and follow-on innovation mode. Bombardier of Canada created a niche for the fifty-seat craft, in contrast to the two European incumbents that retained their existing product lines covering seventy to 120 seats. The rise of the Brazilian Embraer against Bombardier was similar because the former also targeted a different niche—for seventy to 120 seats—by developing a new product line and using more advanced technology than that used for existing products.

In the **steel** sector, the rise of Japan against the United States was path-creation along the adoption and follow-on innovation mode. Japan adopted and further improved the Austrian-invented BOF method, whereas the United States was stuck with the old open hearth furnace (OHF) method (Lee and Ki, 2017). South Korean POSCO rising against Japanese Nippon Steel is an example of stage-skipping leapfrogging because the former adopted state-of-the-art technologies for its second mill from the mid-1980s to the 1990s.

Finally, the rise of new world **wine** producers can also be regarded as path- creation targeting new markets with differentiated products. Morrison and Rabellotti (2017) indicated that the new production pattern developed by new world producers was characterized by technological modernization, product upgrading, and marketing innovations. These innovations were largely market-driven, and they aimed to solve problems related to output variability, quality, and adaptation to international taste.

In summary, all **eleven cases** of leadership change tend to involve an element of either leapfrogging I or II, including path-creation I or II or stage-skipping, but none of path-following. This verifies leapfrogging as one of the necessary conditions for leadership changes.

Incumbent Responses: Lock-Ins, Incumbent Traps, and Delayed Investments

We now examine the role of incumbent responses in industrial leadership changes. We are interested in determining whether or not and to what extent any lock-in or delayed response by incumbents, such as firms and systems, contributes to the rise of late entrants. Table 5–1 shows that various types of incumbent reactions that can be classified as ex-ante lock-ins and complacency or ex-post delayed responses tend to be present in ten out of eleven leadership change events or rises of late entrants.

In the **cell phone** sector, Motorola largely invested in improving the analogue system despite the emergence of digital telecommunication technologies adopted by Nokia, which is a perfect example of the incumbent trap. Thereafter, Nokia stayed with its own old mobile operating system (Symbian) rather than switching to the Android OS that was custom-built to support the touch interface in smart phones.

In the two leadership change incidents in the **memory chip** sector, incumbents tend to be highly cautious or conservative in investing during downturns, when late entrants largely invest in preparation for next generation technologies (Shin, 2017).

In the **camera** industry, the mid-1950s leadership change from German to Japanese firms also involved complacency and lock-in factors among incumbents. Leading German firms continued to focus on the RF and disregarded the SLR introduced by the Japanese, which significantly solved the two critical problems of the old RF, namely, parallax and limited lens interchangeability (Donze, 2014).

The **steel** sector has another example of the incumbent trap because American firms did not immediately adopt the new BOF method, unlike the Japanese. By contrast, POSCO outperforming Japanese firms did not involve any apparent mistake by the latter or incument, other than their willingness to transfer technology to POSCO (upon payment) at its early stages.

In the remaining cases of **regional jets** and **wine** sectors, any mistake by incumbents tended to involve a slow response to changing or newly rising market demands. Such a pattern is possible because these events tend to involve the demand rather than the technology window. For example, in the leadership shift from European firms to the Canadian Bombardier, the former continued with their strategy of addressing the fifty-seat market with turboprops instead of jets because of sunk costs in their seventy- to 120-seat jet and fifty-seat turboprop product line. However, the demand for the Bombardier fifty-seat regional jets in the 1990s significantly exceeded the demand for its seventy- to 120-seat regional jets. A similar story unfolded after another shift in market demand in the early 2000s, involving the incumbent Bombardier against Embraer, its rising rival from Brazil.

The cases of the sectors addressed in this study indicate that the sources of the incumbent trap and slow response are diverse and include misjudgment, the presence of costly equipment with a relevant economic life, and high uncertainty about the future of economic variables. Misjudgments may occur in estimating the potential of new technologies or new markets vs. those in existing markets. In other cases, such as those in the steel sector, one of the reasons American steel firms did not adopt BOF is because of the number of mills constructed on the basis of the old OHF method before the mid-1950s, and the useful economic life of their OHFs did not end when BOF was introduced to commercial operations in the mid-1950s (Yonekura, 1994). The incumbent inevitably falls into the trap whenever an innovation emerges before the end of a current life cycle. When Bombardier performed strategic actions in response to the demand window opened to small regional jets at the end of the 1980s, BAe and Fokker, the incumbent regional jet producers, had a valid reason not to follow suit. Given that outlooks for low oil prices were uncertain, a fair assumption was that airlines, which are price sensitive in the increased competition because of liberalization in air transport services, would buy more low-priced fifty-seat turboprops than jets. The significant decrease in the development costs of their existing product line adds to the difficulty in questioning the rationale of Bombardier to maximize the economic life cycle of existing products (Vertesy, 2017).

Thus, the extent to which such a decision-making process is a mistake or is rational remains an interesting issue. For example, the trap may only be in an ex post sense regarding whether or not to adopt new technologies. In the early days, new technologies were often costlier, less productive, and less reliable than previous ones, which is why incumbents who command the highest productivity from existing technologies are hesitant to adopt new technologies. The incumbent trap concept can be sufficiently broad to include the "innovator's dilemma," which is the case of whether or not to introduce innovations detrimental to the current business of the incumbent (Christensen, 1997). An example case of this broad definition of the incumbent trap is when Motorola attempted to further improve existing analogue telecommunication technologies despite the arrival of digital ones. Giachetti (2013) and Häikiö (2001) observed that even when digital standards rapidly circulated to many countries because of their superior technical performance with respect to analogue standards, Motorola persisted in investing heavily in analogue mobile phone technologies. The company believed that customers would accept the technological trajectories imposed by its leadership.

5.6 SYSTEM-LEVEL RESPONSES FOR LEADERSHIP CHANGES

Role of the Sectoral Innovation System

This section discusses sector-level responses, including aspects beyond firm level, to consider institutional dimensions (e.g., facilitating government roles), misalignments, and macro-variables (e.g., wage and exchange rates). Responses are highly diverse depending on which sectors in which distinct forms of sector-level responses and events tend to be involved. Therefore, identifying several regularities or stylized facts is difficult.

From the latecomer point of view, broad system-level responses vary. For example, the Japanese forging ahead in the memory chip sector triggered by large increases in investment was facilitated by the government-coordinated VLSI program. The development and progress of Japanese cameras in the 1950s and steel in the 1970s, regional jets in Brazil, and steel in Korea became possible with the active promotion of corresponding governments, although significance level varied depending on the case. In the rise of the Japanese camera, the role of close interfirm cooperation and sharing of key technologies were evident. For example, Nikon helped Canon by providing RFs and lenses (Donze, 2014), and the cooperation between the two specialized firms facilitated technological advancements and economies of scale in the catch-up process (Kang and Song, 2017). In the case of Korean steel, the government promoted the new sectors to consume steel, such as shipbuilding and automobile sectors (Lee and Ki, 2017). Finally, for new world wine producers, the government, particularly that of Australia, played a significant role.

Among the incumbents, slow responses or misalignments of sectoral systems were present in several cases. For example, in the first case of leadership change in the wine industry, extensive EU regulation massively constrained the ability of old world incumbents to respond to market changes. A similar system-level misalignment led to the decline of the United States against Japan in the memory chip sector. Shin (2017), supported by Borrus et al. (1983) and Langlois and Steinmuller (1999), observed that the structure of the US semiconductor industry was peculiar because of its strong anti-trust regulations. The regulation did not allow AT&T and IBM to sell their chips in the open market, which resulted in the emergence and dominance of merchant producers in the US semiconductor industry. However, these merchant producers had more structural disadvantages in sustaining long-term investments than Japanese integrated keiretsu manufacturers. The former tended to cut down investments during the downturn of business cycles, whereas the latter was able to maintain its investments with earning from other businesses. The last example is the case of UK shipbuilders, who did not immediately adopt the new technology (i.e., the welding block method) because of opposition by the trade union. The old rivet method requires four workers, whereas the new method only necessitates one (Lim, Kim, and Lee, 2017). Delayed adoption resulted in the inability of UK firms to compete with Japanese shipbuilders, who realized reduced delivery time and improved productivity after adopting the welding block method (Cho and Porter, 1986).

Finally, the economic success of a country tends to bring changes to its macro variables (e.g., exchange or wage rates), which may work adversely and result in the decline of domestic sectors and their firms. Wage rates or local currency values tend to appreciate if a country succeeds and expands its industrial production and exports. Certain countries prefer to maintain their undervalued exchange rates as an implicit subsidy to boost exports. However, currency values are expected to appreciate if a country succeeds in its exportation and trade surplus is recorded. This situation implies that even macro-variables are endogenous to a certain extent, particularly when a sector is considerably large in a national economy and directly affects overall market wage and exchange rates.

Therefore, long-term changes in macro-variables may be a factor in the eventual decline of a sector in a country. An example is the memory chip sector, where foreign exchange rates became one of the game-changing variables in the competition between Japan and South Korea, particularly when the Japanese yen went into a long-term rapid appreciation against the South Korean won after the Plaza Accord in the mid 1980s. This case served as a critical factor in the rise of South Korean industries and the fall of the Japanese industry. The yen–dollar exchange rate was $227 per yen in 1980, and it decreased to $128 in 1988 (after the Plaza Accord) and below $100 in 1995.[23] In terms of relative rates between the South Korean won and the Japanese yen, 1 yen was equal to 2.7 won in 1980, 5.8 won in 1988, 7.4 won in 1996, and 10 won in 2000.

---

[23]   Data sources are the World Bank and the World Development Indicators.

In the meantime, the rapid increase in wage rates in South Korea may potentially cause the decline of its industries, and then other latecomer countries such as China may catch up. For instance, in the mid-1990s, the South Korean wage rate was less than half that of Japan. However, the former steadily increased in the 2000s, reaching 74% in 2004 and in the range of 90%–110% in the late 2000s (source: International Labor Organization, World Bank).

Interaction among Windows and the Responses by Firms and Systems

The discussion in the preceding sections explained the contingent nature of the effects of windows of opportunity on changes in leadership. Whether or not a window results in leadership change depends on the responses of incumbents and latecomers and their systems. The point connects directly with an aspect of original insight from the concept of windows of opportunity by Perez and Soete (1988: 476), who emphasized the contingent role of technological windows and of knowledge and human resource that are mostly available in public organizations, such as universities, in catching windows of opportunity. The current discussion confirms the general idea of this contingent role and extends it from technological to demand and institutional windows to broad responses related to the sectoral system.

First, we determined that the required capabilities may not only be the generic human capital available in the public domain but also firm capabilities and system responses, as discussed in previous sections.

Second, although Perez and Soete (1988) tended to treat technological windows as exogenous, the cases discussed in the present study refer to the possibility for windows to be "endogenously created" by sectoral system actors. A possible case involves technology windows emerging from firm R&D investments in completely new technologies. One lesson learned from sectoral studies is that considering such "endogenously created windows" as firm responses is better than viewing them as windows. Explanations are presented in the following paragraphs.

We realize that the degree of exogeneity or endogeneity of innovation may depend on who initiates changes in technology. From the perspective of current leaders, innovations must be led toward the direction of competence enhancement when faced with several alternative directions for technical changes. Thus, leaders may "endogenize" technological change in a beneficial direction; the cases of Canon and Nikon illustrate this point. Therefore, they have maintained leadership since the 1980s despite the rise of digital technologies. If these leaders succeed in this direction and are able to transform their successes into industry standards, then they are likely to maintain their leadership positions in future generations. In this way, the memory chip business of Samsung has maintained leadership since 1993 (Shin, 2017).

Accordingly, we propose that innovations created by endogenous actions of firms should not be considered as windows of opportunity. By contrast, changes in technology may be exogenous for latecomers who are below frontiers. Thus, they may have to choose alternative technologies or standards. However, the boundary between exogeneity and endogeneity is ambiguous in several cases. As discussed in the case of the cell phone sector, Google developed a completely new OS for smartphones (i.e., Android). The decision to adopt this standard depends on the endogenous decision-making of firms. While Samsung adopted such an exogenous window to generate success in the new smartphone market, Nokia refused to adopt it and maintained its own OS, which then became the major cause of its downfall. Given that Google also manufactures and sells smartphones, the same technology (i.e., a new OS) is considered endogenous technology for this company but exogenous for Samsung and others. This case suggests that whether or not a new technology can be considered exogenous or endogenous is determined on a case-by-case basis. In general, exogeneity is justified for latecomers.

Third, another related issue concerns the distinction between "competence-destroying" and "competence-enhancing" innovations

(Tushman and Anderson, 1986). This distinction is useful for developing the hypothesis that only competence-destroying innovations may serve as windows of opportunity. This hypothesis is consistent with the case of leadership change from the United States to Japan in the steel sector. The new BOF can thus be considered as competence-destroying for the incumbent US firms. Meanwhile, the camera industry shift to digital technology in the 1980s is an example of a competence-enhancing innovation which did not lead to leadership change (Kang and Song, 2017). The DSLR design was developed primarily on the basis of the SLR design, with the only crucial difference being that film-related parts have been substituted with image sensors. However, this same innovation can be regarded as competence-destroying if one focuses exclusively on the compact camera.[24]

Fourth, we realize that considering the exogeneity or endogeneity of institution and public policy windows is also controversial. Several government actions and measures are simply exogenous to firms, whereas a few others may have been lobbied for by firms in a particular sector. An extreme case is when the government establishes an SOE to enter a sector, such as in the POSCO case in South Korea. This government action was exogenous, but it cannot be regarded as a window of opportunity for firms because the government itself attempted to create a window for its own firm or for the sector of a country. In general, the role of the government in early and later catch-up stages should be discussed separately. Therefore, the role of the government is seemingly critical during the entry and gradual catch-up stages, which is the so-called the infant industry argument that infants need protection until they grow into an adult. The example include the entry of an SOE into the steel sector (South Korea), the shipbuilding industry in Korea (Lee, Lim, and Kim, 2017), and regional jets in Brazil (Vértesy, 2017). The gradual catch-up of Samsung in the

---

[24] In this argument, as presented by Tripsas and Gavetti (2000), the transition to digital may be considered a radical change if one views the camera industry as a whole, without making a distinction between built-in and interchangeable-lens cameras.

cell phone sector was motivated by the public–private joint R&D efforts to develop CDMA and by the exclusive standard policy in mobile phones implemented by the South Korean government (Lee and Lim, 2001). However, the later forging ahead of Samsung during the 2000s to surpass Nokia was predominantly achieved by the firm alone.

From the eleven leadership change cases, those identifying the significant role of institutional and government windows were limited to only two, namely, the rise of Nokia in the cell phone sector and the rise of Japan in the steel sector in the 1970s. In these cases, the role by the government affected the decision and speed of adopting new technologies. In general, latecomers have a greater incentive than incumbents in adopting new technologies because their productivity levels tend to be lower than those of leading firms. However, the risk that latecomers take often requires initial government support. Without subsidies or incentives, few latecomer firms adopt emerging technologies because these technologies often coincide with uncertainty and low productivity at the early stages of development.

Fifth, although the preceding paragraph explains that "follow-on innovation" capabilities are often necessary at the forging-ahead stage of catch-up cycles, building such capabilities as preconditions often takes a long time. An extreme example is the case of Embraer, which has been present in the sector for several decades, beginning with the period of state-owned and intensively state-directed development of aircraft production in the 1960s. Japan became able to dominate the United States in the steel sector in the 1980s because the steel industry of the former had a significantly early start, dating back to the prewar period. POSCO also took almost thirty years to surpass Nippon Steel in 1998, at least in terms of steel gross output. Such a struggle is evident even in IT-based sectors, such as the memory chip manufacturing sector. The Samsung Electronics Corporation took approximately twenty years after its establishment to surpass Japanese firms in 1993. The time span required to build innovation capabilities from production capabilities may be short in the case of sectors based on explicit knowledge (Jung and Lee, 2010) and of those with a short cycle of technologies (Lee, 2013a).

5.7 EXTENSION TO CHINA AND THE SERVICE SECTOR AS THE NEXT CATCH-UP CYCLE

China Leading the Next Catch-Up Cycle

Although the preceding analysis does not consider China, many sectors are now witnessing its rise as the new leader. For instance, in cell phone market in China, Samsung used to be ranked first or second until early 2010 but is no longer one of the top ten firms. Such catch-up is also prevalent in global markets. First, Chinese firms such as Xiaomi and Oppo have recently unseated Samsung, which used to be number one in the cell phone market in India. In the global smartphone market, Chinese firms led by Huawei are ranked third, after Samsung and Apple. Assessing China's achievement from the catch-up cycle perspective is worthwhile. A study of four sectors in China—mobile phones, telecommunication systems, automobiles, and semiconductors—was recently conducted.[25] One of the findings is that the catch-up by China tends to use the large and segmented domestic market as the initial nurturing ground for indigenous firms and their eventual global expansion.

This factor can be explained in terms of the role of market regimes in the sectoral system framework. If markets feature segmentation or the existence of low segments, such conditions play an important role, as seen in the three successful cases of cell phones, telecommunication systems, and automobiles, in contrast to the slow catch-up in memory chips without such features. Chinese firms managed to achieve initial success from a low-end market in segmented market conditions (e.g., telecom equipment and mobile phones) and in a government-protected market (e.g., telecom equipment). Conversely, latecomers in markets with no such segmentation (e.g., memory chips) find entering such a sector difficult. This difficulty is

[25]   See Lee, Gao, and Lee (2016).

one of the reasons behind the slow progress of Chinese firms in the memory chip sector. This finding implies that one of the most difficult challenges faced by latecomers is identifying their initial entry point or niche market, such as low-end or inland markets.

One interesting aspect of the rise of China is the importance of the institutional window. This can be seen in the active role of government ministries, combined with the large size of domestic markets, which have served as sources of large bargaining power in dealing with MNCs for technology transfer and licensing. For instance, Huawei is a privately owned global IT company from China, and its initial growth momentum was the government promotion of domestically produced fixed-line telephone switches (Mu and Lee, 2005). The Ministry of Postal and Telecommunications requested that service providers use domestically produced products when their performance was equal to that of MNC products. In 1996 and 1999, the Ministry organized two coordination meetings to encourage the use of domestically produced switches. These two meetings were the turning point at which indigenous firms began to replace MNCs in Chinese markets.

After successful catch-up in fixed-line switches, the Chinese government became confident and ambitious, and promoted the indigenous standard of TD-SCDM for 3G wireless telecommunication. According to Gao (2014), the government offered support for the TD-SCDMA standards, such as establishing the TD-SCDMA Alliance and providing financial support to facilitate collaboration among Alliance member firms and technical service. This was done to verify TD-SCDMA system's reliability as a stand-alone network rather than as a complement to WCDMA. The government also implemented an administrative order by requesting China Mobile Company to adopt this standard in January 2009. These initial forms of support in the domestic market helped Huawei purse globalization in mobile telecom systems later and entered cell phone markets. Huawei has thus far first achieved successful catch-up with Ericsson in the telecom system market and, later, with Samsung in the cell phone market.

Huawei has accelerated its market shares since the mid-2000s, and in 2012 it finally overtook Ericsson in terms of annual sales revenue.

Joo, Oh, and Lee (2016) have shown that the catch-up of Huawei in the global market of telecom systems involved an important leap-frogging role or path-creation strategy. Our study investigated Huawei and Ericsson patents and their citations, and found that Huawei relied on Ericsson as a knowledge source in its early days by citing patents of the latter. Huawei subsequently reduced this reliance (i.e., citing less of patents owned by Ericsson) and increased its self-citation ratio to become independent. The results of analysis of mutual (direct reliance), common (indirect reliance), and self-citation data of Huawei and Ericsson provide strong evidence that Huawei has caught up with or overtaken Ericsson by taking a different path from, rather than following, Ericsson. The citation results of nonpatent literature and citation lags show that Huawei has conducted extensive exploration of basic research and maintained up-to-date technologies to accomplish its technological catch-up. Overall, our study suggests that Huawei tried leapfrogging in that it explored a technological path new and different from that of its forerunner, Ericsson.

Although the role of the government window in the catch-up of China was important in many sectors, its final effect also tended to be different depending on its interaction with other factors, such as the regime of technologies and markets. For instance, the catch-up record of China in the memory chip sector has been slow despite government efforts. One reason for the slow catch-up is the fact that the market regimes of memory chips are different from typical consumer markets; they are not segmented into low and high ends. Instead, only one segment exists. Old and new generations of chips do not coexist in the market, as new chips quickly replace old ones with enhanced power at similar prices. Such a feature is generally unfavorable for latecomers, as they cannot use low-end markets as leverage for late entry. This condition implies that latecomers should simultaneously develop current and next generations of chips, which is what Korean firms did in their catch-up effort with Japanese firms. The consortium of

Korean firms and the government attempted to overcome difficulties posed by specific market regimes and technologies in the memory chip sector by sharing knowledge and risks. However, such joint effort does not always produce success, as many other factors are involved.

In the case involving Korea and China, different catch-up stories about memory chips imply that technologies with short cycles provide latecomers a good chance to catch up only when they have already accumulated certain absorption capabilities from starting early. Otherwise, frequent changes in technologies become additional barriers against catching up, which is the case of China. Therefore, sectors with short-cycle technologies often require leapfrogging to target and jump to emerging or next-generation technologies, as exemplified by the TD-SCDMA standard in China and by the memory chip sector in Korea. Now China is doing excellent leapfrogging in other emerging sectors, such as cloud computing, mobile banking, mobile shopping, fin-tech, drone, and electric car sectors, including share economy businesses. These rises have been led by the three IT service giants, namely, Alibaba, Tencent, and Baidu, which are the Chinese counterparts to Amazon, Facebook, and Google, respectively.

Overall, these stories are consistent with the main thesis of the catch-up cycle framework, which states that catch-up dynamics can be explained by the interaction of technological and market regimes with responses by actors, including firms and governments. Details of dynamics diverge, reflecting the heterogeneity of sectors. In some cases, the technological regime looms heavily without the government playing much of a role in its domination. In other cases, proactive responses by firms and the government succeed or fail in overcoming difficulties induced by technological and market regimes.

Leapfrogging of India in IT Service[26]

We can extend the catch-up cycle framework to the IT service industry. With India as a prime example, latecomer entry into the IT service

---

[26]   This subsection is a summary of Section 8.3 in Lee (2013a).

industry makes sense because it is a short-cycle, technology-based sector, which indicates frequent emergence of new business opportunities and a low entry barrier in terms of required capital. The IT service industry is a leading growth engine in the Indian economy. This industry is currently led by three giants, namely, TCS, Wipro, and Infosys, which have competed with equally advanced IT service firms in the United States and the EU. The success of the IT service industry in India makes an interesting catching up growth case that is based on services instead of manufacturing. This subsection discusses windows of opportunity available to Indian firms, as well as the nature of leapfrogging strategies that these firms have adopted to take advantage of available opportunities.

The first window of opportunity for India surfaced when a new techno-economic paradigm or business model emerged, and the second surfaced when the government intervened by changing policies on foreign firms. This techno-economic paradigm shift can happen to other latecomer countries and firms. Thus, additional factors specific to Indian firms are identified. We then emphasize that Indian firms have created their own unique path or business model in IT service. Indian firms are responsible for reinventing the offshoring model and for later inventing the global delivery model (GDM), which has now become a global industry standard.

Among the three leading IT firms, Wipro exhibited the most typical example of leapfrogging. Wipro was established as an agro-business company that produced and sold vegetable oil products (Hamm, 2007). However, as it entered the personal computer era, Wipro engaged in the business of assembling and selling personal computers as well. Shortly, the firm realized its weak competitiveness against foreign products and thus switched to PC maintenance and repair service. The Y2K panic brought a decisive boost to the business of Wipro, transforming the firm into a global IT service company listed on the New York Stock Exchange. The historical evolution of Wipro illustrates the leapfrogging of a company from a vegetable oil company into an IT service company, bypassing the manufacturing stage.

Moreover, we identify three upgrading stages in Indian IT service firms, namely, body shopping, offshoring, and GDM, that are similar to the three upgrading steps in manufacturing discussed in Chapter 4 (i.e., OEM, ODM, and OBM). Upgrading enables Indian IT service firms to move into high value-added segments of the industry. These services contain elements common to an IT service value chain, at the top of which are consulting and planning; followed by system integration; then application design, development and maintenance; and programming (coding) at the bottom. Indian IT service firms previously provided low value-added services, such as application development, maintenance, and testing. These firms have increasingly delivered strong performances in high value-added services, such as system analysis and design, system integration, and consultation, and have ventured into business process outsourcing.

Two Windows of Opportunity for India[27]

The first window of opportunity for the IT service sector in India was the rise of the new techno-economic paradigm and business models. In the 1980s, American firms introduced a new production arrangement called offshoring as an alternative to downsizing. According to Grossman and Rossi-Hansberg (2006), the production chain of the global economy has embraced a new paradigm called "vertical integration of production across borders" or "trade in tasks," in which "tasks," "end-products," and "components" are subject to international trade through offshoring. In this case, cost advantage instead of high-quality service was the main reason why multinational firms designated India as their offshore center for reaching countries such as Ireland, Israel, and Singapore. Other reasons were the English language skills of Indian nationals and the zonal time difference of about twelve hours, providing American firms a twenty-four-hour work environment.

---

[27]   This part is a summary of a section in Lee, Park, and Krishnan (2011) written by the current author. Taken from Lee (2013: Chapter 8).

The shift from hardware technology to client-server systems in the late 1980s presented another opportunity for India. This shift created a new and huge source of demand for customized software, enabling firms to migrate from the mainframe to client-server systems. Thus, system integration between the existing mainframe and the new client-server became a significant new market that Indian companies such as TCS, which had a pool of qualified software manpower, exploited.[28] As a result, American firms turned to Indian firms in areas of low value-added and labor-intensive services, such as coding, testing, and software maintenance.

The Y2K problem on the arrival of the year 2000 and the "dotcom boom" were two important market booms for Indian IT service firms in the late 1990s. Addressing the Y2K problem entailed ensuring that existing programs would not suffer glitches in the new millennium. During this time, multinational companies extensively used Indian companies to solve their Y2K problems. India received considerable business deals because of its abundant workforce, which is capable of writing many lines of codes. The dotcom boom also saw the rise to prominence of Indian technology executives as successful entrepreneurs, chief technical officers, and venture capitalists in Silicon Valley. This rise brought an overall positive effect on the Indian IT service industry in terms of its reputation and ability to generate businesses. The presence of qualified Indian technophiles in senior customer firm positions also helped Indian IT service firms secure business deals from American firms.

The second window of opportunity was the change in government regulation. The policy lines of India have been inward-looking, particularly along the lines of import substitution industrialization, since its independence from England in 1947. A stellar example is the Foreign Exchange Regulation Act (FERA) of 1973, which is one of the policies that helped regulate foreign exchange transactions and securities with the objective of conserving the foreign exchange resources

---

[28] For details, see Athreye (2005) and Krishnan and Vallabhaneni (2010).

of India. In protest of the discriminatory effects of the policy on foreign companies, IBM decided to leave India because FERA required it to dilute its equity holdings to 60%.[29] The exit of IBM was a window of opportunity as the Indian government acquired India-IBM, nationalized it, and renamed it CMC, which TCS acquired in 2002. As a result, various capabilities previously monopolized by India-IBM, such as the mainframe support system, infrastructure, skills, and human resources, were transferred to many Indian firms and subsequently to TCS during the nationalization period. The acquisition of CMC by TCS was a major milestone in the technical progress of the latter.

As India faced the foreign exchange crisis of 1991, it veered toward liberalization. With this came the move to replace the drastic measures of FERA with a set of liberal foreign exchange management regulations. This Indian deregulation policy coincided with the accelerated demand for software programming services, as large multinational firms moved from mainframe to client-server systems. At the same time, the Indian government reduced duties on imported software from 1992 to 1995 and provided income tax exemptions from 1993 to 1999. In 1988, the Vajpayee administration also launched a campaign with the slogan, "Being an IT superpower until 2008." With this campaign, the administration (1) reformed tax regulations; (2) sold state firms; (3) reduced financial deficits; (4) expanded social infrastructure; (5) promoted foreign investments; (6) increased software development funds; (7) formed a task force to establish a long-term IT strategy; and (8) created the Ministry of Information Technology.

Path-Creation of Indian Firms: The Body Shop Model → Offshoring → GDM[30]

The OEM–ODM–OBM path shows the three observed stages in the typical catch-up process of latecomers in manufacturing industries.

---

[29] Information in this regard is based on Mizuho Corporate Bank (2008).

[30] This part is a summary of a section in Lee, Park, and Krishnan (2011) written by the current author.

Indian IT service firms also followed catching-up and upgrading processes through several stages or business models. The catch-up stage of these firms includes three models: body shopping, offshoring, and GDM. These three steps can be explained using TCS as an example, as it is the oldest of the three firms involved in the IT service business.

The opportunity for body shopping (i.e., dispatching Indian firm manpower to clients) emerged because of the growing shortage of computer engineers in the United States and Europe since the 1970s. The exit of IBM from India also necessitated the outsourcing of application development work for Indian companies. At that time, TCS provided services to American customers in the form of body shopping or body staffing; that is, TCS only dispatched Indian manpower to clients who did not have any responsibility in managing and controlling them. From the late 1960s to the 1970s, TCS served as a subcontractor of multinational IT firms such as Burroughs, IBM, and ICL. TCS also supplied manpower for low value-added jobs, such as computer hardware code programming produced by multinational IT firms. Thus, the catch-up process of TCS during this period is similar to that of OEM because TCS depended largely on multinational firms.

However, at that time, offshoring centers served mainly as subsidiaries or captive development centers that MNCs established overseas. Although these subsidiary/offshoring MNC models were deemed effective in terms of cost savings, MNCs had to invest a substantial amount of capital and resources and struggled with local regulations and cultural differences in operating their respective subsidiaries. Indian IT service firms, specifically Infosys, carefully observed IT captive centers and pursued their respective niches. Infosys finally found that it could deal with all these concerns on behalf of MNC offshoring subsidiaries, such that MNCs would no longer have to establish and operate them. Thus, Infosys and other Indian IT service firms reinvented the existing offshoring concept into an independent business model, which spread worldwide. Offshoring is a business model that enables the offsite utilization of cheap labor, with Indian firms being responsible for managing and controlling manpower. However, TCS marketing activities still relied on multinational IT firms. Such dependence is similar to that of ODMs in terms of relying on multinational companies for marketing and distribution. Similarly, TCS developed its own software and established a new business model that performed additional tasks beyond coding.

The GDM first emerged in the mid-1990s, when TCS upgraded its offshore model to a highly advanced business model effectively combining onsite, offshore, and nearshore businesses. This model emerged as MNCs saw great demand for a globally standardized IT service for their offices located around the world. These changes in client firms motivated IT service firms to maximize the use of standardized jobs employing cheap offshore manpower and to minimize interaction with clients on site. Thus came the emergence of so-called nearshore centers, which are service delivery centers in locations where cultures and languages are similar to those of clients, thereby making them more responsive to customer needs than offshore companies. The GDM maximizes efficiency and reduces costs by combining onsite, offshore, and nearshore activities at a proper ratio. Indian IT service firms mainly used to provide low value-added services, such as ADM (application design, development, and maintenance) and testing, in the offshoring model. However, they gradually climbed the value chain through consultation and system integration. The full-service range of Indian IT service firms provides customers various choices. Although client MNCs continue providing certain design functions, such a high degree of independence and comprehensiveness in business activities is similar to that characterized by OBM firms.

In summary, Indian firms created their own unique paths or business models within the IT service industry, thereby leapfrogging to advanced development phases. These firms first reinvented the offshoring model and then, ahead of Western companies, created the GDM that has become the global industry standard.

5.8 SUMMARY AND POLICY IMPLICATIONS

The previously discussed stories on leadership changes provide support for our initial hypothesis that leapfrogging is involved in most leadership change cases, thus becoming a necessary condition for the successful rise of latecomers to positions of hegemony within sectors. Typical cases of leadership changes also tend to involve certain variants of the incumbent trap behavior. These hypotheses are supported because we find that all eleven cases of leadership changes in Table 5–1 involve an element of leapfrogging I or II, including path-creation I or II or stage-skipping, but none of path-following. Various types of incumbent reactions that can be classified as ex-ante lock-ins, complacency, or ex-post delayed responses are also present in ten out of eleven leadership change events or rise of late entrants.

The phenomenon of factory relocation to emerging countries with low wages or cost conditions that Vernon discussed can be considered as serving learning and building capabilities as a precondition for leapfrogging. Cost differences are favorable initial conditions for latecomers to familiarize themselves with existing technologies (i.e., learning by doing) and to eventually generate revenue for further investment in production technologies. Therefore, gradual catch-up in market shares by latecomers is often realized in the low-end segment of sectors, such as in the cases of steel and software. Although this type of catch-up based on factor cost advantages is not rare, it does not easily lead to the eventual reversal of market shares between incumbents and latecomers, which often requires an increased level of technological capabilities combined with local ownership of production and R&D. If a latecomer economy fails to generate a full cycle by decisively moving into the forging-ahead stage, then the catch-up cycle is aborted. This result is consistent with the state of being stuck in the MIT, in which a latecomer economy fails to upgrade to high value-added products and is confined to performing low-valued activities in the GVC.

Despite the possibility of the MIT that the cycle will be aborted, we can say that leadership change is always possible for prepared latecomers because diverse windows of opportunity always eventually and unexpectedly emerge, although with different frequencies across sectors. Thus, we conclude that latecomers should not be discouraged and are instead advised to prepare for the opportunity to catch up. Latecomer countries should be prepared in terms of building sector-specific capabilities, networks, and institutions to conduct adaptive or follow-on innovations, bearing in mind that doing so may take a long time. Thus, we may consider several useful policy ideas to help middle-income developing countries transcend that stage or escape the MIT, which are quite different from ideas from the old product life cycle theory.

In the product life cycle theory, industrial leadership is implicitly assumed to remain with advanced economies, whereas the catch-up cycle assumes continuous movement to other late-emerging economies. In product life cycle, a latecomer inherits mature industries from advanced economies, whereas in the catch-up cycle they leapfrog into new or emerging industries. Product life cycle also suggests trade-based specialization founded on the resource endowments of a country, whereas the catch-up cycle suggests technology-based specialization anchored in created/dynamic technological capabilities. The sources of competitiveness in product life cycle are low costs in human or natural resources, whereas those in the catch-up cycle are product differentiation and fast/first mover advantages. Finally, regarding policy tools, product life cycle tends to adopt the tariff or undervaluation of currency as a policy tool, whereas the catch-up cycle proposes adopting technology policies. Among these are public–private joint R&D, R&D subsidies for early entrants, innovation procurements, and standard policies. In summary, the key policy agenda should be to develop technological capabilities or at least the ability to conduct follow-on innovations for companies to seize windows of opportunity.

This chapter focused on the power of leapfrogging in first-tier emerging economies. However, leapfrogging is also a potential development strategy for low and middle-income countries in Africa and Latin America. We discuss this issue in Chapter 7 on policies.

6 Recapitulation of the Art

6.1 HUMAN CAPACITY-BASED VIEW ON ECONOMIC DEVELOPMENT

One of the motivations for this book is the idea that there are different mechanisms of economic growth in countries at varying stages or income levels, as well as a narrow transition passage in between. Difficulties in making this transition indicate the existence of poverty or MIT. A theoretical prediction of traditional growth theory is the eventual convergence in the income level of countries around the world, given the so-called catch-up effect in which a low-income country tends to grow faster and its growth rate gradually decreases as the country comes closer to high-income levels. However, a strong assumption behind such prediction of global convergence is that the production functions of countries, including their technology and productivity, are identical and that the only difference is the initial level of capital (per capita). If this assumption is not true, which must be the case, then global convergence is not possible. Once we abandon this assumption of uniform production functions, we arrive at different production functions and different growth mechanisms in different groups of countries. Thus, discussing poverty traps and MIT becomes meaningful.

Based on certain studies that find more incidents of MIT than of a poverty trap, this book focuses on MIT or how to cross the narrow transition path from the (upper) middle- to high-income groups.[1] However, before this book concludes, the two traps and the issue of economic growth in different stages, such as low-, middle-, and high-income stages, should also be considered.

---

[1]   World Bank (2012).

Discussions about different factors for economic growth at different stages can begin by referring to the basic production function and its factors. A simple idea for production function in economics suggests that output (economic growth) is a function of land, labor, capital, and knowledge. Here, land may represent all unchangeable factors such as natural endowments, weather, and geography, which are not policy concerns. Knowledge, which includes innovation, is a separate factor that is often attached to or is a work of human beings (unless we think of artificial intelligence). It depends on how the labor factor can be conceptualized and differentiated further, such as simple manual labor, skilled labor, intellectual labor, or labor equipped with a primary or secondary education or a college or higher-education degree. Therefore, other than the unchangeable factor of land, economic growth is basically accomplished by labor and capital. However, physical capital investment is also an embodiment of innovations made by human beings and the actions they take to increase labor productivity. Thus, we delve into labor, which can be differentiated further into simple, skilled, and intellectual.

We can combine this idea of different mechanisms of economic growth with diverse types of labor or diverse aspects of human capabilities, such as physical labor power, simple human capital corresponding to primary and secondary education, and a higher level of brain power enabling invention and innovations. These different forms of human capability have already been associated with economic growth at different stages in the literature, as has been discussed in the preceding chapters. A simple synthesis is that at the low- or lower-middle income stage, what matters or is binding is primary and secondary education, whereas at the upper-middle or high-income stage, high education and innovation are the binding factors.[2] We should also consider the special conditions of the so-called least developed countries, which have very low levels of development and where basic health and food is also an issue. The binding

---

[2] Lee and Kim (2009) and Bulman, Eden, and Nguyen (2014) are examples.

importance of basic health and nutrition in low-income countries has already been verified in some growth empirics at the cross-country level.

The consideration of this additional context leads us to realize that to pursue economic growth along the stages of economic growth, we have to enhance/improve the conditions under which human beings live and cultivate the means by which they can enrich their capabilities. For those at the low-income stage, these means include providing health care and nutrition; for those at the next, or lower-income stage, primary and secondary education; and finally, for those at the upper-middle income stage, higher education and technological innovations. In other words, economic growth at any level is the work of human capabilities. Thus, human capabilities are fundamental to economic development. Simply put, economic growth will occur if people are well-fed and healthy, if they are provided with a good education and training, and if innovation is encouraged by sharing risks and supplying funds.

The long-term process of economic development in Korea since the 1960s is a good fit with the idea of the human-centered perspective on economic development.[3] Korean economic growth started by first taking care of basic food and education. In the 1950s or after the civil war, South Korea was poor and the people were starving, making it difficult to start any kind of industrialization. Thus, the initial emphasis was on solving the food shortage through an agricultural revolution via a new rice variety, as well as providing universal education to the entire population. This well-fed and well-educated population served as an effective initial condition for building the capabilities of private firms for subsequent industrialization. The deepening of industrialization in the late stages or since the mid-1980s is the work of human beings, led by the higher- education revolution in the mid-1980s and big business-led innovations.[4]

---

[3]   See Lee (2017b) for more on the early days of economic development in Korea.

[4]   On the turning point of the mid-1980s, when Korea got out of MIT, see Lee (2013b).

The importance of different human capabilities at varying stages also has firm-level evidence. Using the World Bank survey data of eight developing countries in the 2000s, my own study, Lee and Temesgen (2009), finds that the growth of firms in developing countries is contributed mainly by relatively basic factors, such as physical capital and a low level of human capabilities, as measured by primary or secondary education. By contrast, the growth of firms in advanced countries is, in a relative sense, driven more by a higher level of human capabilities, such as managerial and R&D capital. The empirical results show that the contribution of tertiary-level-educated workers is not that significant in firm growth in low-income economies. These results stand in sharp contrast with the findings on advanced countries (e.g., as applied in Denmark), in which the proportion of workers with tertiary education is related significantly and positively to firm growth as measured by job growth (Laursen et al., 1999). However, the results are consistent with findings from studies on other developing economies, such as Guatemala, indicating that secondary education is more important for growth (Loening, 2005) than primary or tertiary education.

Another interesting finding is the two measures between human capital, that is, generic knowledge versus specific knowledge. The variable of specific human capital, represented by a dummy variable indicating whether workers had received training from the firm, turns out to be non-significant, which implies that firms tend to utilize the general knowledge of workers more than firm or industry-specific knowledge in developing countries. This finding is also consistent with the nature of production in these countries, that is, the basic assembly type involving a simple production process that uses technology embodied in machinery.

This different growth mechanism in the low stage of development does not have to stay at such a level, or to rely on a low level of human capabilities and simple assembly production. The important thing is to achieve a transition from one level to another, namely, from the lower level of growth mechanism to the higher-level ones. Two transitions can be regarded, one from the low- to middle-income stage and the other from the middle- to high-income stage. Each transition requires solving different problems and thus using different strategies, but a common element would be building and upgrading the capabilities of human beings. Also, these two transitions are related in the sense that approximately 70% of the poor around the world live in middle-income rather than low-income countries, and today's low-income countries will be tomorrow's middle-income countries. Thus, this book focuses more on the issue of how to realize the upgrading transition from middle- to high-income economies and attempts to identify the key transition variables.

6.2   FROM FAILURES AND BARRIERS TO DETOURS AND LEAPFROGGING

In an effort to identify the transition variables, we studied existing literature on other determinants of growth at different stages of development. These include the role of political institutions, human capital, and innovation; of big businesses in middle- or high-income countries; of minor (petit patents) vs. regular (regular patents) forms of IPR; and of openness and exports.[5] Our focus is on the different factors of growth at the high- vs. the middle-income groups; examining the literature leads to the following summary on growth determinants at different stages.

We find that for economic growth at the low- and lower-middle income levels of development, the relevant variables include political institutions (democracy), basic human capital (primary and secondary education), minor forms of IPR protection (utility models), and sustaining exports. For economic growth at

---

[5]   On political institutions, human capital, and innovation, see Lee and Kim (2009), and on the different extent and forms of IPR protection, see Kim et al. (2012); both are widely cited. On the roles of big businesses, see Lee et al. (2013), which finds that the existence of these businesses is the dividing factor between high- and middle-income economies. On the diverse measures of openness and sustaining exports, see Ramanayake and Lee (2015), which finds that sustained exports are more robust than other measures of openness, and also matter in both developed and developing countries.

the upper-middle or higher-income stages, the important variables are a higher level of human capital (tertiary education), innovation capabilities, big businesses, a higher level of IPR protection (patent rights), and sustaining exports. In addition to the variable of sustained export growth, which is common to both groups, the differences are simply the existence of big businesses and innovation capabilities (comprising high levels of IPR and tertiary education). Clearly, latecomer upper-middle income economies should try to improve on these aspects (innovation and big businesses). Considering that innovation and big businesses are the targets—namely, the final destination point—the key is determining how to reach this point. That is, identifying the specific path of the transition toward being innovative and having big businesses.

To find the key transition strategies, we look into the experiences of successful countries, mostly in East Asia, that have made such a transition. In other words, the secrets are not in the "average" but in the successful "outliers." Therefore, conventional growth empirics cannot discover the secrets, because most empirics have attempted to estimate the average rather than to identify the outliers. This book finds that these outlier countries, in terms of innovation, have taken three detours, different from the rest of the group. The first detour is to promote minor innovations via petit patents rather than the high level of innovation via regular patents. The second detour is to specialize in short-cycle technologies rather than long-cycle technologies. The final detour is to increase the share of domestic value-added in exports rather than rely on GVCs with a low level of domestic value-added. The detour regarding big businesses is to promote diversified business groups, which are often under family control, rather than specialized and stand-alone companies run by professional managers. However, the latter are typical forms of businesses in advanced economies.

These experiences of going through the detours of successful outliers suggest that these countries did not replicate or emulate the practices of advanced economies; rather, they went in the opposite direction, which makes sense because that means avoiding direct competition in the same markets and business models. As the term outlier indicates, the passage from middle- to high-income is narrow. This is because of the need to adopt a different production function with higher level of technologies, as well as the presence of two failures (capability and size failures) and one barrier of IPR protection in the North and the small space for intervening policy under the WTO regime.

Although consolidation of technological capabilities has long been suggested as being vital for economic catch-up, not enough details have been provided. This book elaborates on the details of the three detours in building capabilities, which are centered around three keywords: imitative to innovation, short-cycle to long-cycle technologies, and foreign to domestic value-added. The process of capability-building via these detours should be designed and implemented carefully within the broad framework of NIS. If one does not take these detours, the process of capability-building might be derailed and delayed. For instance, regarding the first detour, capability-building would be less effective if a latecomer economy provided a high level of IPR protection from the beginning. Moreover, regarding the issue of choices over technologies, the process would be derailed if a latecomer attempted to enter first into sectors/segments with long-cycle time, which means high entry barrier sectors. Finally, the detour in opening to GVC emerges because all latecomer economies should be open to learning from outside at the initial stage. At the same time, the final goal of learning is being able to stand alone with one's own learning and innovation mechanism, similar to how a child who learns to walk should be able to walk alone eventually. Likewise, participation in the GVC should go together with the effort to build a local knowledge base, and thereby increase domestic value-added at the intermediate stage.

In addition to detours, this book emphasizes the role of leapfrogging as the final stage of catching up or overtaking. The thesis of leapfrogging and windows of opportunity means that newly emerging generations of technologies, particularly competence-destroying innovations, may allow latecomer countries to have a head start. This is because, in the competition within a new techno-economic paradigm, both incumbents and latecomers begin from the same starting line and incumbents often stick to the existing technologies from which they derived supremacy. Therefore, in our dynamics of economic catch-up, the role of leapfrogging is like "flying on a balloon when the conventional ladder to catch up is kicked away." A precondition to try flying includes having built up capabilities, often in big businesses; otherwise, one might fall through the "windows" rather than fly upward. In sum, detour and leapfrogging are the core theoretical concepts in the theory of economic catch-up. The detours refer to latecomers doing different things from those done by the forerunners, whereas leapfrogging refers to latecomers doing something new ahead of the forerunners, thereby leaping over the incumbent.

Then, we have a comprehensive theory of economic catch-up, consisting of "late entry→ three detours→ leapfrogging." Such sequential dynamics are needed because of "two failures and one barrier," and leapfrogging is necessary because the detours are not enough and should be tried only with the arrival of exogenous windows of opportunity. Leapfrogging involves risk but is the only way to forge ahead and overtake the forerunners; thus, leapfrogging is a necessary condition to make the transition possible. In sum, this theory of catch-up is framed with three paradoxes. The first paradox is that "to be similar, be different." The second paradox is that "a detour can be faster than a straight road." The third paradox is that "you may fly or fall through the window."

6.3 TWO BLACK BOXES IN THE ECONOMICS OF CATCH-UP

As discussed, building capability and engaging in innovation are the enabling factors to manage successfully the process of economic catch-up and transition toward a high-income economy. Given that firms are carriers of capabilities and agents of innovations, another important issue in the economics of catch-up is the nature and types of internal organizations and governance of the firms. Basically, organizational innovation is another source of raising productivity from the same inputs of labor and capital, aside from technological innovations. Such a view on innovation in terms of both technological and organizational dimensions originates from Schumpeter (1943: 73). He considered a new method of production and forms of industrial organization that an enterprise creates as fundamental impulses of economic change. However, both technological and organizational innovations are treated as black boxes in neoclassical economics, and as something residual or exogenous. In contrast, in the Schumpeterian economics of catch-up proposed in this book, the two black boxes hold a central position because they contain the key solution to economic problems, namely, various failures and barriers facing the latecomers.

As we recognize the different mechanisms of growth involved in different levels of development, we expect that the characteristics and behavior of latecomer firms should also vary at different stages. In terms of the transition path from middle- to high-income economies, this book argues that a certain type of firm would be a more effective device to overcome the two failures and one barrier, that is, the BGs—a collection of firms that is bound together under family ownership but is often diversified into several business areas.

BGs are a natural response and solution to market and capability failures prevalent in developing economies. The classical literature on BGs has long considered them to be an organizational solution to market failure associated with high transaction costs. In particular, scarcity of financial capital and weak capital market conditions tend to justify the internal capital market role of BGs. The role of BGs in overcoming capability failure can be discussed by reference to a resource-based theory of the firm proposed by Penrose (1959). She defined firm as a collection of resources (meaning competences) under administrative control. However, in contrast to the firms in advanced economies, many resources are quite lacking in latecomer firms.

The advantages of BGs are that they facilitate the sharing of a lack of resources during the initial entry and growth stages, while subsidizing losses during the entry into new business areas. Such organizational forms are also advantageous in sharing the costs to build, and the efficient utilization of, lumpy intangible (not available in market) assets, including R&D unit and brands. In addition, they facilitate innovation by allowing a high level of within-group spillovers of knowledge. Furthermore, fast decision-making in family-controlled BGs can be an additional source of advantages in some sectors, such as ITs, where technological and product market cycles tend to be short and thus are regarded as niche for latecomer firms (Chapter 3).

Such advantages of BGs make it somewhat natural to consider them a legitimate method to promote big businesses and realize a jump from middle- to high-income economies. Big businesses are needed to overcome the size failure in developing economies, which tend to only have SMEs, because these alone are not sufficient to lead economies toward the path of high-income economies. Thus, this book points out the promotion of BGs as a means to grow big businesses in an environment full of market and capability failures.

In the context of East Asia, core competences of BGs have evolved from simple project execution capabilities at the earliest stage to vertical or horizontal integration at the middle stage, and finally to innovation capabilities at the final stage. BGs in Asia have been the carrier of dynamic diversification in the form of successive entries into new sectors. In the 1950s and 1960s, such firms in Korea, including Samsung, specialized in labor-intensive (low value-added) industries, such as apparel or footwear industries. These firms then moved to the short- or medium-cycle sectors of low-end consumer electronics, chemicals and plastics, and automobile assemblies in the 1970s and 1980s. In the late 1980s, they moved on to the short-cycle sector of telecommunication equipment and finally to memory chips, cell phones, and digital televisions in the 1990s. Therefore, such BGs have been a perfect example for the dynamics of catch-up framed along the stages of entry -> detour -> leapfrogging. The transaction-cost saving (and thereby overcoming of market failure) attribute of BGs qualifies them as an effective organizational device for late entry, and their resource-sharing advantage qualifies them as a device for capability-building via detours. Finally, all these advantages, as well as risk-sharing, within-group knowledge spillover, and building intangible assets, would qualify the firms as a device to manage leapfrogging cum diversification by quickly riding new techno-economic paradigms.

6.4   DISTINCTION, CONTRIBUTION, AND LIMITATIONS

Before concluding the book, the art of economic catch-up should be compared with the existing recipe of economic development by latecomers. We will sort the distinction, contribution, and limitations of this book. In what follows, the three main schools of thought are considered, starting with the literature on the Gerschenkron-Amsden framework, the convergence thesis of the GVC revolution, and the literature on structural transformation.

The Gerschenkron-Amsden Framework

The art of economic catch-up shares a common motivation with the so-called Gerschenkron-Amsden framework but takes a different focus and offers different suggestions in terms of concrete policy agenda.[6] The two main arguments of the so-called Gerschenkron-Amsden framework are as follows. First, late industrializing economies would have a distinctive pattern of institutional innovation so that the latecomers may find substitutes for the institutions or practices already found in advanced countries. Second, the latecomers would have their own advantage of adopting up-to-date technologies and the associated catch-up effect, thereby enabling faster growth than the incumbents.

---

[6]   Mathews (2018) provided a compact exposition of the Gerschenkron-Amsden framework. Discussion with him led me to write this subsection.

Regarding the first argument, the institutional innovation—development states and state banks—has been discussed in the literature. However, there are many cases of state failure, and one of the sources of such failure is the lack of effective guidance for state intervention or industrial policy. Given this state of play, a distinctive focus of the current book is to provide more concrete guidance in terms of development policy centered on the three detours. This guidance includes a dynamic shift from imitation to innovation, from short- to long-cycle sectors, and from more to less GVC involvement; none of these are discussed in the early literature. In addition, as a different kind of institution innovation, this book goes beyond the role of state banks to suggest BGs as an organizational device to realize economic catch-up, emphasizing the role of internal capital market (intra-group financing of new projects and entries into new business areas), as well as of intra-group resource- (competence-) sharing to loosen the resource constraint.

Regarding the second argument, this book is concerned with the possibility that a natural catch-up effect may slow down as one comes close to the frontier. This issue is not treated in the original Gerschenkron-Amsden framework, which focuses on the early stage of late industrialization. In contrast, this book proposes detours to build capabilities and leapfrogging to find a new and different path somewhere in the middle before coming close to the frontier. The slowdown and eventual exhaustion of the catch-up effect is natural, as long as the latecomer tries to catch up with the forerunning incumbents along the same production function. Leapfrogging is a switch to a new and different production function with a steep slope. However, leapfrogging comes with risks and thus should be tried when a new window of opportunity emerges, such as new or disruptive innovations and techno-economic paradigms. This window of opportunity leapfrogging thesis is the Schumpeterian addition to the discourse on late industrialization. This thesis has been suggested by Perez and Soete (1988). This book extends the thesis into the catch-up cycle framework that considers the technological, market, and institutional windows, and discusses the match between the diverse windows and the response and varying strategies of latecomers, such as path-following, stage-skipping, and path-creation. Therefore, this book suggests a theoretical alternative to the old product life cycle theory by Vernon (1966), which failed to see the leadership shift from advanced to latecomer economies.

Global Convergence via the GVC

The Gerschenkron-Amsden framework proposed late industrialization by industrial policy. A more recent and mainstream view, including that supported by Baldwin (2016), noted that global convergence becomes possible because of GVC revolution (or the so-called second unbundling or new international separation of factories). Scholars in this group commonly noted the declining share of G7 in manufacturing or world GDP, from above 60% before the 1990s to less than 50% in the 2010s or an approximately 15% decline over the last twenty years. The decline of G7 is contrasted with the rise of late industrializers (the so-called I6), such as China, India, Korea, Poland, Indonesia, and Thailand. This decline is attributed to the GVC revolution and the benefiting of later industrializers from the relocation of manufacturing and knowledge.

This contrast between G7 and I6 might give the impression of global convergence, although this is somewhat misleading because approximately 90% of the reversal is simply owing to the rise of a single country, China. The China share in the world GDP has increased from less than 2% in the 1990s to more than 15%.[7] The share of India increased from 1.5% to approximately 3% by the late 2010s. Therefore, simply a catch-up by China and partly India, rather than a global convergence, occurred. Moreover, many countries are stuck in the MIT. One example is that, despite joining the NAFTA and consequently the GVC, the Mexican share in world GDP declined from close to 2% in the 1990s to less than 1.5% in the 2010s, and its

---

[7] Figures on various economies in this part are all calculations using International Monetary Fund statistics.

per capita GDP in purchasing power parity decreased from more than a 40% level of the United States in the 1990s to nearly 30% in the late 2010s. More importantly, during the rapid catch-up period in the 2000s, the degree of China's participation in the GVC, as measured by the share of foreign value-added in its gross exports, reversed its trend to peak at 37% in the early 2000s and decline to 31% in the late 2000s.[8] This pattern of declining foreign share but increasing domestic value-added in China replicated the similar reversal in Korea and Taiwan from the mid-1980s to the mid-1990s. That is the secret to the catch-up.

Convergence via the GVC revolution misses this important catch-up mechanism. This is one of the essential ingredients of the art of catch-up, which is exactly why this book is called the detour of "more, less, and more" GVC again (see Chapter 3 and Section 4.4). The latecomers learned know-hows and technologies by joining the GVC in the early stage of late industrialization. However, rapid catch-up was realized only after the latecomers localized certain value segments, such as intermediate capital goods of parts and supplies. Otherwise, whenever the latecomers export, they have to import more foreign capital goods and become stuck in trade deficits. Without stable trade surplus and foreign currency earning, the latecomers cannot import investment goods and economic catch-up cannot be sustained at the middle-income stages. In this sense, Gerschenkron has proven to be correct in his emphasis on the need for latecomers to focus on producer rather than consumer goods. However, a detour of first exporting consumer goods and later turning to producer goods was the essential aspect of upgrading within the GVC, without which initial catch-up cannot be sustained.

Unsurprisingly, even Korea still had trade deficits during most of its first round of late industrialization from the early 1960s to the late 1980s. Korea first recorded trade surplus in the late 1980s. Until then, it was not much of a catch-up in terms of per capita GDP

---

[8] This figure is a by-product of the author's research on the GVC contained in Lee et al. (2017).

compared with Japan or the United States, although Korea recorded fast growth rates. This first-time trade surplus was sustained because of the continued localization of high-end goods and segments in the GVC, or basically the substitution of imported high-end goods with domestic goods, which consolidated the domestic value chains to a certain degree. It has only been since the 2000s that the share of foreign value-added increased again. This occurred as Korea relocated more of its factories (low-end segments) abroad due to high domestic wage rates and went for radical globalization via FTAs with the United States, the EU, China, and India.

Structural Transformation in Kaldor, Structural, and Neoclassical Development Economics

Another strand of the economic literature places emphasis on the structural transformation in the course of economic development by latecomers. This emphasis is shared by several economics groups, such as the neoclassical development economics of Rodrik, as well as new structural economics initiated by Justin Lin, former VP of the World Bank, in addition to Kaldor.[9] In general, the desired pattern of structural change is the expansion of higher productivity sectors over others, in particular, the expansion of the share of the manufacturing and reduction of the share by agriculture. This idea goes back to the classical work of Kaldor. Many developing countries initially faced labor abundance and were advised to move into or specialize in labor-intensive manufacturing sectors in the early stage of development.[10]

Undoubtedly, having such structural change in any economy is desirable, and the economic problems of latecomers keep changing at different stages of development, especially once they reach the middle-income stage or after the first wave of industrialization. The next stage of structural transformation is focused on the choice of sectors within manufacturing, which often involves movement into those sectors with high capital intensity and value-added per work or labor

[9]   Refer to Kaldor (1967), Rodrik (2010, 2013), and Lin (2012, 2011).
[10]   See Kuznets and Murphy (1966).

productivity. The current problem is the existence of many capital-intensive and high value-added sectors, and economics has so far provided no theoretical criteria to choose among the many capital-intensive sectors. The concept of produce space by Hidalgo et al. (2007) provides some help in determining what step to take next, but not in choosing among the many neighboring spaces.[11] Latecomers need to obtain additional help on which directions to go among the many neighboring spaces. Furthermore, the product space cannot help making "long jumps" to faraway spaces, which is equivalent to leap-frogging in our terminology. Rather, Lin's (2012) concept of latent comparative advantage does a better job of pinpointing the sector of a country that a latecomer can target in terms of low entry barrier, although such action is not much about leapfrogging.

Schumpeterian economics can provide answers to choices among sectors, because one key thesis of this school is that all sectors are heterogeneous in terms of technological regime, such as technological opportunity, knowledge tacitness, cycle times, cumulativeness, and so on. This book and a previous book of mine confirm that latecomers at the middle-income stage are advised to choose sectors with higher growth prospects but lower entry barriers, which is consistent with short-cycle, technology-based sectors involving more explicit than tacit knowledge.[12] First, the short-cycle times mean the dominance of incumbents is often disrupted (namely, low entry barrier). Second, the continuous emergence of new technologies can generate new opportunities. In addition, this criterion does not discriminate service in favor of manufacturing; for instance, IT services and software are also short-cycle sectors and thus are a potentially good choice for latecomers.

Summary, Limitations, and Way Ahead

The art of catch-up expressed in this book contends that the growth mechanisms of rich and poor nations differ, and that a "narrow

[11] See Hidalgo et al. (2007)   [12] See Chapter 3 and Lee (2013a).

passage" exists between these nations. Such transition is possible by taking detours and leapfrogging, given the presence of two failures (e.g., firm capability and size failures) and one barrier of IPR protection from the North. Building capabilities have three detours. The first detour is from imitation to innovation, the second is from short- to long-cycle sectors, and the third is from more to less and more again regarding GVC. Apart from these detours, this book emphasizes the role of leapfrogging at the final stage of catch-up or overtaking, namely, when latecomers do something new ahead of the forerunners and leap over them. We can only fly balloons under favorable weather conditions and, hence, economic leapfrogging only becomes successful when exogenous windows of opportunity are available. By combining these concepts, we devise a comprehensive theory of economic catch-up consisting of "late entry→ detours→ leapfrogging." In sum, the art of catch-up is rather paradoxical because one can never catch up if they keep catching up, where the former "catch up" means closing the gap or overtaking and the latter "catching up" means imitation.

One limitation of this book is the fact that leapfrogging is discussed mostly at the sectoral level in Chapter 5 rather than at the country level, and assumes that country-level catch-up performance is often driven by the rise and decline of certain sectors. The chapter only briefly mentioned the role of macro-level factors, such as exchange rates and wage levels. The economic success of a country tends to bring changes to its macro variables (e.g., appreciation of currency and rising wage rates), which may work adversely to the advantage of domestic sectors and their firms. This situation implies that such macro variables are endogenous to a certain extent, and thus should be considered in the full dynamics of a country to explain their catching up, forging ahead, and falling behind. We require a macro-level economic model of leapfrogging that goes beyond the early one by Krugman.[13] In this regard, a new stream of works by Dosi et al.

---

[13]   Krugman discussed a model of leapfrogging in a coauthored article with Brezis et al. (1993).

For the Schumpeter–Keynes synthesis, see Dosi et al. (2010).

doing agent-based modeling of the Schumpeter–Keynes synthesis appears to be a promising road, especially when considering explicitly open economy models.

From this perspective, one possible hypothesis is that country-level dynamics in latecomers are determined not only by innovation capabilities (NIS) of countries but also whether they achieve trade surplus or deficits. While Schumpeterian economics, including this book, focus on the former, the latter is equally important for latecomers that do not have the privilege of reserve currency and therefore cannot simply print money to pay for imported goods. Without strong export performance to afford imported capital goods, investments cannot be sustained; the same is true for economic growth and catch-up. Although the book entitled *Balance* by Hubbard and Kane (2013) pointed out that fiscal balances are determinants of the rise and the decline of super powers, external balance (trade) may matter more than internal balance in the case of latecomer open economies that tend to face foreign currency earnings as the binding constraint. Macro-level modeling of latecomer economies should have this balance of payment as an essential ingredient.

Before modeling, we need qualitative or "appreciative theorizing" studies of the long-term dynamics of more latecomer economies struggling with various development traps at different stages. In this regard, another limitation of this book is that examples of catch-up and leapfrogging are mostly from Asian economies. However, it was unavoidable because Asia is where successful catch-up has tended to happen more than on other continents.

At the same time, it is thus to be noted that the main focus of the book has been the transition from middle-income to high-income economies. The transition from low- to middle-income economies is also discussed, but mostly in terms of capability-building. Also to be noted is that both transitions are affected not only by economic but also non-economic factors, such as geo political factors, which was particularly important in the cases of success in Korea and Taiwan in terms of the role of the postwar world order. However, a more recent success, that of China under the different world order, indicates the importance of national efforts and strategies to overcome any constraint imposed by international factors. That is why in the next chapter we discuss in some detail how to practice the "art" in current late-latecomer activity and about the size of the policy space under the WTO regime.

7 Practicing the Art in Late Latecomers

Since the 2012 UN Conference on Sustainable Development, this concept has been the overarching theme of development in UN and was used to formulate the details of the sustainable development goals (SDGs) after the end of the millennium development goals in 2015. SDGs call for "socially inclusive and environmentally sustainable economic growth" (Sachs, 2015: 3). In other words, sustainable development involves three dimensions, namely, economic, social, and environmental. Economic sustainability is concerned with spreading prosperity and consequently reducing poverty. The social aspect is concerned with equity and emphasizes inclusive development. The environmental aspect focuses on the current ecological and resource crises that threaten the developmental prospects of countries worldwide. Sachs pointed to "good governance'" by major social actors, such as governments and businesses, as the key enabler of achieving these aspects together. In contrast, this book pays attention to science, technology, and innovation (STI), which hold the key to link these three aspects and thus can serve as effective solutions to problems in the three areas together.[1]

STI can identify and promote new technologies that can solve or alleviate environmental challenges and may bring new innovative and affordable products and services that address the needs of the poor. An example is increasing agricultural productivity, which will consequently lower food prices. In addition, without STI capabilities that

---

[1] The term "innovation" hereafter refers to science, technology, and innovation (STI). This paragraph and the next rely on Lee and Mathews (2013).

may help differentiate and upgrade products to increase their value, sustaining economic growth to create additional jobs is not feasible. Economic growth in numerous developing countries is short-lived because their products rely on cheap labor or minerals, which are subject to price volatility or the so-called adding-up problem. This adding-up problem occurs when developing countries flood the market with similar goods they are good at producing, thereby decreasing the relative prices of these goods and consequently the profitability of these sectors.[2]

Given the global consensus toward sustainable development, we propose leapfrogging as an effective way to switch to an environment-friendly, sustainable mode of development. Figure 7–1 that

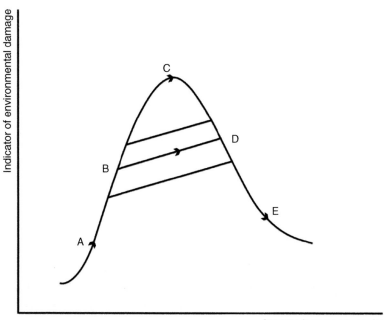

FIGURE 7–1. Leapfrogging and the Environmental Kuznets Curve (Redrawn by the author following the graph in Jackson and Roberts, 2000).

***

[2]   This problem of adding-up is also mentioned in Spence (2011).

follows shows the so-called Environmental Kuznets Curve, where the degree of environmental damage is measured along the vertical axis and per capita income on the horizontal axis. The idea of this curve is that a bigger environmental damage is expected with the initial rise of per capita income. Environmental damage may be mitigated after a certain point of growth of income levels. Given this path of the forerunning economies, if all current latecomer economies continue to follow the path of the existing economic model of growth, the global goal to reduce carbon emission would be impossible and cause further substantial damage to the global environment. A better alternative is to skip a middle point, such as Point C, by jumping or leapfrogging to Point D from B. With the proper composition of economic activities and the use of better technologies, such leapfrogging becomes a possibility.[3]

Leapfrogging remains highly relevant because it promises to bring newly industrializing countries up to the level of advanced countries and propels them to lead in certain sectors, such as greening technologies that are in use today in Africa and elsewhere. If the advanced countries see their path blocked by "carbon lock-in" (excessive dependence on fossil fuel systems), then latecomer countries can bypass such blockages by leapfrogging to cleaner and greener technologies. Mathews (2017, 2018) calls this alternative "green development," based on a green industrial system free from fossil fuels and extensive resource throughput. Actually, a green window of opportunity has opened with the rise of various renewable energy technologies. These enable the production of solar panels, wind turbines, new smart grid devices, electric vehicles, and recharging stations, among others.

Thus, considering this green window of opportunity, late latecomers (those economies other than several East Asian economies that are already achieving significant catch-up) are in an appropriate position to attempt leapfrogging into an environment-friendly trajectory of development. Certainly, such leapfrogging requires the pre-

---

[3] This remark was also made in Lee and Mathews (2013, 2018).

existence or building up of a certain level of capabilities. In the next section, we explore the possibility of leapfrogging via the detour of capability-building in late latecomer economies in Africa, Latin America, and Southeast Asia. Finally, the issue of policy space under the WTO regime is also discussed.

7.2   FROM DETOURS TO LEAPFROGGING IN AFRICA

This section first discusses ways by which low-income countries, or least-developed countries (LDCs), particularly those in Africa, can build the innovation capabilities necessary to address sustainability. The section also focuses on the role of learning mechanisms and the channels of access to foreign knowledge in augmenting domestic capabilities as part of innovation systems. In the framework of late entry -> detours -> leapfrogging, the following section elaborates the first stage, namely, late entry.

Two Modes of Building Productive Capacities in LDCs

Generally, productive capacity development in LDCs is classified into two modes on the basis of whether the abundant resource of the country is labor or natural resources.[4] The first mode is evident in a predominantly manufacturing sector that involves OEM, in which LDC firms manufacture products according to foreign buyers' specifications under diverse contractual arrangements, including FDI (Hobday, 2000). The second mode typically involves resource-based sectors, such as mining, which evolve as extensions of and upgrade into backward or forward linkage sectors as part of GVCs commonly led by foreign companies (Morris et al., 2012). The following section discusses each mode briefly in sequence.

A conventional mode of developing productive capacity in LDCs occurs through contractual arrangement with foreign countries in the form of OEM or FDI. This arrangement is a specific form of subcontracting under which a completed product is made exactly

---

[4]   These two modes of upgrading were also suggested in a draft form to the Committee for Development Policy of the UN by the author.

according to its buyer's specifications. Examples of OEM- or FDI-based assembly-type products include clothing, consumer electronics, automobiles, and telecommunication equipment. These arrangements are typical in low- or middle-income countries. From the 1970s to the early 1990s, OEM accounted for a significant share of the electronic exports of Taiwan and South Korea and facilitated technological learning (Hobday, 2000). An example is textile products, which latecomers produce for export markets via OEM arrangements with firms from advanced countries.

OEM does not simply mean production and job creation in the host countries but naturally involves learning and building certain capabilities. Learning under the OEM mode can be divided into two stages. During the first stage of development, latecomer firms learn skills or operational know-how while producing final products according to foreign-supplied manuals on foreign-made plants or production lines. In other words, an operation manual is available, and tacit knowledge (know-how and skills) is created during the process. Therefore, the process can be called skill formation and leads to an increase in productivity. This productivity increase through learning by doing is the main source of catching-up during this stage. In terms of catching-up patterns, this stage corresponds to path-following catching-up (Lee and Lim, 2001). This stage involves simple assembly production and, hence, the production responsibility borne by local or latecomer firms or entrepreneurs is small.

The second stage is an advanced form of OEM and involves the acquisition of processing technology, such that the latecomer firms now bear the responsibility of production. In this stage, latecomer firms acquire processing technology while producing goods according to designs provided by the foreign firms, which are usually the final producers. The designs can be those of the products, the production facility, or both. Acquisition of processing technology means the latecomer firms become capable of *setting up their own production facility and bear the responsibility of production*. The foreign firms not only provide designs but also consistently dispatch personnel who provide technical guidance in setting up production facilities and/or producing the goods. In terms of the catching-up pattern, this stage still corresponds to a path-following catching-up because it allows latecomers to imitate the forerunning firms. Thus, this stage can be described as "duplicative imitation" according to the framework discussed by Kim (1997).

In this mode of OEM-based learning by doing or exporting, the by-products are job creation and foreign exchange earnings. Policy tools frequently include tariffs and undervaluation of currencies. An asymmetric tariff structure may be desirable. For example, high tariffs can be implemented for sectors being promoted, and low tariffs can be established for imported capital goods. Such asymmetric tariff structures increased the world market share of Korean products in the 1970s (Shin and Lee, 2012). Alternately, other forms of horizontal interventions are necessary to build physical infrastructure.

The second mode of productive capacity development in LDCs aims to build productive capacities in related segments while LDCs are engaged initially in resource-based (minerals) production under foreign leadership (Morris et al., 2012). New perspectives have emerged, and arguments have been made that LDCs may escape the resource curse under certain conditions. In particular, the changing strategies of industrial organizations, such as focusing on the efficiency of GVCs, have led commodity firms to emphasize the virtues of external supply of inputs into their operations, initially from the lowest-cost global supplier and subsequently from the lowest-cost local supplier. Linkages and upgrading transformation may emerge from lead commodity producers in the commodities sector to input suppliers (backward linkages) and commodity processors (forward linkages or downstream activities).

Several promising examples include the following. Botswana rose from being a low-income to a middle-income country because of its diamond sector, which since the 1980s has enabled local firms to evolve from simple commodity producers to diamond-cutting and polishing processors.[5] The rise of Botswana took a long time. Progress had been slow until 2005, when the government and De Beers, a global diamond jewelry company, entered into a significant deal to promote local processing industries. Having gained considerable bargaining power in 2005 with the impending renewal of the 25-year mining license of De Beers that year, the government persuaded the jewellery company to help Botswana create a viable and globally competitive cutting and polishing industry to enable the renewal of their license for another 25 years. Until then, De Beers previously opined that Botswana had no comparative advantage in the processing sector. However, after the new contract was sealed, the government invited the world's leading cutting and polishing companies (sixteen in total) to establish factories in Botswana and subsequently transfer cutting and polishing skills to local citizens. Although the current situation in Botswana is considerably better than before, the long-term challenge is to continue moving up the value chain from the current crude diamond production, cutting, and polishing to polished dealing, jewellery manufacturing, and marketing and sales, which occupy a big part of the pie in the chain.

A similar challenge in upgrading exists in the mode that starts from OEM. Despite the effectiveness of OEM as a method of catching up at the early stage of economic growth, this mode is a somewhat uncertain long-term strategy because foreign vendor firms may move their production orders to other low-wage production sites (Lee, 2005; Lee and Mathews, 2013). Currently, a similar trend is under way among flower producers in East Africa because foreign vendor firms buy flowers not only from Kenya but also from neighboring countries that are catching up with Kenya. In this respect, OEM firms should prepare long-term plans in their transition to ODM and finally to OBM. ODM firms carry out most of the detailed product design, and their customer firms continue with marketing functions. Meanwhile, OBM firms undertake manufacturing, design of new products, R&D

---

[5]   This story of diamond sector is from Morris et al. (2012).

for materials, processing of products, and sales and distribution for their own brands. The path from OEM to ODM to OBM has become the standard upgrade process for latecomer firms.

The transition to OBM is difficult and rare even in East Asia, as discussed in Chapter 4 (Section 4). However, a successful case can be found in Uganda in Africa. Good African Coffee, a company established by an entrepreneur from Uganda named Rugasira (2013), has been successful in the global market with its brands and sales network in Europe and North America. This case is very unusual and exceptional in Africa, because this company exports not crude or unprocessed coffee but high-valued processed branded coffee. An interesting aspect of this case is that the company skipped the OEM stage and attempted OBM from the beginning. In a sense, this case is also an instance of leapfrogging that bypassed the earlier stage of OEM. Actually, the company started by selling its own brand of coffee in retail supermarkets in foreign countries, with packing also performed abroad. Only after several years had the company gained the capacity of packaging in Uganda. This case is similar to several Korean companies, such as Hyundai Motors. It started selling cars with its own brands, but with foreign-made engines and transmissions, and only later progressed to localizing engines and transmissions. This case may imply that the agro-food industry and processing segment of the primary-sector industry can also be a compelling option for industrial development in Africa.

Modified examples of such upgrading by African flower firms include producing long-lasting flowers with specific scents and using a small amount of pesticides, which require innovation. A transition to OBM in the flower industry will require African firms to enter into marketing and set up their own outlets with their own brands in Europe. Such a transition to ODM or OBM is difficult but serves as a narrow path to middle- or even high-income status. Another model available for African countries, which are endowed with rich resources, is the combination of "black" and "green" development, in which cash from exports of natural resources can be utilized to finance entry into green industries (Lee and Mathews, 2013). Transitioning to the middle-income stage generally calls for sector-specific or vertical-intervention policies. This condition is necessary because the country must identify its niche between low-income countries with cost advantages in low-end goods and high-income countries with quality advantages in high-end goods. To illustrate, Botswana is attempting to find a niche by targeting the middle-level quality of diamond cutting and polishing, which lies above that of the small stones produced in China and India and below that of the highly specialized stones produced in Belgium and Israel (Morris et al., 2012).

In this stage, public policy should focus on two kinds of upgrading: entry into new industries and upgrading to high-valued segments in existing industries, which involves upgrading the overall industrial structure. Short-cycle, technology-based sectors are candidate niches for latecomers. The main issue is determining how to break into medium short-cycle technology-based products or the high-valued segment of existing sectors. Effective targets for such import substitution entry are the products that these countries used to import at high prices because of the oligopolistic market structure dominated by incumbent exporting countries or firms. A compelling example is China's telephone switch development in the 1980s and 1990s (Lee et al., 2012). The lessons learned from these cases have implications for African countries, such as Nigeria, which produce oil without refining and exporting the latter mostly as crude oil. They can build additional oil refineries, which are sectors corresponding to mature or medium short-cycle technologies. This task is possible because the technology required to build oil refineries is old, mature, and easily available at a cost. The process resembles Korea's entry into steel-making through a state-owned enterprise in the early 1970s.

The abovementioned technological development models share the common element of accessing foreign knowledge through diverse channels. Foreign knowledge is critical; latecomers' catching-up effort frequently becomes risky, time consuming, and costly without it. The diverse channels of knowledge, access, and learning generally include such modes as (1) training in foreign firms and institutes, (2) OEM, (3) licensing, (4) joint ventures, (5) co-development with foreign specialized R&D firms, (6) hiring of individual scientists or engineers, (7) reverse brain drain, (8) overseas R&D centers, (9) strategic alliances, and (10) international mergers and acquisitions (Lee, 2005). Successful technological development by latecomers involves government support, access to foreign knowledge, and private firms' effort. The weights and specific roles of the three elements differ by sector and level or stage of economic development.

Development Trap and Challenges Facing Africa

The suggested entry techniques into and the promotion of manufacturing sectors presented by the preceding subsection face numerous challenges in implementation in the specific context of Africa. The typical situation in Africa is characterized by weak manufacturing, premature tertiarization leading to numerous microenterprises, and weak export bases. Thus, several countries in Africa at the low-income stages have had trade deficits for many years because of their weak export capabilities and ever-strong demand for imported goods. Such difficulties must be caused by unfavorable initial conditions, such as colonial experiences, frequent civil wars, and political instability, as well as food shortage and hunger. However, Korea previously experienced similar conditions in the 1950s before its economy took off. South Korea underwent several decades of colonial rule in the early twentieth century, several years of civil war (1950–1953), a period of hunger and food shortage, and, consequently, reliance on US food aid in the 1950s and even in the 1960s. South Korea was worse off than Africa in terms of resource endowments because all the minerals were in North Korea.

South Korea also went through three decades of trade deficits until it recorded its first trade surplus in 1986; since then, it has maintained a trade surplus (Lee, 2013b). In the early 1960s, Korea had a 1:9 export-to-import ratio, which was considerably worse than that of a typical country in Africa. Thus, Korea had a big savings gap, with domestic savings and gross investment only at 9% and 15%, respectively, of the GDP. Consequently, the country relied on foreign borrowing to fill the gap. This condition illustrates the importance of exports and their role as critical binding constraints for the growth of economies at low- or middle-income stages.

Recovering from a trade deficit may take several decades; thus, a country at a low-income stage may find implementing transitory measures necessary in managing the balance of payments.[6] Korea's past experience can be useful in the search for specific policy tools. In the 1960s and 1970s, Korea maintained a tight centralized control on foreign exchanges within the economy; all export earnings (foreign currencies) of the country were initially placed under the control of the government (Bank of Korea) and subsequently allocated for "justifiable uses," such as payment for imported capital goods (Amsden, 1989). Foreign exchanges were under tight control in the closed capital market in the early period because export promotion and free capital mobility cannot work together. Export promotion often involves the undervaluation of currencies (similar to typical economic conditions in emerging economies involving frequent depreciation), which is a signal or incentive for people to take their money abroad or deposit it into foreign currency-dominated bank accounts.

In these practices, imports of non-necessities, such as luxury consumer goods, were discouraged by high tariffs, diverse non-tariff barriers, or social campaigns. Moreover, permission to use dollars was difficult to obtain. For example, even imports of foreign fruits (e.g., bananas) was discouraged by high tariffs or non-tariff barriers in Korea. Tariffs were generally low for capital goods and high for consumer goods, which Korea aimed to promote as exportable goods; this tactic was termed by Shin and Lee (2012) as asymmetric protection. Such protection had a significant impact not on the total factor productivity changes but on the volume and market shares of Korean export products. These practices also meant tight control of capital outflow or

---

[6] The several transitory policy measures are discussed in detail in Lee (2017b).

capital flight. For example, ordinary people were not permitted to have bank accounts in foreign countries, and foreign banks were not allowed to open businesses in Korea until the late 1980s.

Despite the low income and low domestic savings, Korea maintained a high investment rate. One of the reasons for this condition was low interest rates, with rate hikes being suppressed by the government. Despite this suppressed interest ratio, the domestic savings ratio in Korea continued to increase because of the growth of income associated with the strong investment over the decades. This experience may have several implications for African countries, such as Uganda. In these countries, interest rates are currently high at over 24%, despite tolerable inflation rates and low interest rates applied to savings deposited into banks. This situation is unfavorable for private investment and reflects the asymmetric power and dominance of the lender over the borrower and of the banking sector over the manufacturing sector. If both sides have equal power, then interest rates for savings should also be high. In other words, financial markets are oligopolistic and imbalanced in terms of the power of supply and demand and may be in a state of market failure. Such a state may justify government intervention, including the regulation of interest rates. In other words, the banking sector is earning extra rents associated with oligopoly, which is the opposite of the desirable state of a productive sector enjoying rents. This is the opposite of the past situation in Korea, when the banking sector "served" the real (manufacturing) sector by providing a stable supply of so-called "growth money" at affordable rates, and the manufacturing or production sector was given priority.

In many African countries, such as Uganda, exports are unresponsive despite competitive exchange rates (undervaluation or depreciation). This situation is expected because competitive exchange rates work only in an economy with a strong manufacturing basis. Moreover, Ramanayake and Lee (2017) found a negative effect of undervaluation on growth in mineral-exporting groups; if the currency is undervalued in countries that depend substantially on natural resource exports, then less income is earned in terms of dollars because natural resource exports are often insensitive or inelastic to exchange rates.

In summary, the typical conditions of already-free capital mobility and already-privatized banking sectors indicate that promoting manufacturing in typical African countries is difficult, except in a few countries (e.g., Ethiopia) that receive FDI flow from Asia, including China. Low valuation of currency leads to capital flight and decreased domestic savings available for investment. Control of interest rates to boost investment in industrial sectors is also not that feasible under the private (or foreign) dominance of commercial banking. The situation of Kenya, which recently implemented an interest ceiling, shows such a dilemma.

If domestic effort to promote exports is limited, then FDI is certainly an option. However, attracting FDI in the manufacturing sector has not been easy in many African countries. In this case, a radical or an innovative idea for a country such as Uganda might be to leapfrog into IT services or smart agriculture and bypass the manufacturing stage. A preceding case of leapfrogging happened in India, which bypassed manufacturing to leapfrog into IT service as its engine of growth (Chapter 7, see Section 5.7). Agriculture is increasingly being recognized as a high-technology sector rather than a traditional industry that belongs to the so-called "sixth industry," which is a combination of primary, secondary, and tertiary industries. The sixth industry is combined with IT or digital technologies as it braces for the benefits of new innovations that have been associated in recent years with the 4IR. A role model is the Netherlands, which is leading in smart farming and dairy. In 2015, the country's export value in agriculture comprised 20% of its total exports and was the second largest in the world, at 438 billion Euros. Agriculture may be a more attractive sector to FDI than manufacturing in several African economies in terms of comparative advantages.

Role of the Public Sector and International Community and the Possibility of Leapfrogging

Any radical upgrading and leapfrogging in Africa generally require the help of government research institutes (GRIs) or public research organizations (PROs) because of the weak capabilities of the private sector. Thus, we may draw a picture of a latecomer model of productive and technological development and leapfrogging (Table 7–1) with a focus on a tripartite G–P–G cooperation involving GRIs (G), private firms (P), and government ministries (G), which had played a key role in such countries as Korea.[7] Under this model, the actors have different roles, depending on their stage of development. A typical division of labor in past examples from East Asia placed government research laboratories in charge of R&D; private firms, of production; and government ministries, of marketing in the form of direct procurement or protection by tariffs and exclusive standards.

The case of the telephone switch in Korea and China is a typical representation of this model (hereafter called GPG1). Under GPG1, R&D is undertaken mainly by GRIs or PROs (Table 7–1). Private firms are in charge of manufacturing, and the government helps in marketing by procuring domestically made products. The model has other variations depending on the level of capabilities of the involved private firms and public agencies. The case of the digital TV and CDMA mobile phones in Korea is another variation (hereafter called GPG2). In the GPG2 model, the costs and risks of R&D are shared between GRIs and private firms. In addition, the GRIs observe technological trends and coordinate to bring diverse actors into the consortium. The GPG2 model is an advanced form of the GPG arrangement and is possible only when the capabilities of private firms are sufficiently advanced to undertake increased R&D.

Another variation of the GRI–private–government (GPG) model, which places government agencies in charge of both R&D and production, is needed when the capabilities of private firms are very low. This

---

[7]   This G–P–G model was first discussed by the author in Lee and Mathews (2013).

Table 7–1. *From Government-Private-Government (GPG) Model to Foreign Actor-Local Firm-Government (FLG) Model*

First stage	GPG0	FLG0
Tech transfer/R&D	GRI/foreign actor	Foreign cooperation partner
Production	*SOEs/private firms	Local firms (private, SOEs)
Market promotion/ protection	Government	Government
Second Stage	GPG1	FL–P–G2 (FLG1)
R&D	GRIs	Joint R&D by foreign and local GRIs/firms
Production	Private firms	Local private firms
Market promotion/ protection	Government	Government
Third Stage	GPG2	G–P–G2 (FLG2)
R&D	Joint R&D by public and private firms	Joint R&D by local public and private firms
Production	Private firms	Local private firms
Market promotion/ protection	Government	Government
Fourth Stage	GPG3 (PG)	G–P–G3 (FLG3)
R&D	Private firms	Local private firms
Production	Private firms	Local private firms
Market promotion/ protection	None	None

*Note: State-owned enterprises (SOEs). *Source:* Lee and Mathews (2013)

variation can be called the GPG0, although it is not GPG but government-government (GG) without the involvement of private firms (P). An example is steel development in Korea by the government-owned enterprise POSCO.

The opposite of the GPG0 model is GPG3 or PG, which has no GRI involvement. An example is the development of the automobile industry spearheaded by Hyundai Motors. In this case, the government or a GRI was not involved in R&D and was limited to providing protection for the infant industry by tariffs (Lee and Lim, 2001). R&D was undertaken by Hyundai Motors or other private firms. Thus, this case illustrates a GP rather than a GGP model in which private firms undertake R&D and production.

The Korean experience shows that state activism for technological development with increasing private-sector participation comes in four models. In the GPG0 or GG model, the government undertakes market provision while SOEs undertake R&D and production. In the GPG1 model, R&D is accomplished by GRIs while production is undertaken by private firms. In the GPG2 model, a considerable number of R&Ds are shifted to private firms, which cooperate with GRIs. Finally, in the GPG3 or PG model, private firms undertake R&D and production. In these variations, the role of the government or ministries involved focus on guaranteeing initial market creation in the form of procurement policies and local market protection by tariffs or the exclusive setting of standards.

The aforementioned GPG model can be modified to form a model of international technological assistance for African countries. This model, which can involve cooperation among foreign actors (such as international research organizations), local firms, and government (FLG), involves foreign research organizations invited by the donor government or the UN in place of the GRI/PRO in the GPG model. This is done to ensure that foreign cooperation partners undertake R&D and transfer the results to local private firms or SOEs in African countries (stage FLG0). In the subsequent FLG1 stage, foreign partners conduct joint R&D with local R&D organizations or firms. In the third stage, the aid-receiving African country can conduct R&D locally through private–public partnerships, which is equivalent to GPG2. The final stage is where all functions are performed by private actors.

The so-called green revolution of the 1960s and 1970s and the system of rice intensification (SRI) method are examples of the FLG model (Lee et al., 2014). The green revolution involved the introduction of high-yielding varieties of rice, wheat, maize, fertilizers, pesticides, irrigation, and new management practices, thereby resulting in a dramatic increase in productivity and production. The green revolution, which was initiated with support from the Ford and Rockefeller Foundations and led by Norman Borlaug, has saved over a billion people from starvation. A substantial amount of the initial research on rice and wheat had been conducted previously in American universities but required adaptation to local conditions; the latter required the creation of new international research institutes, initially the International Maize and Wheat Improvement Center in Mexico and the International Rice Research Institute in the Philippines (Juma, 2011). These institutions were later brought under the auspices of the Consultative Group on International Agricultural Research, which is currently a consortium of fifteen research institutes working on agroforestry, biodiversity, dry areas, food policy, fish, forestry, livestock, maize, wheat, potato, rice, semi-arid tropics, tropical agriculture, and water. As required by this international initiative, local authorities expanded roads, improved irrigation systems, and provided electrical power to support farmers in adopting new technologies. International lending was also offered to promote the package. International research collaboration led to the birth and expansion of national agricultural research institutes tasked with adapting the internationally developed varieties of rice and wheat to local conditions.

In the case of India, the government played a key role in the diffusion of new seed varieties (Lee et al., 2014). With financial support from the World Bank and technical assistance from the Rockefeller Foundation, the government established state seed corporations in most major states in the 1960s, thereby leading to the creation of the seed industry in India (Juma, 2011). SRI was started in the early 1980s, after participating groups from forty countries assembled in Madagascar in 1983 and spread rapidly to additional countries with the assistance of Cornell University. India is one of the biggest beneficiaries of this initiative.

In a certain context and under certain conditions, such as the availability of foreign assistance and access to knowledge and funding, latecomers may attempt to leapfrog into newly emerging sectors, such as renewable energy. An example is the use of solar power in desert grasslands in rural areas in Jigawa, Nigeria (Lee and Mathews, 2013). This semi desert area has no water supply. The traditional option was to open wells with ropes and buckets, hand pumps, or government-supplied, diesel-powered pumps that worked until they broke down or until villagers ran out of money to buy the expensive diesel. This problem was solved through solar-powered pumps designed to run maintenance-free for at least eight to ten years.

Another example is the O&L Group in Namibia (Lee et al., 2014). Established by Mr. Shilongo, this company started in retail and brewery and then diversified into dairy and solar energy. O&L survived and expanded quickly with government support (against a South African company's effort to sabotage it by price dumping), with sales reaching approximately 4% of the GDP of Namibia. O&L plans to enter the energy business, including wind power, because Namibia imports electricity from South Africa and Angola. However, the company must first solve the hurdle of a government-imposed grid monopoly.

Another notable example of leapfrogging is the M-Pesa in Kenya, which serves as an efficient and convenient mobile banking and payment system for African people without access to offline banking.[8] M-Pesa's founders were looking for a method to apply their mobile payment system to solve other problems. Thus, they started another company called M-Kopa Solar to provide solar energy to rural households in Africa. Their system uses three readily available technologies, namely, solar generation and low-energy LED lights, mobile payments similar to those of M-Pesa, and the SIM cards embedded in the M-Kopa control unit. M-Kopa's innovation is to package these technologies and combine them with a mobile payment

---

[8]   This story of M-Pesa and M-Kopa relies on Shapshak (2016).

system, thereby providing solar energy products at affordable prices. M-Kopa is an effective off-the-grid solar system for Africa, which suffers from poor land-based infrastructure and a frequently erratic electricity supply. M-Kopa enabled children in rural areas to study after school, and relieved their mothers from the burden of fetching firewood and burning kerosene late into the night. Thus, the process is a leapfrogging out of kerosene-based lighting, bypassing the grid-based electricity into off-grid renewable energies. This system is an innovation not only in technological terms but also in terms of business models suited to African conditions.

A few example cases in LDCs may pertain more to the adoption of new technologies than to local innovations. However, adoption is a beginning, or stepping stone, for learning and eventual innovation. Learning is not possible without adoption. Manufacturing firms in East Asia, such as Samsung and Hyundai Motors in Korea, all started from adopting foreign technology for production, learning from using, enhancing productivity by mastering production technologies, and finally acquiring design technology (Lee, 2005, 2013a). Recent examples can be found in the renewable energy markets of China, Brazil, and India, which involve the transition toward low-carbon economies. Options for LDCs in low-carbon technologies include wind, solar, biogas, and geothermal energy sources. In this case, coordinated initiatives and incentives for early adopters are essential in reducing the risks associated with weak initial markets.

7.3 TO LEAPFROG BEYOND THE RESOURCE CURSE IN LATIN AMERICA

The Double Curse of Resources

This section discusses possible policy ideas for resource-rich middle-income countries, particularly those in Latin America. The economies of many countries in this region (e.g., Brazil) are richly endowed with mineral resources. However, these apparent advantages have often been turned into disadvantages associated with the so-called resource curse. This implies not only a weaker imperative to the development of manufacturing but also negative impacts on the appreciation of national currency caused by the inflows of money from exports.

Ramanayake and Lee (2017) found that undervaluation has a negative effect on the growth of mineral-exporting economies, such that the dollar income is reduced if currency is undervalued in countries that depend heavily on natural resource exports; such exports are often insensitive or inelastic to exchange rates. Thus, these mineral-exporting economies face the growth-impeding and procyclical effects of undervaluation during periods of weak economic performance, along with the typical balance-of-payment crisis. These effects of undervaluation underscore the difficulties facing economic growth in mineral-exporting economies and the dilemma of the resource-based development model. Therefore, the nature of the resource curse is being stuck in the resource-based sector, with a weak chance or insufficient incentive for entry into manufacturing as a result of the countercyclical effects of the low valuation of currencies. In other words, even if they try to get around the curse by undervaluing their currency, such undervaluation does not help but instead hurts the economy in terms of reduced dollar incomes.

In addition to this resource curse, a negative legacy of the colonial period exists. In particular, aboriginal slaves and slaves from Africa were freed without land ownership. Being separated from their lands, the slaves became the urban poor in the informal sector. The lack of land reform in Latin America is a radically different initial condition from that in East Asia. In East Asia or South Korea and Taiwan, government reforms provided land to tillers. This situation not only set an equal initial condition for the population but also enabled peasants to sell their lands later to pay for the education or business start-ups of their children. Therefore, land reform was one of the enabling factors of the rapid increase of educational attainment in East Asia and worked to supply educated workers for manufacturing development.

The preceding discussion emphasizes the triple traps or legacy of Latin America, namely, the resource curse, the colony legacy, and weak human capital. This initial condition inevitably leads to weak manufacturing development unless manufacturing is by FDI or MNCs. Several governments in Latin America (particularly in Brazil) have also attempted industrial policies, which remained import-substituting, that is, not extending to export orientation. Such policies have not been pursued consistently and long enough to have an impact. The implementation of these policies was often stopped because of unstable macroeconomic conditions or liberalization movements along the Washington Consensus. Several governments, such as Lula in Brazil, attempted to implement several pro-poor policies. However, they were not inclusive enough because they failed to effect radical change of the weak educational attainment of the big segment of the population.

Given this historical legacy, the NIS in a typical Latin American country is characterized commonly by a weak industrial sector stemming from weak indigenous firms. These firms are either weak in manufacturing or are successful exporting firms but subsidiaries of MNCs.[9] These firms have led to a weakened collaboration with public institutions or universities. This is because the focus of the science sector on basic academic research is irrelevant to the industrial sector due to the low demand for the latter. Despite this overall picture, several successful cases exist, such as the salmon sector in Chile and the biofuel, soybean, and mid-sized jet sectors in Brazil, as noted in several studies.[10] Interestingly, the development in these sectors all involved certain forms of private and public collaboration.

Implementing Leapfrogging While Avoiding Design Failure

Despite such successful cases being few and far between, they can be employed as a basis for increased leapfrogging attempts. Several scholars, including Perez (2008), have argued that Latin America should

---

[9]   See Pack (2001), Alcorta and Peres (1998), Katz (2001), and Velho (2004).
[10]   See Suzigan and Albuquerque (2011) and Albuquerque et al. (2015).

utilize resource-based development as a starting point from which its countries can leapfrog into emerging technologies that combine renewable energies, nanotechnology, bioelectronics, and new materials. Similarly, resource-rich Latin American economies can use their current resource exports as a platform for and source of funding with which to enhance their capabilities in preparation for entry to the next technological revolution. Other than manufacturing-based leapfrogging, IT service may also be a promising sector for Latin America to consider because it also depends on short-cycle technology and thus could leapfrog into service while bypassing manufacturing. The advantages of IT services, such as low-entry barriers, have earlier been exploited in India to promote these services; this is an example of leapfrogging over to IT.[11] Furthermore, the software sector has had success with public–private collaboration in Latin America, such as that of the ARTech Consultores in Uruguay.[12]

In this leapfrogging effort, identifying the sector or business items is an important issue. The third chapter of this book suggests the criterion of short-cycle technologies. In the actual implementation, we can think of a method consistent with the idea of entrepreneurial discovery, which is suggested by the smart specialization framework.[13] This outline states that policy makers should organize a joint public–private task force that includes representatives from the private sector. In addition, they should administer a survey to existing private firms and entrepreneurs on the nature of business items or technological areas, near-future areas of potential, opportunities, risks, and bottlenecks related to entering or starting out. These business areas include those in which the private sector sees certain market potential and short-cycle times, but with technological, financial, and related environmental or regulatory uncertainties. Private firms may know where the next markets are but may be unsure of

---

[11]   Explained in Section 5.7 in this book and also in Lee (2013a, Chapter 8 on India).
[12]   Noted in Sabel et al. (2012, Chapter 10).
[13]   A pioneering reference on smart specialization is Foray (2015). The following two paragraphs rely on Lee's chapter in a recent edited volume (Radosevic et al., 2017).

their capability to develop the necessary and proper technologies and to raise funds for R&D and initial marketing. In other words, new business or technology areas with highly certain market potential but technological, financial, and regulatory uncertainties are the target areas. Policy intervention promotes these areas by mobilizing public and private resources and competencies that correct market and coordination failures.

An example is the Korean electronics industry in the early 1990s. The TV industry was a globally fast-growing market. Moreover, new technologies, such as high-definition (HD) TVs, were emerging. HD TV technologies came in two forms, namely, analogue HD technologies pioneered by Japanese firms and digital technology-based HD TVs by Western firms. Thus, the Korean latecomer firms were certain that there was a market, but they faced three choices: continue producing the old (non-HD) analogue TV, follow the Japanese firms and license analogue HD TV technologies, or leapfrog into digital TV technologies. Lee et al. (2005) explained that the public–private R&D consortium chose the third option and developed their own digital TV technology. Meanwhile, Japanese firms were locked in for a while with their own analogue HD TVs. Thus, Korean firms (e.g., Samsung) experienced a turning point by becoming the leader in digital TVs and surpassed Japanese firms (e.g., Sony) in the display industry.

The aforementioned case in Korea can be contrasted with one in South Africa where an electric car called "Joule" was developed but failed to become a commercial venture. Swart (2015) explained that the South African government provided the initial funding and established Optimal Energy in 2005. Optimal Energy was a start-up business with the objective of "establishing and leading the electric vehicle industry in South Africa." The company was initially successful and had four roadworthy prototypes by December 2010. The Joule was a "born electric" five-seat passenger car with an entirely novel vehicle design that incorporated a locally developed battery, motor, and software technologies. However, the company closed in June 2012 despite their technical success and extensive network of partners and suppliers. The government, as the company's major shareholder, decided to stop the funding required to start the large-scale production of the electric cars because of uncertainties in marketing success.

The failure of the Joule was caused by the lack of involvement of indigenous private companies in volume production and sales. Extant foreign multinational companies and local auto companies did not want this new "disruptive innovator," a state-owned company, to become another rival in car sales. From the outset, the government should have formed a public–private consortium with a plan for volume production to be performed by private actors after the development of the prototype. Thus, this South African case is more of a design failure than a targeting failure.

Caution against government activism often does not indicate whether failure arises from targeting or design because the sources are often mixed together. In reality, numerous public initiatives fail not because of target failure but because of design or capability failure, which indicates low execution capabilities. Uncertainty diminishes if the private sector, which has knowledge about the markets, is involved in the process of targeting in relation to identifying potential or existing markets. Targets may often be obvious for latecomers that are not on the frontier, as a clear benchmark case often exists for them. Then, the identification of niches between existing firms and projects may be attempted.

The automobile sector in Brazil, one of the biggest markets in Latin America, is currently dominated by foreign imported cars or foreign joint-venture cars with local assembly. If Brazil is determined to remedy this situation and attempt leapfrogging into new sectors, electric cars can be an option. Given its favorable weather and long sunny days, an expansive domestic market, and a decent cumulated stock of scientific and technological knowledge, Brazil has a high chance of success if the government has political will and determination, combined with appropriate tax incentives. The case of South Africa demonstrates that developing electric cars is no longer difficult and the manner of implementation is crucial for avoiding design failure. Korea's Hyundai took seven years to develop their own engines, and Malaysia's Proton failed because of the lack of local engine technologies, among other reasons. Engines represent one of the most difficult and high-tech items in conventional cars, but electric cars do not have them because they can run without engines and only with batteries. In other words, producing electric cars involves low technological barriers.

Emerging economies, such as Brazil, can attempt to implement a "green industrial policy" and endeavor to leapfrog into both electric cars and diverse renewable energies, including solar energy.[14] Renewable energies represent a new techno-economic paradigm and thus provide new windows of opportunity for leapfrogging. Such a direction also corresponds to sustainable development that adopts environment-friendly technologies. Wealthy countries became industrialized through their early and easy access to energy sources of unprecedented power (i.e., steam power and then electric power based on fossil fuels) and the availability of resources at unprecedented levels of exploitation (largely through exploitation of extraterritorial colonial possessions). The latecomers in East Asia deployed the same industrial model but did so by exploiting latecomer advantages and accessing export markets through cost-driven mass production capacities.

Earth's resources are currently being spread thin because of the actions of the early industrializers. The answer to this problem is to build a new type of industrial system, that is, a "green" industrial system, as argued by Mathews (2017). Such green development strategy is the inevitable choice because newly emerging economies are lagging in conventional fossil-fueled technology but can leapfrog to and lead with green technology. Actually, Brazil has been implementing strategies to build renewable power industries, including an indirect local sourcing requirement imposed outside the trading system (so

[14]   Mathews (2017) elaborates strategies for such leapfrogging in emerging countries. For green industrial policy, see Altenburg et al. (2017).

as to avoid trade disputes) but financed by the Brazil National Development Bank.[15]

Learning WTO Rules through Two Contrasting Cases

Green development can be a safe choice even considering the WTO rules on the space for industrial policy. Previously, the WTO had rules on permitted (so-called "green light") subsidies, which included those for R&D, regional development, and environmental compliance. Without such rules, several industrial policies might have led to disputes under the WTO regime. An example is the case of Indonesia, which attempted a late entry into the automobile industry but failed because of the interference of incumbent countries, such as Japan and the United States. A brief introduction of this case follows.[16]

In the 1990s, the Indonesian government attempted to specialize in several specific industries that require a higher technological level than low-degree primary resource-based skills. The government decided to develop its automobile sector as a national strategic industry, considering the nation's relatively abundant labor resource. At that time, Japanese automotive companies nearly monopolized the market with over 90% of market shares. Such new entry attempts were therefore sensible economically because they promote competition and reduce market failure. The Indonesian national car program, initiated in February 1996, aimed to develop an indigenous automotive industry by reducing dependency on foreign brand owners and increasing local industrial capacity. National automotive companies were required to use increasing amounts of local materials in their automobiles. PT Timor Putra Nasional (TPN) was the only company to satisfy the requirements for obtaining the national car status granted by the Indonesian government. Unfortunately, PT TPN was unable to produce a car independently. Thus, a Presidential Decree was issued in 1996 to allow PT TPN to

---

[15]   See Mathews (2017: 98).

[16]   This section relies heavily on the last section of Lee, Shin, and Shin (2015), a reprint of Lee, Shin, and Shin (2014).

form a partnership and import automobiles either in completely knocked-down or completely built-up form from South Korea while securing time to develop its own technology. Kia Motors in South Korea agreed to incorporate the technology transfer clause in the outcome of its business-to-business negotiations with Japan. Japan did not transfer technology even though it operated in the Indonesian market for over twenty years. Moreover, the national car program provided significant benefits to PT TPN for the Timor car project through duties and taxes, which accounted for over 60% of the show-room price of their sedans.

However, the joint venture between Kia Motors and PT TPN for producing the Timor brand of national motor vehicles resulted in disputes in the WTO, particularly regarding complaints from market incumbents excluded from the government incentives, namely, local firms controlled by other foreign companies (e.g., Japanese and American firms). The EU, Japan, and the United States alleged that the exemption of national vehicles from customs duties, luxury taxes, and related measures on imports and the components thereof violated the obligations of Indonesia under the GATT (MFN and NT), SCM (Subsidies and Countervailing Measures) Agreement (specific subsidies), TRIMs (local content requirement), and TRIPs (NT with respect to the use of trademarks).[17] The WTO panel investigated the case and decided in July 1998 that Indonesia violated the rules. Therefore, the country abolished the 1996 national car program and instituted a new automotive policy (the 1999 automotive policy) that implemented the recommendations of the WTO. Consequently, imports from Japan, the EU, and the United States encroached upon the Indonesian automobile market. The R&D efforts of the National Agency for Technological Research regarding automotive products either could not be used or remained as prototypes, including the development of machinery and car parts.

Contrary to the preceding case, which involved serious difficulties, some countries have conducted industrial policy successfully

[17] Indonesia – Certain Measures Affecting the Automobile Industry, WT/DS54/R, WT/DS55/R, WT/ DS59/R, and WT/DS64/R, adopted July 1998.

even under the WTO regime. The first case involves the wind power sector in China.[18] The Chinese government promoted wind power development through the local contents requirement policy in the 1990s. The initial target for local contents was set at 40% and subsequently reached 70%, which resulted in local value chains. However, because of serious international complaints through the WTO, China stopped the program in 2009. By that time, the program had already achieved success in making China a global player in wind power development. This case indicates the importance of a decisive and swift move with targeted industrial policy to achieve the threshold level of results before the case is brought to the WTO dispute panel.

Another case involving China and solar panels demonstrates a country escaping the constraints of the WTO system because subsidies were spread widely across many countries.[19] The price of solar panels dropped significantly because of the competition seemingly driven by Chinese firms, which were increasing market shares from 8% in 2008 to 55% in the last quarter of 2010 (Baldwin, 2011). This was counteracted by the US government (US Department of Commerce), which charged anti-dumping duties and countervailing duties; similar complaints were also filed by the EU. However, China requested a consultation with the United States and the EU under the WTO dispute settlement body (DSB) to rebut their claims. Moreover, China requested the WTO to investigate the subsidies subject to domestic content restrictions and feed-in tariff programs in the renewable energy sectors in the United States and in EU countries. Consequently, China was freed from this dispute. In fact, promotion and subsidies have been common in the solar panel sector in the United States and in many European countries.[20]

---

[18]   For details on China's wind power development, see Mathews (2017: 96–97).

[19]   This case of the solar panels is also from Lee, Shin, and Shin (2015), which is a reprint of Lee, Shin, and Shin (2014).

[20]   As an example, Lee et al. (2015) discuss the case of Solyndra, a private company that received various forms of financial support from the US government. This included a $535 million loan guarantees obtained by Solyndra in September 2009 under the Loan Guarantee Program of the Department of Energy. The guarantee was financed through the Federal Financing Bank. The loan interest rate was 1.025% per quarter,

7.4 INDUSTRY 4.0 AND THE PROSPECT OF LEAPFROGGING IN SOUTHEAST ASIA

Manufacturing has been the main feature of the catch-up stories discussed in the preceding chapters, particularly in the discussions on East Asian economies, including China. Countries in Southeast Asia, such as Thailand, Malaysia, and Indonesia, have pursued a similar development strategy of export-based manufacturing. However, manufacturing businesses are experiencing challenges because domestic wages increase while products remain at the low-end segment. Thus, several Southeast Asian economies are showing signs of being stuck in MIT.

Furthermore, the challenge with the arrival of the 4IR (4th Industrial Revolution), as noted by Schwab (2016) at the 2016 World Economic Forum, is whether the late latecomers—Southeast Asian economies in particular—can still use export-based manufacturing as a path to prosperity.[21] The existing mode of economic catch-up is encountering numerous problems with the arrival of the 4IR in several aspects. First, the 4IR is rewriting the rules of manufacturing. As the cost of automation plummets, low-cost labor is becoming a decreasingly effective strategy for attracting manufacturing investment. Second, a trend of reshoring manufacturing to the developed world (e.g., Apple in the United States and the shoe manufacturing of Adidas in Germany) is emerging with the 4IR. Third, global supply chains are expected to flatten further and become increasingly regional, and even national, to reduce delivery times and render manufacturing progressively responsive to local tastes and demands.

Originally, the 4IR referred to the new wave of innovations consisting of several technologies, such as 3D printing, the Internet

which was excessively low and accounted for only a third or a fourth of the interest rate of other government-supported projects. Furthermore, the California state government reduced the sales tax of Solyndra through a sales and use tax exclusion in 2010 by the amount of $25.1 million.

[21] This challenge in Southeast Asia is dealt with in more depth in other work by the author, such as Lee et al. (2018). What follows also draws from this work.

of Things, artificial intelligence, smart cars, big data, and on-demand economy (sharing economy). However, the scope of the 4IR is extremely broad, and many of the related technological revolutions are not present in Southeast Asia. Thus, the concept of Industry 3.0 (automation) and Industry 4.0 (smart factory) may be more relevant when one is concerned with manufacturing in Southeast Asia. In fact, typical Southeast Asian factories are at the Industry 2.0, or the mass production, stage. Hence, even Industry 3.0 (automation) has not progressed much, let alone transformed into Industry 4.0 or a smart factory (ILO, 2016a: 4 and ILO, 2016b: 3). Accordingly, we can state that industrial upgrading is a more important concern in this region. This is in line with the view, such as that of UNCTAD, that robot-based automation per se does not invalidate the traditional role of industrialization as a development strategy, but that the great difficulty lies in attaining sectoral upgrading and productivity growth (UNCTAD, 2017: 50).

Preliminary results of my own studies (Lee et al., 2018) on the electronic cluster in Malaysia and the automobile cluster in Thailand suggest a positive possibility of upgrading into high-end segments and thus getting out of the MIT. In both cases, local institutions that have enabled training and upskilling of their local force constitute a key factor for this positive scenario. For instance, in Penang, Malaysia, such institutions include the PSCD, a not-for-profit institution that provides technical knowledge and training programs to engineers, and the CREST, which hosts multinationals and local firms, universities, and research institutes. In the automobile cluster in Thailand, the corresponding institutions include the AHRDP, a joint collaboration between Thailand, Japanese firms, and public agencies to train workers and engineers in auto parts manufacturing. In other words, the 4IR could be a blessing (window of opportunity) for countries like Malaysia and Thailand facing labor shortages, and it may compel FDI firms to introduce factory automation (smart factory) or other labor-saving technologies toward upgrading into higher segments with local spillovers.

Hence, the big wave called the 4IR may expedite the transition from mass production to automation or leapfrogging into the smart factory system in Southeast Asia. The issue of policy responses to these new challenges may also be considered in terms of the NIS framework and the Schumpeterian idea of leapfrogging and windows of opportunity. Newly emerging technological paradigms serve as a window of opportunity for a latecomer or developing country not to be locked into old technological systems, and to be able to leapfrog into new technologies or industries. If the Third Industrial Revolution or the first-generation digital technologies were windows of opportunity for first-tier East Asian economies, then the 4IR can be such window for next-tier latecomer economies in Southeast Asia. The way latecomer economies ride with and respond to these innovations determines their economic fortune. Depending on these conditions, the innovations can be either a new window of opportunity or a window through which to fall behind (destruction) and be stuck in the MIT. Even if leapfrogging is adopted, this approach should be managed carefully because it comes with both potentials and risks. As discussed in Lee et al. (2015), those risks come in two forms: the risk of making the wrong choices among several alternative technological trajectories and standards and that of whether an initial market exists for the first movers.

Most 4IR technologies are currently initiated not only by latecomers but also by advanced economies. Thus, these technologies could be reinforcing factors for the continuing or returning dominance of advanced economies. Despite this reality, several possible sources of opportunities are available for latecomers in this new era. These can be conceived in the following four manners. First, windows of opportunity can open because the 4IR causes diverse forms of disaggregation and disintegration of the manufacturing process (Schwab, 2016: 62). Existing firms and consumers or clients will disintegrate, thereby possibly opening new entry points for latecomers. Second, a window of opportunity can open with the emerging shift from mass production to individualized or distributed production, which could likely open new entry points for latecomer firms targeting niche production (and decreasingly subject to scale economy). Third, the rise of the sharing economy is a related window of opportunity in that it corresponds to low entry barriers in relation to the required size of initial stocks of capital and knowledge (Choudary, 2015). Moreover, the rise of new financial tools (such as crowdfunding, P2P loans, and block chains) may serve as a new source of funding for start-ups and their eventual growth. Fourth, the speed of progress with regard to the 4IR is uneven in advanced economies and their firms, thereby leading to the likelihood of incumbent trap behavior (Lee and Malerba, 2017). This is associated with the vested interests of current incumbents from these economies and firms. For instance, several countries forbid UBER or AirBnB from their areas. The possibility of the incumbent trap-like situation in several advanced economies is a source of opportunity for latecomers attempting to maximize their advantages and minimize their disadvantages.

However, to realize these potentials, coordinated and strategic responses are required from the public and private sectors in the region. For example, business models in the platform or in the sharing economy may require new forms of soft infrastructure, including big data and proper standards in its usage in connection with balancing public interests and privacy. In addition, although a young population is a major advantage for several latecomer economies, their educational systems are often insufficient to be effective because their contents become outdated soon after students graduate. An e-learning approach involving new forms and a space for interactive teaching should therefore be promoted. Desirable policy responses can be considered and designed within the conceptual framework of the NIS. This framework entails the relationship among the actors involved in creating, diffusing, and utilizing knowledge and innovations, including firms, public laboratories, government ministries, financial actors, and IPR and educational systems. The effectiveness of each nation's NIS determines the innovative and economic performance of countries in response to the challenge of the 4IR.

In this regard, the business group style of firms noted as an organizational catch-up device in Chapter 4 is useful given its suitability for diversification, which, in turn, is needed during the 4IR. Currently, firms in advanced economies switch to conglomerates or business groups as they embrace or lead diversification, while borders among business areas are blurred and crossed. For instance, Google has turned into a holding company called Alphabet to facilitate diversification. It currently has numerous affiliates, although the holding company owns 100% of the shares of its affiliates. Tesla, Amazon, and Facebook in the United States and Alibaba, Tencent, and Baidu (the three IT service giants) in China have become highly diversified and have taken on multidivisional forms of either a conglomerate or a business group.

New innovations in the 4IR also seem to require new modes of public policy and public–private partnerships. The comprehensiveness and across-the-board nature of this era require not just one policy response by a specific government ministry but consultation with and responses by multiple ministries, with the cooperation of the prime minister's office. Innovation-related uncertainties arise from the supply and demand sides. Joint private–public R&D projects are typical responses to supply-side uncertainty (how technologies can be developed). Conversely, countries may also consider the public procurements of innovations in Europe and attempt to adopt such policy tools into their own contexts to address demand-side uncertainty. Only with the proper responses will latecomer economies realize the potential of the 4IR. Furthermore, responses should be timely because several negative impacts of 4IR can occur earlier than expected, including loss of certain assembly and business process outsourcing jobs.

A premise in policy response is that latecomer economies cannot employ all varieties of 4IR-related technologies but should find niches considering their local readiness, complexities, different time horizons of the tipping points for diverse technologies, and varied heights of entry barriers. In addition, although slightly advanced local firms in latecomer economies may attempt to find niches in existing or related segments of the manufacturing industry, laggard firms may try to find niches in the 4IR-related transformation of resource-based sectors, such as agriculture and agribusinesses. The convergence of IT software and services with newly emerging fields of the 4IR can be a niche for a broad spectrum of economic agents that cannot produce and try new technological innovations but can simply apply new business models, as what has been happening often in China. The 4IR era will also disrupt and reshape the current GVC. Thus, new forms of insertion into the new GVC can emerge, not necessarily at the firm level but definitely at the individual level. Therefore, education and training should be emphasized, the labor market should be integrated at international levels, and start-ups by young entrepreneurs should be promoted by sharing resources on successful role models and cases.

7.5   SIZE OF POLICY SPACE UNDER THE WTO REGIME

This section is to discuss the possibility of industrial policy under the WTO constraint, relying on the existing works by this author.[22] Diverse forms of industrial policy have been attempted by developed and developing countries throughout the world and are currently being revived (Wade, 2012). This is particularly true since the 2008 financial crisis, during which many US companies were bailed out by subsidies. However, few such cases have been brought to the WTO for arbitration. By contrast, numerous cases have been raised against former attempts at industrial policy implementation by middle-income countries. This situation raises the concern of possible asymmetries regarding the use or abuse of industrial policy between developed and developing countries under the WTO regime. Girvan and Cortez (2013) noted that issues of asymmetric power related to WTO governance are reflected particularly in the use of the dispute settlement mechanism, certainly not with respect to the transparency

---

[22]   Thus, what follows relies heavily on the last section of Lee, Shin, and Shin (2015), which is a reprint of Lee, Shin, and Shin (2014).

of the process and the independence of its rulings but because of issues related to access and actual use of remedies or retaliatory measures against faulty parties who are unable or unwilling to act on a given ruling.

In practice, the possibility of imposing retaliatory measures is limited from the point of view of developing countries, especially those with small markets. In addition, more than half of disputes are settled during consultations, and few decisions are reached and lead to countermeasures.[23] For example, bananas are the major export of Ecuador. Although the country won three WTO dispute cases related to this product from 1996 to 2008 against the EU, the only WTO-authorized option for Ecuador was the implementation of retaliatory measures against the EU. Such action was not beneficial for Ecuador because the EU was one of the major markets for their banana exports.

Under the WTO regime, governmental policies must be formulated and implemented in a manner that is non-discriminatory to exporters on the border (most-favored nation) and within the domestic market (national treatment, [NT]). Moreover, instead of being industry-specific, policy instruments for production subsidies should be generic for all producers regardless of their affiliation. The WTO regime generally restricted the pursuit of industrial policy space and the flexibility of achieving policy objectives that used to be granted to developing countries under the previous trade regime.[24] Other scholars argue that several regional integrations and bilateral approaches, including free trade agreements (FTAs), enable developing countries to expand their policy space and market access to a certain degree.[25] However, the expansion and effectiveness of the policy space under the FTA framework is ambiguous.

For instance, R&D subsidies by government entities were permitted as non-actionable subsidies, that is, as allowable under the

---

[23]   Mentioned in Girvan and Cortez (2013).

[24]   This concern is raised by Dicaprio and Gallaher (2006), UNCTAD (2006), Wade (2003), and Cimoli, Dosi, and Stiglitz (2009).

[25]   This view is expressed by Mayer (2009) and Shadlen (2005).

SCM (Subsidies and Countervailing Measures) agreement. However, defining subsidies involves some degree of ambiguity itself, and some are regarded as permissible if they are "not specific to certain firms and sectors," which is also a matter of definition.[26] In other words, if a subsidy is provided on the basis of objective criteria or conditions, it may be considered as "not specific."[27] Types of subsidies provisionally permitted include R&D subsidies, regional development subsidies, and subsidies for complying with environmental requirements.

Practices of the Current WTO Rules and Size of the Policy Space

The following points summarize the current practices under the WTO rule.

First, developed countries have used WTO rules effectively and predominantly for their legal and economic interests. More than half of the 419 WTO dispute cases and the 86 SCM dispute cases were raised by developed countries. Half of the SCM dispute cases are related closely to industrial policies and involved developed countries. A quarter of such cases were between developed and middle-income countries. Only 17.44% of the SCM cases were raised by middle-income countries against developed countries, and 4.65% of the cases involved middle-income countries. Southern countries use the WTO system minimally because the trade flows of developing countries are usually small; thus, the expected benefit from WTO disputes is also minimal. Southern countries usually have insufficient legal capacities, such as limited access to international lawyers or

---

[26] This provision for R&D was terminated in January 2000 on the basis of Article 31 of the SCM agreement, which defines what subsidies are. The continuation of the provision reached an impasse because its extension was not negotiated. Thus, whether R&D subsidies are still allowed is somewhat ambiguous (Lee et al., 2015; Shin and Lee, 2013). Moreover, if a government provides goods and services at market prices, then no benefit is conferred; therefore, no subsidy exists (Sykes, 2005). In considering market prices, the market to be used as a benchmark remains unclear.

[27] However, subsidies may be considered de facto specific if a subsidy is limited to certain enterprises in a particular region. See the SCM Agreement Article 2.1., Shin and Lee (2013), and Lee et al. (2015) for details.

specialists in international trade and law, thereby discouraging them from initiating disputes (Horn, Mavroidis, and Nordstrom, 1999).

Second, none of the 419 WTO cases and 86 SCM cases were against low-income countries, implying that such countries may not have to be too concerned with the use of various tools of industrial policies. Unless they are successful and competitive enough to threaten the interests of developed countries, low-income nations are unlikely to face complaints by the WTO. In fact, Article 27 of the SCM Agreement permitted export subsidies by the South, especially those with incomes of less than $1,000. Although this article expired in 2003, countries may still ask for its extension, subject to approval by the WTO Ministerial Conference. As of 2015, export subsidies have been permitted for more than fifteen countries, including Barbados, Belize, Costa Rica, Dominica, El Salvador, and Fiji.[28]

Third, many developed countries use various industrial policies, but few cases have been brought to the WTO by developing countries. Even in such cases, developing countries cannot remedy the situation effectively because they have limited resources and retaliatory power to enforce the remedies. This finding is consistent with the argument that executing retaliatory measures against large countries, such as the United States, is practically impossible or has a negligible effect when initiated by developing countries with small domestic markets. Furthermore, even if developing countries win WTO disputes against developed countries, executing the remedies will not be beneficial because the allowed retaliatory action is generally an exemption from the WTO commitment or an import restriction against developed countries. These remedies are not feasible because developing countries are usually dependent on imports from developed countries, such as capital and consumer goods. The exports of developing countries also often depend heavily on developed markets, as shown by the banana dispute between Ecuador and the EU.

---

[28] For details, refer to Article 27.4 of the Agreement on Subsidies and Countervailing Measures (WT/L/691)

Fourth, the significant number of claims by developed countries against middle-income countries indicates that the current WTO rules create MIT by frustrating the industrial development efforts of middle-income countries. Banning export subsidies while allowing R&D subsidies is difficult to justify. A remote reason might be that R&D is likely to involve market failure. If this is the case, then market failure caused by monopoly or oligopoly in international markets should also be corrected by encouraging the market entry of subsidized firms from the South. An example is the case discussed in the preceding section of the failed attempt by Indonesia to promote its local automobile industry against foreign carmakers that nearly monopolize the industry through their market share of approximately 90%.

The problems of the WTO pertain not only to the rules themselves but also to the arbitrariness and asymmetry of the implementation of the rulings. Implementation is important because the WTO DSB(dispute settlement body) system can be problematic if the system fails to induce compliance with the rulings. The following gambling case illustrates this point.[29] It presents a prominent example of how small countries, such as Antigua and Barbuda in Latin America, cannot resort to WTO rules effectively and may feel powerless when retaliating against large economies, such as the United States.

The United States is one of the largest online gaming markets in the world, though online gaming accounts for only 8%–9% of the entire gaming sector. However, other countries such as Canada and many small countries in Latin America (including Antigua and Barbuda, Curacao, and Gibraltar) have also been promoting this sector by offering friendly licensing regulations because the industry can be a major source of jobs in these small countries. This dispute in the case example involved the measures applied by the US central, regional, and local authorities for controlling the cross-border supply of

---

[29]   This case is from Lee, Shin, and Shin (2015). Refer also to United States – Measures Affecting the Cross-Border Supply of Gambling and Betting Services, WT/DS285/AB/R, adopted April 20, 2005.

gambling and betting services. Antigua and Barbuda claimed the United States violated the WTO General Agreement on Trade in Services (GATS) because it committed to full market access and full national treatment of the cross-border supply. The WTO panel confirmed in 2005 that the three federal laws (the Wire Act, the Travel Act, and the Illegal Gambling Business Act) in the United States were inconsistent with WTO GATS rules. The panel gave the country the option of either allowing all Internet gambling or repealing the related US laws that prevented Internet gambling services from abroad. Nevertheless, the United States kept delaying the implementations of the rulings of the DSB by requesting additional time for actual compliance.

Thus, on June 8, 2006, Antigua and Barbuda requested consultations, and the panel concluded that the United States failed to comply with the recommendations and rulings of the DSB. However, instead of implementing its laws in accordance with WTO rules, the United States announced in May 2007 that it would withdraw gambling from its services and closed market access. The WTO panel ruled that Antigua and Barbuda were entitled to $21 million per year in compensation for being excluded from the US online gambling market. The award was far from what Antigua and Barbuda demanded ($3.44 billion in cross-retaliation). After nearly a decade of disagreement with and refusal by the United States to comply with the WTO rulings, the DSB meeting on January 28, 2013, allowed Antigua and Barbuda to seek compensation outside the original service sector, thereby suspending concessions and obligations to the United States with respect to IPR. However, several observers were concerned that this retaliation regarding IPR not only damages the tourism sector of Antigua but also its economy, reputation (because the country would be considered a "pirate"), and investment and innovation environments.

What Can Be Done to Change the Current Global Rules

First, reducing asymmetries and arbitrariness is imperative with regard to access and actual use of remedies (retaliatory measures) against faulty parties unwilling to act on a given ruling. One way to accomplish this is to establish a third party that will enforce remedies not only through the resources of the involved parties but also through resources and penalties at the international level. Otherwise, the WTO may have to consider introducing a rule that can restrict a country with a large market size (representing the size of retaliatory power) from complaining against a considerably smaller country when the size difference between the two exceeds a certain level. A committee should be established to conduct a prereview of submitted cases.

Second, the situation of the developing countries not receiving the promised technology transfer in return for their concurrence with the strict IPR protection rules under the TRIPs should be improved.[30] Otherwise, high-income countries that fail to deliver their promises or their official development assistance commitments (0.7% of GNI) should not be allowed to complain against developing countries that use R&D or other subsidies to enhance their technological capabilities.

Third, the WTO rules on permitted ("green light") subsidies, such as those for R&D, regional development, and environmental compliance, expired in 2000. To extend these rules and/or establish new rules on such subsidies, the interests of developing countries should be considered broadly. Although expiration means those subsidies are no longer viable, taking no explicit action after the expiration date can also be interpreted as implicitly retaining the permitted subsidies unless one party raises a serious objection. If this is the case, then clarifying these rules on subsidies via new agreements is preferred so that these subsidies can be extended for a longer or infinite period.

---

[30] TRIPs Article 66.2 requires the developed members to implement technology transfer for the LDCs by providing incentives to enterprises or institutions. The developed countries' efforts on this provision are supposed to be reported to the WTO in pursuance of their commitments under the Article. However, few developed countries appear to have followed the rule properly (see http://wto.org/english/tratop_e/trips_e/techtransfer_e.htm in detail), and, thus, the technology gap between the North and the South remains substantial (Shin, Lee, & Park, 2014).

Fourth, the late entry of emerging countries into product markets characterized as near-monopolies or oligopolies should be treated in a special manner under the WTO rules because they can promote competition and efficiency by correcting market failures and distortions associated with monopoly. In such cases, promoting late entry by subsidies or SOEs may be justified. Furthermore, a strong international agency, such as a global fair trade commission, should be established for monitoring the market dominance of or distortion caused by a few major players. This agency should also have authority over international mergers and acquisitions, which can have anti-competition implications.

Fifth, international guidelines on subsidies or government assistance should be established in areas where public intervention may be justified. The case of international dispute over escalating subsidies in the solar panel industry demonstrates that although the subsidies may be justified in terms of environmental factors, internationally agreed-upon guidelines are needed. Such guidelines would prevent subsidies from escalating across countries—such a situation is not optimal from a global perspective. Bailouts during financial crises in developed countries also require certain guidelines because bailouts may be justified when firm failure is not caused by the firm itself but rather by transitory and global or external factors beyond the control of the firm.

Sixth, as noted by Girvan and Cortez (2013), despite the formal equality in terms of decision-making rights, decisions in practice are made through consensus-building, which is dominated by a few major industrial countries; thus, most nations that have been excluded from consensus-building are dissatisfied. Hence, improved procedures should be established for small and issue-based meetings with authorization from all members, and the meetings should be governed by transparent rules. All meetings, such as the Green Room or mini-ministerial ones, should be called by all members and be inclusive and transparent (Khor & Ocampo, 2010).

Seventh, measures for enhancing the resources and capabilities of the South to understand and use WTO rules and procedures should be implemented, such as providing training sessions and technical assistance. A pool of international experts and lawyers can be mobilized and should be available to the South when it needs WTO-specific legal services to defend various cases. A promising move in this regard is the establishment of the Advisory Center on WTO Law for providing legal service, support, and training to developing countries. Increased effort from governments and the industry in learning how to utilize the WTO DSB system is a crucial factor (Davis & Bermeo, 2009).

Permissible Alternatives under the Current Rules

First, developing countries, especially low-income ones, are advised not to consider the WTO restriction on industrial policies as an excuse for precluding industrial policy; members can deviate from WTO disciplines provided that no other member initiates legal action (and makes the case) against that measure. Such objection is possible only when industrial policies become significantly successful. Developed countries have been exploiting this feature, and, thus far, low-income countries have never been the target of a dispute raised with the WTO.

Second, R&D subsidies are not restricted or classified as "green light" subsidies. Although subsidies on exports are prohibited, those on production (for domestic consumption) are "green light" subsidies, or have not been prohibited unless deemed specific and cause adverse effects on other member countries, as noted by UNIDO/UNCTAD (2011). Moreover, the SCM does not prevent governments from subsidizing activities, particularly through regional, technological, and environmental policies, provided they have sufficient ingenuity to present such subsidies as WTO-compatible (UNCTAD, 2006). Developing countries may generally attempt to exploit the loopholes or opportunities for flexible interpretation in many of the rules in the WTO SCM as the term "yellow light," under which certain types of subsidies are classified. Even if a country is brought into the WTO process, the process is lengthy and the enforcement sometimes dubious.

Third, the South may be able to use several non-specific subsidies because they are not prohibited by the WTO. In other words, when subsidies are not limited to certain enterprises or industries but are available on the basis of objective criteria or conditions, they are regarded as non-specific. Accordingly, an industrial policy based on evolutionary targeting, "Program Portfolio Profile," proposed by Avnimelech and Teubal (2008), was formulated for innovators to leverage domestic market forces and local demand, thereby stimulating the development of indigenous technology. The proposed evolutionary targeting concept is an alternative approach to firm-specific targeting and focuses on the specification of the selection mechanisms. Evolutionary targeting involves the design and implementation of targeted programs for the development of a multi agent structure.

Finally, as noted by Cornia and Vos (2013), developing countries can use a stable and competitive exchange rate as an effective alternative to tariffs. Helleiner (2011) revealed that this strategy has significantly greater protective effects on the import-competing domestic manufacturing sector than does tariff rates of 30% or above. Specifically, countries can combine subsidies on production to targeted sectors, which is allowed by the WTO, with the general undervaluation of their currencies and this will have the same effect as that of export subsidies on targeted sectors.

References

Abernathy, W. J., and J. M. Utterback. (1978). "Patterns of Industrial Innovation." *Technology Review*, 80(7): 40–47.

Abramovitz, M. (1986). "Catching Up, Forging Ahead, and Falling Behind." *Journal of Economic History*, 46(2): 385–406.

Acemoglu, D., S. Johnson, and J. A. Robinson. (2002). "Reversal of Fortune: Geography and Institutions in the Making of the Modern World Income Distribution." *Quarterly Journal of Economics*, 117(4): 1231–1294.

——— (2001). "The Colonial Origins of Comparative Development: An Empirical Investigation." *American Economic Review*, 91(5): 1369–1401.

Acemoglu, D., and J. Robinson. (2012). *Why Nations Fail*. New York: Crown Business.

Adams, S. (2009). "Foreign Direct Investment, Domestic Investment, and Economic Growth in Sub-Saharan Africa." *Journal of Policy Modeling*, 31(6): 939–949.

Aiyar, M. S., M. R. A. Duval, M. D. Puy, M. Y. Wu, and M. L. Zhang. (2013). "Growth Slowdowns and the Middle-Income Trap." *IMF Working Paper*, No. 71.

Albuquerque, E., W. Suzigan, G. Kruss, and K. Lee. (2015). *Developing National Systems of Innovation: University–Industry Interactions in the Global South*. Cheltenham, UK: Edward Elgar Publishing.

Alcorta, L., and W. Peres. (1998). "Innovation Systems and Technological Specialization in Latin America and the Caribbean." *Research Policy*, 26(7–8): 857–881.

Alexander, J. (2002). "Nikon and the Sponsorship of Japan's Optical Industry by the Imperial Japanese Navy, 1917–1945." *Japanese Studies*, 22(1): 19–33.

Alfaro, L., A. Chanda, S. Kalemli-Ozcan, and S. Sayek. (2004). "FDI and Economic Growth: The Role of Local Financial Markets." *Journal of International Economics*, 64(1): 89–112.

Altenburg, T., C. Assmann, D. Rodrik, E. Padilla, S. Ambec, M. Esposito, A. Haider, W. Semmler, D. Samaan, and A. Cosbey. (2017). *Green Industrial Policy: Concept, Policies, Country Experiences*. Geneva; Bonn: UN Environment; German Development Institute.

Amsden, A. H. (1989). *Asia's Next Giant: South Korea and Late Industrialization.* New York; Oxford: Oxford University Press.

Amsden, A. H., and W. W. Chu. (2003). *Beyond Late Development: Taiwan's Upgrading Policies.* Cambridge, MA: MIT Press Books.

Amsden, A. H., and T. Hikino. (1994). "Project Execution Capability, Organizational Know-How and Conglomerate Corporate Growth in Late Industrialization." *Industrial and Corporate Change*, 3(1): 111–147.

Amurgo-Pacheco, A. (2008). *Patterns of Export Diversification in Developing Countries.* Washington, DC: World Bank Publications.

Anderson, K., and S. Nelgen. (2011). "Wine's Globalization: New Opportunities, New Challenges." *Wine Economics Research Centre Working Paper*, No. 111.

Arocena, R., and J. Sutz. (2001). "Changing Knowledge Production and Latin American Universities." *Research Policy*, 30(8): 1221–1234.

Arrow, K. J. (1962). "The Economic Implications of Learning by Doing." *Review of Economic Studies*, 29(3): 155–173.

Athreye, S. S. (2005). "Indian Software Industry and Its Evolving Service Capability." *Industrial and Corporate Change*, 14 (3): 393–418.

Au, K., M. W. Peng, and D. Wang. (2000). "Interlocking Directorates, Firm Strategies, and Performance in Hong Kong: Towards a Research Agenda." *Asia Pacific Journal of Management*, 17(1): 29–47.

Avnimelech, G., and M. Teubal. (2008). "Evolutionary Targeting." *Journal of Evolutionary Economics*, 18(2): 151–166.

Awokuse, T. O., and H. Yin. (2010). "Does Stronger Intellectual Property Rights Protection Induce More Bilateral Trade? Evidence from China's Imports." *World Development*, 38(8): 1094–1104.

Balasubramanyam, V. N., M. Salisu, and D. Sapsford. (1996). "Foreign Direct Investment and Growth in EP and IS Countries." *Economic Journal*, 106 (434): 92–105.

Baldwin, R. (2016). *The Great Convergence.* Cambridge, MA: Harvard University Press.

  (2011). *Trade and Industrialisation after Globalisation's 2nd Unbundling: How Building and Joining a Supply Chain Are Different and Why It Matters.* New York: National Bureau of Economic Research.

Baldwin, C., and K. Clark. (1997). "Managing in an Age of Modularity." *Harvard Business Review*, 75(5): 84.

Bebchuk, L. A., R. Kraakman, and G. Triantis. (2000). "Stock Pyramids, Cross-Ownership, and Dual Class Equity: The Mechanisms and Agency Costs of Separating Control from Cash-Flow Rights." In Morck, R. (Ed.),

Concentrated Corporate Ownership, pp. 295–318. Chicago: University of Chicago Press.

Beck, T., A. Demirguc-Kunt, and R. Levine. (2005). "SMEs, Growth, and Poverty: Cross-Country Evidence." *Journal of Economic Growth*, 10(3): 199–229.

Bell, M., and P. N. Figueiredo. (2012). "Building Innovative Capabilities in Latecomer Emerging Market Firms: Some Key Issues." In Amann, E. and J. Cantwell (Eds.), *Innovative Firms in Emerging Market Countries*, pp. 24–109. Oxford; New York: Oxford University Press.

Beneito, P. (2006). "The Innovative Performance of In-House and Contracted R&D in Terms of Patents and Utility Models." *Research Policy*, 35(4): 502–517.

Bently, L., and B. Sherman. (2001). *Intellectual Property Law*. Oxford; New York: Oxford University Press.

Bergek, A., S. Jacobsson, C. Bo, S. Lindmark, and A. Rickne. (2008). "Analyzing the Functional Dynamics of Technological Innovation Systems: A Scheme of Analysis." *Research Policy*, 37(3): 407–429.

Berle, A. A., and G. C. Means. (1932). *The Modern Corporation and Private Property*. New York: Macmillan.

Bernardes, A. T., and E. D. M. E. Albuquerque. (2003). "Cross-over, Thresholds, and Interactions between Science and Technology: Lessons for Less-Developed Countries." *Research Policy*, 32(5): 865–885.

Besedeš, T., and T. J. Prusa. (2006). "Product Differentiation and Duration of US Import Trade." *Journal of International Economics*, 70(2): 339–358.

Blackford, M. G. (1998). *The Rise of Modern Business in Great Britain, the United States, and Japan*. Chapel Hill: University of North Carolina Press.

Borensztein, E., J. D. Gregorio, and J. W. Lee. (1998). "How Does Foreign Direct Investment Affect Economic Growth?" *Journal of International Economics*, 45(1): 115–135.

Borrus, M., J. Millstein, and J. Zysman. (1983). "Trade and Development in the Semiconductor Industry: Japanese Challenge and American Response." In Zysman, J., and L. Tyson (Eds.), *American Industry in International Competition: Government Policies and Corporate Strategies*. Ithaca: Cornell University Press.

Brenton, P., C. Saborowski, and E. Von Uexkull. (2010). "What Explains the Low Survival Rate of Developing Country Export Flows?" *World Bank Economic Review*, 24(3): 474–499.

Brezis, E. S., P. R. Krugman, and D. Tsiddon. (1993). "Leapfrogging in International Competition: A Theory of Cycles in National Technological Leadership." *American Economic Review*, 83(5): 1211–1219.

Bulman, D., M. Eden, and H. Nguyen. (2014). "Transitioning from Low-Income Growth to High-Income Growth: Is There a Middle-Income Trap?" *Policy Research Working Paper*.

Cadot, O., C. Carrère, and V. Strausskahn. (2011). "Export Diversification: What's Behind the Hump?" *Review of Economics & Statistics*, 93(2): 590–605.

Carkovic, M. V., and R. Levine. (2002). "Does Foreign Direct Investment Accelerate Economic Growth?" In Moran, T. H. et al. (Eds.), *Does Foreign Direct Investment Promote Development?* Washington, DC: Institute for International Economics, Center for Global Development.

Cassis, Y. (1997). *Big Business: The European Experience in the Twentieth Century*. Oxford; New York: Oxford University Press.

Chaminade, C., P. Intarakumnerd, and K. Sapprasert. (2012). "Measuring Systemic Problems in National Innovation Systems. An Application to Thailand." *Research Policy*, 41(8): 1476–1488.

Chandler, A. D. (1990). *Strategy and Structure: Chapters in the History of the Industrial Enterprise*. Cambridge, MA: MIT Press.

Chandler, A. D., F. Amatori, and T. Hikino. (1997). *Big Business and the Wealth of Nations*. Cambridge; New York: Cambridge University Press.

Chandy, R. K., and G. J. Tellis. (2000). "The Incumbent's Curse? Incumbency, Size, and Radical Product Innovation." *Journal of Marketing*, 64(3): 1–17.

Chang, H.-J. (2002). *Kicking Away the Ladder: Development Strategy in Historical Perspective*. London: Anthem Press.

Chang, S.-J. (2003). *Financial Crisis and Transformation of Korean Business Groups: The Rise and Fall of Chaebols*. Cambridge: Cambridge University Press.

Chang, S. J., and U. Choi. (1988). "Strategy, Structure and Performance of Korean Business Groups: A Transactions Cost Approach." *Journal of Industrial Economics*, 37(2): 141–158.

Chang, S. J., and J. Hong. (2000). "Economic Performance of Group-Affiliated Companies in Korea: Intragroup Resource Sharing and Internal Business Transactions." *Academy of Management Journal*, 43(3): 429–448.

Cheong, K. S., K. Choo, and K. Lee. (2010). "Understanding the Behavior of Business Groups: A Dynamic Model and Empirical Analysis." *Journal of Economic Behavior & Organization*, 76(2): 141–152.

Chi, S. (1996). *Zhongguo Qiyejituan Yanjiu (Studies on the China Corporate Group)*. Jinan, China: Jinan Publishing House.

Cho, D. S., and M. E. Porter. (1986). "Changing Global Industry Leadership: The Case of Shipbuilding." In Porter, M. E. (Ed.), *Competition in Global Industries*, pp. 539–567. Boston: Harvard Business School Press.

Choi, J.-P., and T. G. Cowing. (1999). "Firm Behavior and Group Affiliation: The Strategic Role of Corporate Grouping for Korean Firms." *Journal of Asian Economics*, 10(2): 195–209.

Choo, K., K. Lee, K. Ryu, and J. Yoon. (2009). "Changing Performance of Business Groups over Two Decades: Technological Capabilities and Investment Inefficiency in Korean Chaebols." *Economic Development and Cultural Change*, 57(2): 359–386.

Choudary, S. P. (2015). "Platform Scale." *Platform Thinking Labs Google Scholar*.

Christensen, C. M. (1997). *The Innovator's Dilemma: When New Technologies Cause Great Firms to Fail*. Boston, MA: Harvard Business School Press.

Cho, D., and M. Porter (1986). "Changing Global Industry Leadership: The Case of Shipbuilding in Competition in Global Industries." In Porter, M. E. (Ed.), *Competition in Global Industries*. Boston: Harvard Business School Press.

Chu, W.-W. (2011). "How the Chinese Government Promoted a Global Automobile Industry." *Industrial and Corporate Change*, 20(5): 1235–1276.

Cimoli, M. (2000). *Developing Innovation Systems: Mexico in a Global Context*. London; New York: Routledge.

Cimoli, M., G. Dosi, and J. Stiglitz. (2009). *Industrial Policy and Development: The Political Economy of Capabilities Accumulation*. Oxford; New York: Oxford University Press.

Cirera, X., and W. F. Maloney. (2017). *The Innovation Paradox: Developing-Country Capabilities and the Unrealized Promise of Technological Catch-Up*. Washington, DC: World Bank Publications.

Cohen, W. M., R. R. Nelson, and J. P. Walsh. (2000). "Protecting Their Intellectual Assets: Appropriability Conditions and Why US Manufacturing Firms Patent (or Not)." New York: National Bureau of Economic Research.

Colpan, A. M., T. Hikino, and J. R. Lincoln. (2010). *The Oxford Handbook of Business Groups*. Oxford; New York: Oxford University Press.

Coriat, B.(2016). "From Exclusive IPR Innovation Regime to 'Commons-Based' Innovation Regime." Working Paper 2016–1. http://EnCommuns.com

Cornia, G. A., and R. Vos. (2013). "Common Elements for Inclusive and Sustainable Development Strategies Beyond 2015." In Alonso, J. A. et al. (Eds.), *Alternative Development Strategies for the Post-2015 Era*, pp. 215–251. New York: Bloomsbury published in association with the United Nations.

Cusmano, L., A. Morrison, and R. Rabellotti. (2010). "Catching-Up Trajectories in the Wine Sector: A Comparative Study of Chile, Italy, and South Africa." *World Development*, 38(11): 1588–1602.

Dalum, B., K. Laursen, and B. Verspagen. (1999). "Does Specialization Matter for Growth?" *Industrial and Corporate Change*, 8(2): 267–288.

Davis, C. L., and S. B. Bermeo. (2009). "Who Files? Developing Country Participation in GATT/WTO Adjudication." *Journal of Politics*, 71(3): 1033–1049.

D'Costa, A. P. (1999). *The Global Restructuring of the Steel Industry: Innovations, Institutions, and Industrial Change*. London; New York: Routledge.

Deere, C. (2009). *The Implementation Game: The Trips Agreement and the Global Politics of Intellectual Property Reform in Developing Countries*. Oxford: Oxford University Press.

Dennis, A., and B. Shepherd. (2007). "Barriers to Entry, Trade Costs, and Export Diversification in Developing Countries." *World Bank Policy Research Working Paper*, 4(368): 1–40.

Dicaprio, A., and K. P. Gallagher. (2006). "The WTO and the Shrinking of Development Space—How Big Is the Bite?" *Journal of World Investment & Trade*, 7(5): 781–803.

Dodgson, M., A. Hughes, J. Foster, and S. Metcalfe. (2011). "Systems Thinking, Market Failure, and the Development of Innovation Policy: The Case of Australia." *Research Policy*, 40(9): 1145–1156.

Donzé, P.-Y. (2014). "Canon Catching up with Germany: The Mass Production of "Japanese Leica" Cameras (1933 until 1970)." *Zeitschrift für Unternehmensgeschichte*, 59(1): 27–46.

Dosi, G., G. Fagiolo, and A. Roventini. (2010). "Schumpeter Meeting Keynes: A policy-Friendly Model of Endogenous Growth and Business Cycles." *Journal of Economic Dynamics and Control*, 34(9): 1748–1767.

Doytch, N., and M. Uctum. (2011). "Does the Worldwide Shift of FDI from Manufacturing to Services Accelerate Economic Growth? A GMM Estimation Study." *Journal of International Money and Finance*, 30(3): 410–427.

Durham, J. B. (2004). "Absorptive Capacity and the Effects of Foreign Direct Investment and Equity Foreign Portfolio Investment on Economic Growth." *European Economic Review*, 48(2): 285–306.

Easterly, W. (2001). "The Lost Decades: Developing Countries' Stagnation in Spite of Policy Reform 1980–1998." *Journal of Economic Growth*, 6(2): 135–157.

Eichengreen, B., D. Park, and K. Shin. (2013). *Growth Slowdowns Redux: New Evidence on the Middle-Income Trap*. Cambridge, MA: National Bureau of Economic Research.

(2012). "When Fast-Growing Economies Slow Down: International Evidence and Implications for China." *Asian Economic Papers*, 11(1): 42–87.

Ernst, D., and P. Guerrieri. (1998). "International Production Networks and Changing Trade Patterns in East Asia: The Case of the Electronics Industry." *Oxford Development Studies*, 26(2): 191–212.

Ernst, D., and L. Kim. (2002). "Global Production Networks, Information Technology and Knowledge Diffusion." *Industry and Innovation*, 9(3): 147–153.

Eun, J.-H., and K. Lee. (2002). "Is An Industrial Policy Possible in China?" *Journal of International and Area Studies*, 9(2): 1–21.

Eun, J.-H., K. Lee, and G. Wu. (2006). "Explaining the 'University-Run Enterprises' in China: A Theoretical Framework for University–Industry Relationships in Developing Countries and Its Application to China." *Research Policy*, 35(9): 1329–1346.

Felipe, J., U. Kumar, and R. Galope. (2014). "Middle-Income Transitions: Trap or Myth?" *ADB Economics Working Paper Series*, No. 421.

Ferris, S. P., K. A. Kim, and P. Kitsabunnarat. (2003). "The Costs (and Benefits?) of Diversified Business Groups: The Case of Korean Chaebols." *Journal of Banking & Finance*, 27(2): 251–273.

Foray, D., P. McCann, and R. Ortega-Argilés. (2015). "Smart Specialization and European Regional Development Policy." *Oxford Handbook of Local Competitiveness*: 458–480.

Foster, R. (1986). *Innovation: The Attackers Advantage*. London: Pan Books.

Fosu, A. K. (1990). "Export Composition and the Impact of Exports on Economic Growth of Developing Economies." *Economics Letters*, 34(1): 67–71.

Foxley, A., and B. Stallings. (2016). *Innovation and Inclusion in Latin America: Strategies to Avoid the Middle Income Trap*. New York: Palgrave Macmillan.

Frankel, J. A., and D. H. Romer. (1999). "Does Trade Cause Growth?" *American Economic Review*, 89(3): 379–399.

Freeman, C. (1987). *Technology Policy and Economic Performance: Lessons from Japan*. New York: Pinter.

Freinkman, L. (1995). "Financial-Industrial Groups in Russia: Emergence of Large Diversified Private Companies." *Communist Economies and Economic Transformation*, 7(1): 51–66.

Fugazza, M., and A. C. Molina. (2009). "The Determinants of Trade Survival." *HEID Working Paper*, No. 05.

Gao, X. (2014). A Latecomer's Strategy to Promote a Technology Standard: Case of Datang and TD-SCDMA. *Research Policy*, 43: 597–607.

Gao, X., and X. Liu. (2004). "Study on the Technology Strategies of Local Automobile Firms in China." *Study of Economic Development*, 17(2): 91–113.

Genba, K., H. Ogawa, and F. Kodama. (2005). "Quantitative Analysis of Modularization in the Automobile and PC Industries." *Technology Analysis & Strategic Management*, 17(2): 231–245.

Gereffi, G. (2014). "Global Value Chains in a Post-Washington Consensus World." *Review of International Political Economy*, 21(1): 9–37.

Gerlach, M. (1989). "Keiretsu Organization in the Japanese Economy." In Johnson, C. et al. (Eds.), *Politics and Productivity*. New York: Harper Business.

Gerschenkron, A. (1962). *Economic Backwardness in Historical Perspective: A Book of Essays*. New York: Praeger.

Ghemawat, P., and T. Khanna. (1998). "The Nature of Diversified Business Groups: A Research Design and Two Case Studies. " *Journal of Industrial Economics*, 46(1): 35–61.

Giachetti, C. (2013). *Competitive Dynamics in the Mobile Phone Industry*. Basingstoke, UK: Palgrave Macmillan.

Giachetti, C., and G. Marchi. (2017). "Successive Changes in Leadership in the Worldwide Mobile Phone Industry: The Role of Windows of Opportunity and Firms' Competitive Action." *Research Policy*, 46(2): 352–364.

Gill, I. S., H. J. Kharas, and D. Bhattasali. (2007). *An East Asian Renaissance: Ideas for Economic Growth*. Washington, DC: World Bank Publications.

Girvan, N., and A. L. Cortez. (2013). "The Enabling International Environment in Alonso." In Alonso, J. A. et al. (Eds.), *Alternative Development Strategies for the Post-2015 Era*. New York: Bloomsbury Academic in association with the United Nations.

Giuliani, E., C. Pietrobelli, and R. Rabellotti. (2005). "Upgrading in Global Value Chains: Lessons from Latin American Clusters." *World Development*, 33(4): 549–573.

Glaeser, E. L., R. La Porta, F. Lopez-de-Silanes, and A. Shleifer. (2004). "Do Institutions Cause Growth?" *Journal of Economic Growth*, 9(3): 271–303.

González-Álvarez, N., and M. Nieto-Antolín. (2007). "Appropriability of Innovation Results: An Empirical Study in Spanish Manufacturing Firms." *Technovation*, 27(5): 280–295.

Goto, A. (1982). "Business Groups in a Market Economy." *European Economic Review*, 19(1): 53–70.

Granovetter, M. (1995). "Coase Revisited: Business Groups in the Modern Economy." *Industrial and Corporate Change*, 4(1): 93–130.

Grant, R. M. (1996). "Toward a Knowledge-Based Theory of the Firm." *Strategic Management Journal*, 17(S2): 109–122.

Greenaway, D., W. Morgan, and P. Wright. (1999). "Exports, Export Composition and Growth." *Journal of International Trade & Economic Development*, 8(1): 41–51.

Greenwald, B., and J. E. Stiglitz. (2014). *Creating a Learning Society: A New Paradigm for Development and Social Progress*. New York: Columbia University Press.

Grossman, G. M., and E. Rossi-Hansberg. (2006). *The Rise of Offshoring: It's Not Wine for Cloth Anymore*. Paper presented at The New Economic Geography: Effects and Policy Implications, Federal Reserve Bank of Kansas City, Jackson Hole, 59–102.

Guillen, M. F. (2000). "Business Groups in Emerging Economies: A Resource-Based View." *Academy of Management Journal*, 43(3): 362–380.

Haggard, S., W. Lim, and E. Kim. (2003). *Economic Crisis and Corporate Restructuring in Korea: Reforming the Chaebol*. Cambridge, UK: Cambridge University Press.

Häikiö, M. (2001). *Nokia: The inside Story*. Helsinki: Edita.

Hamm, S. (2007). *Bangalore: How Indian Tech Upstart Wipro Is Rewriting the Rules of Global Competition*. New Delhi: Tata McGraw-Hill.

Han, X., and S.-J. Wei. (2015). "Re-Examining the Middle-Income Trap Hypothesis: What to Reject and What to Revive?" *ADB Economics Working Paper Series*, No. 436.

Hanson, E. M. (2008). *Economic Development, Education and Transnational Corporations*. London; New York: Routledge.

Hausmann, R., J. Hwang, and D. Rodrik. (2007). "What You Export Matters." *Journal of Economic Growth*, 12(1): 1–25.

Helfat, C. E., and M. A. Peteraf. (2003). "The Dynamic Resource-Based View: Capability Lifecycles." *Strategic Management Journal*, 24(10): 997–1010.

Helleiner, E. (2011). "Understanding the 2007–2008 Global Financial Crisis: Lessons for Scholars of International Political Economy." *Annual Review of Political Science*, 14: 67–87.

Hermes, N., and R. Lensink. (2003). "Foreign Direct Investment, Financial Development and Economic Growth." *The Journal of Development Studies*, 40(1): 142–163.

Hesse, H. (2009). "Export Diversification and Economic Growth." In Newfarmer, R. S. et al. (Eds.), *Breaking into New Markets: Emerging Lessons for Export Diversification*, pp. 55–80. Washington, DC: World Bank.

Hidalgo, C. A., B. Klinger, A.-L. Barabási, and R. Hausmann. (2007). "The Product Space Conditions the Development of Nations." *Science*, 317(5837): 482–487.

Hobday, M. (2000). "East Versus Southeast Asian Innovation Systems: Comparing OEM- and TNC-Led Growth in Electronics." In Kim, L., and R. R. Nelson (Eds.), *Technology, Learning, and Innovation: Experiences of Newly Industrializing Economies*, pp.129–169. Cambridge, UK: Cambridge University Press.

(1995). *Innovation in East Asia: The Challenge to Japan*. Hants, UK: Edward Elgar.

(1994). "Export-Led Technology Development in the Four Dragons: The Case of Electronics." *Development and Change*, 25(2): 333–361.

Hoopes, D. G., T. L. Madsen, and G. Walker. (2003). "Why Is There a Resource-Based View? Toward a Theory of Competitive Heterogeneity." *Strategic Management Journal*, 24(10): 889–902.

Horn, H., P. C. Mavroidis, and H. Nordström. (1999). *Is the Use of the WTO Dispute Settlement System Biased?* London: Centre for Economic Policy Research.

Hsiao, C., and Y. Shen. (2003). "Foreign Direct Investment and Economic Growth: The Importance of Institutions and Urbanization." *Economic Development and Cultural Change*, 51(4): 883–896.

Huang, Y., Q. Gou, and X. Wang. (2013). "Institutions and the Middle Income Trap: Implications of Cross-Country Experiences for China. " Paper presented at the International Conference on the Inequality and the Middle Income Trap in China, China Center for Economic Research, Peking University.

Hubbard, G., and T. Kane. (2013). *Balance: The Economics of Great Powers*. New York: Simon & Schuster Paperbacks.

Hummels, D., J. Ishii, and K.-M. Yi. (2001). "The Nature and Growth of Vertical Specialization in World Trade." *Journal of International Economics*, 54(1): 75–96.

Hurmelinna, P., K. Kyläheiko, and T. Jauhiainen. (2007). "The Janus Face of the Appropriability Regime in the Protection of Innovations: Theoretical Re-Appraisal and Empirical Analysis." *Technovation*, 27(3): 133–144.

ILO (International Labor Organization). (2016a). *ASEAN in Transformation: How Technology is Changing Jobs and Enterprises*. Geneva: ILO.

ILO. (2016b). *ASEAN in Transformation: The Future of Jobs at Risk of Automation*. Geneva: ILO.

Im, F. G., and D. Rosenblatt. (2013). "Middle-Income Traps: A Conceptual and Empirical Survey." *World Bank Working Paper*, No. 6594.

Ito, T. (2017). "Growth Convergence and the Middle-Income Trap." *Asian Development Review*, 34(1): 1–27.

Ivus, O. (2010). "Do Stronger Patent Rights Raise High-Tech Exports to the Developing World?" *Journal of International Economics*, 81(1): 38–47.

Jackson, T., and P. Roberts. (2000). *A Review of Indicators of Sustainable Development*. Dundee, Scotland: Geddes Centre for Planning Research, University of Dundee.

Jaffe, A. B., and M. Trajtenberg. (2002). *Patents, Citations, and Innovations: A Window on the Knowledge Economy*. Cambridge, MA: MIT Press.

Jaffe, A. B., M. Trajtenberg, and R. Henderson. (1993). "Geographic Localization of Knowledge Spillovers As Evidenced by Patent Citations." *Quarterly Journal of Economics*, 108(3): 577–598.

Joh, S. W. (2003). "Corporate Governance and Firm Profitability: Evidence from Korea before the Economic Crisis." *Journal of Financial Economics*, 68(2): 287–322.

Joo, S. H., and K. Lee. (2010). "Samsung's Catch-Up with Sony: An Analysis Using US Patent Data." *Journal of the Asia Pacific Economy*, 15(3): 271–287.

Joo, S. H., C. Oh, and K. Lee. (2016). "Catch-Up Strategy of an Emerging Firm in an Emerging Country: Analysing the Case of Huawei Vs. Ericsson with Patent Data." *International Journal of Technology Management*, 72(1–3): 19–42.

Juma, C. (2011). *The New Harvest: Agricultural Innovation in Africa*. Oxford: Oxford University Press.

Jung, M., and K. Lee. (2010). "Sectoral Systems of Innovation and Productivity Catch-Up: Determinants of the Productivity Gap between Korean and Japanese Firms." *Industrial and Corporate Change*, 19(4): 1037–1069.

Jwa, S.-H. (2002). *The Evolution of Large Corporations in Korea: A New Institutional Economics Perspective of the Chaebol*. Cheltenham, UK: Edward Elgar Publishing.

Kaldor, N. (1967). *Strategic Factors in Economic Development*. The Frank W. Pierce Memorial Lectures, October 1966, Cornell University. Ithaca, NY.

Kali, R. (1999). "Endogenous Business Networks." *Journal of Law, Economics, and Organization*, 15(3): 615–636.

Kang, H., and J. Song. (2017). "Innovation and Recurring Shifts in Industrial Leadership: Three Phases of Change and Persistence in the Camera Industry." *Research Policy*, 46(2): 376–387.

Kang, R., T. Jung, and K. Lee. (2017). "What Do the Diverse Forms of Intellectual Property Rights Say About the Economic Development in Korea?: The Trends of the Patents, Utility Models, and Trademarks, 1962 to 2009." Working Paper.

Katz, J. (2001). "Structural Reforms and Technological Behavior: The Sources and Nature of Technological Change in Latin America in the 1990s." *Research Policy*, 30(1): 1–19.

Keister, L. A. (1998). "Engineering Growth: Business Group Structure and Firm Performance in China's Transition Economy." *American Journal of Sociology*, 104(2): 404–440.

Khanna, T. (2000). "Business Groups and Social Welfare in Emerging Markets: Existing Evidence and Unanswered Questions." *European Economic Review*, 44(4–6): 748–761.

Khanna, T., and K. Palepu. (2000a). "The Future of Business Groups in Emerging Markets: Long-Run Evidence from Chile." *Academy of Management Journal*, 43(3): 268–285.

(2000b). "Is Group Affiliation Profitable in Emerging Markets? An Analysis of Diversified Indian Business Groups." *Journal of Finance*, 55(2): 867–891.

Khor, M., and J. A. Ocampo. (2010). "The Unsettled Global Trade Architecture." Paper presented at the Conference on Global Economic Governance, Washington DC.

Kim, C. (2002). "Is the Investment of Korean Conglomerates Inefficient?" *Korean Economic Review*, 18(1): 5–24.

Kim, E. (2006). "The Impact of Family Ownership and Capital Structures on the Productivity Performance of Korean Manufacturing Firms: Corporate Governance and the 'Chaebol Problem.'" *Journal of the Japanese and International Economies*, 20(2): 209–233.

Kim, L. (1980). "Stages of Development of Industrial Technology in a Developing Country: A Model." *Research Policy*, 9(3): 254–277.

Kim, L. (1997). *Imitation to Innovation: The Dynamics of Korea's Technological Learning*. Boston: Harvard Business School Press.

Kim, C. W., and K. Lee. (2003). "Innovation, Technological Regimes and Organizational Selection in Industry Evolution: A 'History Friendly Model' of the Dram Industry." *Industrial and Corporate Change*, 12(6): 1195–1221.

Kim, H., R. E. Hoskisson, L. Tihanyi, and J. Hong. (2004). "The Evolution and Restructuring of Diversified Business Groups in Emerging Markets: The Lessons from Chaebols in Korea." *Asia Pacific Journal of Management*, 21(1–2): 25–48.

Kim, Y. K., and K. Lee. (2015). "Different Impacts of Scientific and Technological Knowledge on Economic Growth: Contrasting Science and Technology Policy in East Asia and Latin America." *Asian Economic Policy Review*, 10(1): 43–66.

Kim, Y.-Z., and K. Lee. (2009). "Making a Technological Catch-Up in the Capital Goods Industry: Barriers and Opportunities in the Korean Case." In Malerba, F. (Ed.), *Sectoral Systems of Innovation and Production in Developing Countries*, pp. 259–286. Cheltenham, UK: Edward Elgar Publishing.

Kim, Y. K., K. Lee, W. G. Park, and K. Choo. (2012). "Appropriate Intellectual Property Protection and Economic Growth in Countries at Different Levels of Development." *Research Policy*, 41(2): 358–375.

Knack, S., and P. Keefer. (1995). "Institutions and Economic Performance: Cross-Country Tests Using Alternative Institutional Measures." *Economics & Politics*, 7(3): 207–227.

Kock, C. J., and M. F. Guillén. (2001). "Strategy and Structure in Developing Countries: Business Groups as an Evolutionary Response to Opportunities for Unrelated Diversification." *Industrial and Corporate Change*, 10(1): 77–113.

Kogut, B., and U. Zander. (2003). "Knowledge of the Firm and the Evolutionary Theory of the Multinational Corporation." *Journal of International Business Studies*, 34(6): 516–529.

Kozul-Wright, R., and B. Rowthorn. (1998). *Transnational Corporations and the Global Economy*. New York: Martin's Press.

Krishnan, T. R., and S. K. Vallabhaneni. (2010.) "Catch-Up in Technology-Driven Services: The Case of the Indian Software Services Industry." *Seoul Journal of Economics*, 23 (2): 263–81.

Krugman, P. (1991). *Geography and Trade*. Cambridge, MA: MIT Press.

Kumar, N. (2002). "Intellectual Property Rights, Technology and Economic Development: Experiences of Asian Countries." Research and Information System for the Non-Aligned and Other Developing Countries Discussion Paper No. 25.

Kuznets, S., and J. T. Murphy. (1966). *Modern Economic Growth: Rate, Structure, and Spread*. New Haven: Yale University Press.

Lall, S. (2000). "The Technological Structure and Performance of Developing Country Manufactured Exports, 1985–98." *Oxford Development Studies*, 28 (3): 337–369.

Langlois, R. N., and W. E. Steinmueller. (1999). "The Evolution of Competitive Advantage in the Worldwide Semiconductor Industry, 1947–1996." In Mowery, D. C., and R. R. Nelson (Eds.), *The Sources of Industrial Leadership*, pp. 19–78. New York: Cambridge University Press.

La Porta, R., F. Lopez-de-Silanies, and A. Shleifer. (1999). "Corporate Ownership Around the World." *Journal of Finance*, 54: 471-517.

Laursen, Keld, V. Mahnke, and P. Vejrup-Hansen. (1999). "Firm Growth from a Knowledge Structure Perspective." DRUID Working Paper No. 99-11.

Lee, J.-W. (1995). "Capital Goods Imports and Long-Run Growth." *Journal of Development Economics*, 48(1): 91–110.

Lee, Keun. (2017a). "Smart Specialization with Short-Cycle Technologies and Implementation Strategies to Avoid Target and Design Failures." In Radosevic, S. et al. (Eds.), *Advances in the Theory and Practice of Smart Specialization*, pp. 201–224. London: Academic Press.

(2017b). "Financing Industrial Policy in Korea: Lessons for Africa." In *The Series: How They Did It*. African Development Bank. Available online.

(2016a). "Industrial Upgrading and Innovation Capability for Inclusive Growth: Experience in East Asia and Its Lessons." In Foxley, A., and B. Stallings (Eds.), *Innovation and Inclusion in Latin America: Strategies to Avoid the Middle Income Trap*. New York: Palgrave Macmillan.

(2016b). *Economic Catch-up and Technological Leapfrogging: The Path to Development and Macroeconomic Stability in Korea*. Cheltenham, UK: Edward Elgar.

(2013a). *Schumpeterian Analysis of Economic Catch-up: Knowledge, Path-Creation, and the Middle-Income Trap*. Cambridge: Cambridge University Press.

(2013b). "How Can Korea Be a Role Model for Catch-Up Development? A 'Capability-Based' View. " In Fosu, A. K. (Ed.), *Achieving Development Success: Strategies and Lessons from the Developing World*. Oxford: Oxford University Press.

(2013c). "Capability Failure and Industrial Policy to Move Beyond the Middle-Income Trap: From Trade-Based to Technology-Based Specialization." In Stiglitz, J. E., and J. L. Yifu (Eds.), *The Industrial Policy Revolution I*, pp. 244–272. Basingstoke, UK: Palgrave Macmillan.

(2005). "Making a Technological Catch-Up: Barriers and Opportunities." *Asian Journal of Technology Innovation*, 13(2): 97–131.

Lee, K., X Gao, and X Li. (2016). "Industrial Catch-Up in China: A Sectoral Systems of Innovation Perspective." *Cambridge Journal of Regions, Economy and Society* 10 (1): 59–76.

Lee, K., and X. He. (2009). "The Capability of the Samsung Group in Project Execution and Vertical Integration: Created in Korea, Replicated in China." *Asian Business & Management*, 8(3): 277–299.

Lee, K., and X. Jin. (2009). "The Origins of Business Groups in China: An Empirical Testing of the Three Paths and the Three Theories." *Business History*, 51(1): 77–99.

Lee, K., and J.-h. Ki. (2017). "Rise of Latecomers and Catch-up Cycles in the World Steel Industry." *Research Policy*, 46(2): 365–375.

Lee, K., and B.-Y. Kim. (2009). "Both Institutions and Policies Matter but Differently for Different Income Groups of Countries: Determinants of Long-Run Economic Growth Revisited." *World Development*, 37(3): 533–549.

Lee, K., and Y. K. Kim. (2010). "IPR and Technological Catch-Up in Korea." In Odagiri, H. et al. (Eds.), *Intellectual Property Rights, Development, and Catch Up*. Oxford: Oxford University Press.

Lee, K., and C. Lim. (2001). "Technological Regimes, Catching-Up and Leapfrogging: Findings from the Korean Industries." *Research Policy*, 30(3): 459–483.

Lee, K., and F. Malerba. (2018). "Economic Catch-Up as Evolutionary Process." In Nelson, R. R. (Ed.), *Modern Evolutionary Economics: An Overview*. Cambridge: Cambridge University Press.

(2017). "Catch-Up Cycles and Changes in Industrial Leadership: Windows of Opportunity and Responses of Firms and Countries in the Evolution of Sectoral Systems." *Research Policy*, 46(2): 338–351.

Lee, K., and J. Mathews. (2018). "How Emerging Economies Can Take Advantage of the Fourth Industrial Revolution." *Agenda Weekly: Expert Edition*. Geneva: World Economic Forum. Accessed at https://www.weforum.org/agenda/2018 /01/

(2013). "STI for Sustainable Development." UN: Committee for Development Policy, Background Paper, No. 16.

(2012). "Firms in Korea and Taiwan: Upgrading in the Same Industry and Entries into New Industries." In Amann, E., and J. Cantwell (Eds.), *The Innovative Firms in the Emerging Market Economies*, pp. 223–248. Oxford: Oxford University Press.

(2009). "Upgrading in the Same Industry and Successive Entries in New Industries for Sustained Catchup." Workshop on Innovative Firms and Catch-Up, Mexico City.

Lee, K., T. Y. Park, and R. T. Krishnan. "Catching-Up or Leapfrogging in the Indian IT Service Sector: Windows of Opportunity, Path-Creating, and Moving Up the Value Chain." *Development Policy Review* 32 (4), 495–518.

Lee, K., and T. Temesgen. (2009). "What Makes Firms Grow in Developing Countries? An Extension of the Resource-Based Theory of Firm Growth and Empirical Analysis." *International Journal of Technological Learning, Innovation and Development*, 2(3): 139–172.

Lee, K., and W. Woo. (2002). "Business Groups in China: Compared with Korean Chaebols." In Hooley, R., and J.-H. Yoo (Eds.), *The Post-Financial Crisis Challenges for Asian Industrialization*, pp. 721–747. Amsterdam: JAI Press.

Lee, K., S.-J. Cho, and J. Jin. (2009). "Dynamics of Catch-Up in Mobile Phones and Automobiles in China: Sectoral Systems of Innovation Perspective." *China Economic Journal*, 2(1): 25–53.

Lee, K., X. Gao, and X. Li. (2016). "Industrial Catch-Up in China: A Sectoral Systems of Innovation Perspective." *Cambridge Journal of Regions, Economy and Society*, 10(1): 59–76.

Lee, K., C. Juma, and J. Mathews. (2014). "Innovation Capabilities for Sustainable Development in Africa." In Monga, C. l., and J. Y. Lin (Eds.), *Handbook of Africa and Economics*. Oxford: Oxford University Press.

Lee, K., B.-Y. Kim, Y.-Y. Park, and E. Sanidas. (2013). "Big Businesses and Economic Growth: Identifying a Binding Constraint for Growth with Country Panel Analysis." *Journal of Comparative Economics*, 41(2): 561–582.

Lee, K., J. Y. Kim, and O. Lee. (2010). "Long-Term Evolution of the Firm Value and Behavior of Business Groups: Korean Chaebols between Weak Premium, Strong Discount, and Strong Premium." *Journal of the Japanese and International Economies*, 24(3): 412–440.

Lee, K., C. Lim, and W. Song. (2005). "Emerging Digital Technology as a Window of Opportunity and Technological Leapfrogging: Catch-Up in Digital TV by the Korean Firms." *International Journal of Technology Management*, 29(1–2): 40–63.

Lee, C. H., K. Lee, and K. Lee. (2002). "Chaebols, Financial Liberalization and Economic Crisis: Transformation of Quasi-Internal Organization in Korea." *Asian Economic Journal*, 16(1): 17–35.

Lee, K., S. Mani, and Q. Mu. (2012). "Divergent Stories of Catchup in Telecom: China, India, Brazil, and Korea." In Malerba, F., and R. R. Nelson (Eds.), *Economic Development as a Learning Process*, pp. 21–71. Cheltenham, UK: Edward Elgar.

Lee, K., D. Park, and C. Lim. (2003). "Industrial Property Rights and Technological Development in the Republic of Korea." WIPO Policy Monograph, Geneva.

Lee, K., W. Shin, and H. Shin. (2014). "How Large or Small Is the Policy Space? WTO Regime and Industrial Policy." In Alonso, J., and J. Ocampo (Eds.), *Global Governance and Rules for the Post-2015 Era*. New York: Bloomsbury Publishing.

Lee, K., W. Shin, and H. Shin. (2014). "How Large or Small Is the Policy Space? WTO Regime and Industrial Policy." *Seoul Journal of Economics*, 27(3).

Lee, K., J. Song, and J. Kwak. (2015). "An Exploratory Study on the Transition from OEM to OBM: Case Studies of SMEs in Korea." *Industry and Innovation*, 22(5): 423–442.

Lee, K., M. Szapiro, and Z. Mao. (2017). "From Global Value Chains (GVC) to Innovation Systems for Local Value Chains and Knowledge Creation." *The European Journal of Development Research*: 1–18. (accessed Online).

Lee, K., C. Y. Wong, P. Intarakumnerd, and C. Limapornvanich. (2018). Is the Fourth Industrial Revolution a Window of Opportunity for Upgrading or Reinforcing the Middle-Income Trap? Work in Progress.

Leff, N. H. (1978). "Industrial Organization and Entrepreneurship in the Developing Countries: The Economic Groups." *Economic Development and Cultural Change*, 26(4): 661–675.

Lim, C., Y. Kim, and K. Lee. (2017). "Changes in Industrial Leadership and Catch Up by Latecomers in the Shipbuilding Industry." *Asian Journal of Technology Innovation*, 25(1): 61–78.

Lin, J. Y. (2013). *Demystifying the Chinese Economy*. Cambridge; New York: Cambridge University Press.

(2012). *The Quest for Prosperity: How Developing Economies Can Take Off*. Princeton: Princeton University Press.

(2011). "New Structural Economics: A Framework for Rethinking Development. *World Bank Research Observer*, 26(2): 193–221.

Lincoln, J. R., M. L. Gerlach, and C. L. Ahmadjian. (1996). "Keiretsu Networks and Corporate Performance in Japan." *American Sociological Review*, 61(1): 67–88.

Linden, G., K. L. Kraemer, and J. Dedrick. (2007). "Who Captures Value in a Global Innovation System? The Case of Apple's iPod." *Communications of the ACM*, 52(3): 140–144.

Linsu, K. (1997). *Imitation to Innovation: The Dynamics of Korea's Technological Learning*. Boston: Harvard Business School Press.

Loening, J. L. (2005). "Effects of Primary, Secondary, and Tertiary Education on Economic Growth: Evidence from Guatemala." World Bank Policy Research Working Paper, No. 3610.

Lundvall, B.-Å. (2012). "One Knowledge Base or Many Knowledge Pools?" In Arena, R. et al. (Eds.), *Handbook of Knowledge and Economics*, pp. 285. Cheltenham, UK: Edward Elgar Publishing.

(1992). *National Systems of Innovation: Towards a Theory of Innovation and Interactive Learning*. London: Pinter Publishers.

Luo, J. (2005). "The Growth of Independent Chinese Automotive Companies." Cambridge, MA: International Motor Vehicle Program, MIT.

Makki, S. S., and A. Somwaru. (2004). "Impact of Foreign Direct Investment and Trade on Economic Growth: Evidence from Developing Countries." *American Journal of Agricultural Economics*, 86(3): 795–801.

Malerba, F. (2009). "Increase Learning, Break Knowledge Lock-Ins and Foster Dynamic Complementarities: Evolutionary and System Perspectives on Technology Policy in Industrial Dynamics." *New Economics of Technology Policy*: 33–45.

(2005). "Sectoral Systems of Innovation: A Framework for Linking Innovation to the Knowledge Base, Structure and Dynamics of Sectors." *Economics of Innovation and New Technology*, 14(1-2): 63–82.

(2004). *Sectoral Systems of Innovation: Concepts, Issues and Analyses of Six Major Sectors in Europe*. Cambridge, UK: Cambridge University Press.

(2002). "Sectoral Systems of Innovation and Production." *Research Policy*, 31(2): 247–264.

Malerba, F., and R. R. Nelson. (2012). *Economic Development as a Learning Process: Variation across Sectoral Systems*. Cheltenham, UK: Edward Elgar Publishing.

Martincus, C. V., and J. Carballo. (2008). "Is Export Promotion Effective in Developing Countries? Firm-Level Evidence on the Intensive and the Extensive Margins of Exports." *Journal of International Economics*, 76(1): 89–106.

Maskus, K. E., and C. McDaniel. (1999). "Impacts of the Japanese Patent System on Productivity Growth." *Japan and the World Economy*, 11(4): 557–574.

Maskus, K. E., and M. Penubarti. (1995). "How Trade-Related Are Intellectual Property Rights?" *Journal of International Economics*, 39(3-4): 227–248.

Mathews, J. A. (2018). "Latecomer Industrialization." In Reinert, E. et al. (Eds.), *Handbook of Alternative Theories of Economic Development*. Cheltenham, UK: Edward Elgar Publishing.

(2017). *Global Green Shift: When Ceres Meets Gaia*. London: Anthem Press.

(2005). "Strategy and the Crystal Cycle." *California Management Review*, 47 (2): 6–32.

(2002a). "Competitive Advantages of the Latecomer Firm: A Resource-Based Account of Industrial Catch-Up Strategies." *Asia Pacific Journal of Management*, 19(4): 467–488.

(2002b). "The Origins and Dynamics of Taiwan's R&D Consortia." *Research Policy*, 31(4): 633–651.

(1997). "A Silicon Valley of the East: Creating Taiwan's Semiconductor Industry." *California Management Review*, 39(4): 26–54.

(1996). "High Technology Industrialisation in East Asia." *Journal of Industry Studies*, 3(2): 1–77.

Mayer, J. (2009). "Policy Space: What, for What, and Where?" *Development Policy Review*, 27(4): 373–395.

Mazumdar, J. (2001). "Imported Machinery and Growth in LCDs." *Journal of Development Economics*, 65(1): 209–224.

Mazzucato, M. (2013). *The Entrepreneurial State: Debunking Public Vs. Private Sector Myths*. London: Anthem Press.

McCalman, P. (2005). "Who Enjoys 'Trips' Abroad? An Empirical Analysis of Intellectual Property Rights in the Uruguay Round." *Canadian Journal of Economics/Revue Canadienne D'économique*, 38(2): 574–603.

Metcalfe, J. S. (2005). "Systems Failure and the Case for Innovation Policy." In Llerena, P. et al. (Eds.), *Innovation Policy in a Knowledge-Based Economy*, pp. 47–74. Berlin; New York: Springer.

Miranda, L. C., and C. A. Lima. (2013). "Technology Substitution and Innovation Adoption: The Cases of Imaging and Mobile Communication Markets." *Technological Forecasting and Social Change*, 80(6): 1179–1193.

Mizuho Corporate Bank. (2008). *Mizuho Industry Research: India-based Globalization in the IT Services Industry 28 (2)*. Tokyo: Industry Research Division, Mizuho Corporate Bank.

Morris, M., R. Kaplinsky, and D. Kaplan. (2012). *One Thing Leads to Another: Promoting Industrialisation by Making the Most of the Commodity Boom in Sub-Saharan Africa*. Cape Town: Cape Town Centre for Social Science Research.

Morrison, A., and R. Rabellotti. (2017). "Gradual Catch Up and Enduring Leadership in the Global Wine Industry." *Research Policy*, 46(2): 417–430.

Mu, Q., and K. Lee. (2005). "Knowledge Diffusion, Market Segmentation and Technological Catch-Up: The Case of the Telecommunication Industry in China." *Research Policy*, 34(6): 759–783.

Nakamura, T., and H. Ohashi. (2012). "Effects of Re-Invention on Industry Growth and Productivity: Evidence from Steel Refining Technology in Japan, 1957-1968." *Economics of Innovation and New Technology*, 21(4): 411–426.

Navas-Alemán, L. (2011). "The Impact of Operating in Multiple Value Chains for Upgrading: The Case of the Brazilian Furniture and Footwear Industries." *World Development*, 39(8): 1386–1397.

Nelson, R. R. (2018). *Modern Evolution Economics*. Cambridge, UK: Cambridge University Press.

Nelson, R. R. (1993). *National Innovation Systems: A Comparative Analysis*. Oxford; New York: Oxford University Press.

Niosi, J. (2000). *Canada's National System of Innovation*. Montreal: McGill-Queen's Press-MQUP.

Nitsch, V. (2009). "Die Another Day: Duration in German Import Trade." *Review of World Economics*, 145(1): 133–154.

Nolan, P. (2003). "Industrial Policy in the Early 21st Century: The Challenge of the Global Business Revolution." In Chang, H.-J. (Eds.), *Rethinking Development Economics*, pp. 299–321. London: Anthem Press.

Nooteboom, B. (2009). *A Cognitive Theory of the Firm: Learning, Governance and Dynamic Capabilities*. Northampton, MA: Edward Elgar Publishing.

North, D. C. (2005). *Understanding the Process of Economic Change*. Princeton: Princeton University Press.

OECD. (1996). *Reviews of National Science and Technology Policy: Republic of Korea*. Paris: OECD.

Pack, H. (2001). "Technological Change and Growth in East Asia: Macro Versus Micro Perspectives." In Stiglitz, J. E., and S. Yusuf (Eds.), *Rethinking the East Asian Miracle*, pp. 95–142. Washington, DC: World Bank.

Pagano, P., and F. Schivardi. (2003). "Firm Size Distribution and Growth." *The Scandinavian Journal of Economics*, 105(2): 255–274.

Palmberg, C., and O. Martikainen. (2005). "The GSM Standard and Nokia as an Incubating Entrant." *Innovation*, 7(1): 61–78.

Park, K.-H., and K. Lee. (2006). "Linking the Technological Regime to the Technological Catch-Up: Analyzing Korea and Taiwan Using the US Patent Data." *Industrial and Corporate Change*, 15(4): 715–753.

Pavitt, K. (1984). "Sectoral Patterns of Technical Change: Towards a Taxonomy and a Theory." *Research Policy*, 13(6): 343–373.

Peng, M. W. (2000). *Business Strategies in Transition Economies*. Thousand Oaks, CA; London: Sage.

Penrose, E. T. (1959, Revised 1995). *The Theory of the Growth of the Firm*. Oxford, UK: Oxford University Press.

Perez, C. (2008). "A Vision for Latin America: A Resource-Based Strategy for Technological Dynamism and Social Inclusion." Globelics Working Paper, No. WPG0804.

Perez, C., and L. Soete. (1988). "Catching up in Technology: Entry Barriers and Windows." In Dosi, G. et al. (Eds.), *Technical Change and Economic Theory*, pp. 458–479. London: Pinter.

Pitelis, C. (2002). *The Growth of the Firm: The Legacy of Edith Penrose*. Oxford, UK: Oxford University Press.

Plümper, T., and M. Graff. (2001). "Export Specialization and Economic Growth." *Review of International Political Economy*, 8(4): 661–688.

Radosevic, S., A. Curaj, R. Gheorghiu, L. Andreescu, and I. Wade. (2017). *Advances in the Theory and Practice of Smart Specialization*. St. Louis, MO: Elsevier Science.

Ramamurti, R. (1987). *State-Owned Enterprises in High Technology Industries: Studies in India and Brazil*. London: Praeger Publishers.

Ramanayake, S. S., and K. Lee. (2017). "Differential Effects of Currency Undervaluation on Economic Growth in Mineral- Vs. Manufacture-Exporting Countries." In Niosi, J. (Ed.), *Innovation Policy, Systems and Management*. (Forthcoming). Cambridge, UK: Cambridge University Press.

(2015). "Does Openness Lead to Sustained Economic Growth? Export Growth Versus Other Variables as Determinants of Economic Growth." *Journal of the Asia Pacific Economy*, 20(3): 345–368.

Rasiah, R. (2006). "Electronics in Malaysia: Export Expansion but Slow Technical Change." In Chandra, V. (Ed.), *The How and the Why of Technology Development in Developing Economies*, pp. 127–162. Washington DC: World Bank.

Reis, A. B. (2001). "On the Welfare Effects of Foreign Investment." *Journal of International Economics*, 54(2): 411–427.

Rodriguez, F., and D. Rodrik. (2000). "Trade Policy and Economic Growth: A Skeptic's Guide to the Cross-National Evidence." *NBER Macroeconomics Annual 2000*, 15: 261–325.

Rodriguez-Clare, A. (1996). "Multinationals, Linkages, and Economic Development." *American Economic Review*, 86(4): 852–873.

Rodrik, D. (2013). "Unconditional Convergence in Manufacturing." *Quarterly Journal of Economics* 128(1): 165–204.

(2010). "Making Room for China in the World Economy." *American Economic Review*, 100(2): 89–93.

(2006). "Goodbye Washington Consensus, Hello Washington Confusion? A Review of the World Bank's Economic Growth in the 1990s: Learning from a Decade of Reform." *Journal of Economic Literature*, 44(4): 973–987.

(1996). "Understanding Economic Policy Reform." *Journal of Economic Literature*, 34(1): 9–41.

(1994). "King Kong Meets Godzilla: The World Bank and the East Asian Miracle." CEPR Discussion Papers, No. 944.

Rodrik, D., A. Subramanian, and F. Trebbi. (2004). "Institutions Rule: The Primacy of Institutions over Geography and Integration in Economic Development." *Journal of Economic Growth*, 9(2): 131–165.

Rogers, E. M. (2003). *Diffusion of Innovations* (5th ed.). New York: Free Press.

Rugasira, A. M. (2013). *A Good African Story: How a Small Company Built a Global Coffee Brand*. London: Bodley Head.

Sabel, C., E. Fernandez-Arias, R. Hausmann, A. Rodriguez-Clare, and E. H. Stein. (2012). "Export Pioneers in Latin America." InterAmerican Development Bank Research Department, No. 421.

Sachs, Jeffrey. (2015). *The Age of Sustainable Development*. New York: Columbia University Press.

Saviotti, P. P. (1998). "On the Dynamics of Appropriability, of Tacit and of Codified Knowledge." *Research Policy*, 26(7–8): 843–856.

Schumpeter, J. A. (1943). *Capitalism, Socialism and Democracy* London and New York: Routledge (2010 edition).

  (1934). *Theory of Economic Development*. Cambridge, MA: Harvard University Press.

Schwab, K. (2016). "The Fourth Industrial Revolution." Geneva: World Economic Forum.

Seo, B.-K., K. Lee, and X. Wang. (2010). "Causes for Changing Performance of the Business Groups in a Transition Economy: Market-Level Versus Firm-Level Factors in China." *Industrial and Corporate Change*, 19(6): 2041–2072.

Shadlen, K. C. (2005). "Exchanging Development for Market Access? Deep Integration and Industrial Policy under Multilateral and Regional-Bilateral Trade Agreements." *Review of International Political Economy*, 12(5): 750–775.

Shapshak, T. (Jan. 28, 2016). "How Kenya's M-Kopa Brings Prepaid Solar Power to Rural Africa." *Forbes*. Accessed at https://www.forbes.com/sites/tobyshapshak/2016/01/28/how-kenyas-m-kopa-brings-prepaid-solar-power-to-rural-africa/#79415e822dbf

Shin, J.-S. (2017). "Dynamic Catch-up Strategy, Capability Expansion and Changing Windows of Opportunity in the Memory Industry." *Research Policy*, 46(2): 404–416.

Shin, H., and K. Lee. (2012). "Asymmetric Trade Protection Leading Not to Productivity but to Export Share Change." *Economics of Transition*, 20(4): 745–785.

Shin, H.-H., and Y. S. Park. (1999). "Financing Constraints and Internal Capital Markets: Evidence from Korean 'chaebols'." *Journal of Corporate Finance*, 5(2): 169–191.

Shin, W., and W. Lee. (2013). "Legality of R&D Subsidies and Its Policy Framework under the World Trading System." *STI Policy Review*, 4(1): 27–53.

Shin, W., K. Lee, and W. G. Park. (2016). "When an Importer's Protection of IPR Interacts with an Exporter's Level of Technology: Comparing the Impacts on the Exports of the North and South." *World Economy* 39(6): 772–802.

Silva, O. (2005). *A Decolagem De Um Sonho: A História Da Criação Da Embraer.* São Paulo, Brazil: Lemos Editorial.

Smith, P. J. (2001). "How Do Foreign Patent Rights Affect US Exports, Affiliate Sales, and Licenses?" *Journal of International Economics,* 55(2): 411–439.

(1999). "Are Weak Patent Rights a Barrier to Us Exports?" *Journal of International Economics,* 48(1): 151–177.

Spence, M. (2011). *The Next Convergence: The Future of Economic Growth in a Multispeed World.* New York: Farrar, Straus and Giroux.

Spender, J. C. (1996). "Making Knowledge the Basis of a Dynamic Theory of the Firm." *Strategic Management Journal,* 17(S2): 45–62.

Steers, R. M., Y.-g. Sin, and G. R. Ungson. (1989). *The Chaebol: Korea's New Industrial Might.* New York: Harper Business.

Stiglitz, J. E., and J. L. Yifu (Eds.). (2013). *The Industrial Policy Revolution I,* Basingstoke, UK: Palgrave Macmillan.

Stiglitz, J. E., J. Y. Lin, and C. Monga. (2013). "Introduction: The Rejuvenation of Industrial Policy." In Stiglitz, J. E., and J. L. Yifu (Eds.), *The Industrial Policy Revolution I,* pp. 1–15. Basingstoke, UK: Palgrave Macmillan.

Strachan, H. W. (1976). *Family and Other Business Groups in Economic Development: The Case of Nicaragua.* New York: Praeger Publishers.

Sturgeon, T. J., and G. Gereffi. (2009). "Measuring Success in the Global Economy: International Trade, Industrial Upgrading and Business Function Outsourcing in Global Value Chains." *Transnational Corporations,* 18(2): 1.

Sturgeon, T., and R. K. Lester. (2004). "The New Global Supply-Base: New Challenges for Local Suppliers in East Asia." In Yusuf, S. et al. (Eds.), *Global Production Networking and Technological Change in East Asia,* pp. 35–87. Washington, DC: World Bank Publications.

Suzigan, W., and E. Albuquerque. (2011). "The Underestimated Role of Universities for the Brazilian System of Innovation." *Brazilian Journal of Political Economy,* 31(1): 3–30.

Swart, G. (2015). "Innovation Lessons Learned from the Joule EV Development." International Association for Management of Technology 2015 Conference Proceedings.

Sykes, A. O. (2005). "Subsidies and Countervailing Measures." In Macrory, P. F. J. et al. (Eds.), *The World Trade Organization: Legal, Economic and Political Analysis,* pp. 1682–1706. New York: Springer.

Szapiro, M., M. A. Vargas, M. M. Brito, and J. E. Cassiolato. (2015). "Global Value Chains and National Systems of Innovation: Policy Implications for Developing Countries." 13th Conferência Globelics, Havana, Cuba.

Teece, D. J. (2007). "Explicating Dynamic Capabilities: The Nature and Microfoundations of (Sustainable) Enterprise Performance." *Strategic Management Journal*, 28(13): 1319–1350.

Teece, D. J., G. Pisano, and A. Shuen. (1997). "Dynamic Capabilities and Strategic Management." *Strategic Management Journal*, 18(7): 509–533.

Tidd, J., J. Bessant, and K. Pavitt. (2005). *Managing Innovation Integrating Technological, Market and Organizational Change*. Chichester, UK: John Wiley and Sons.

Tripsas, M., and G. Gavetti. (2000). "Capabilities, Cognition, and Inertia: Evidence from Digital Imaging." *Strategic Management Journal*, 21(10/11): 1147–1161.

Tushman, M. L., and P. Anderson. (1986). "Technological Discontinuities and Organizational Environments." *Administrative Science Quarterly*, 31(3): 439–465.

Tybout, J. R. (2000). "Manufacturing Firms in Developing Countries: How Well Do They Do, and Why?" *Journal of Economic Literature*, 38(1): 11–44.

UNCTAD. (2017), *Trade and Development Report*: Chapter 3. Robots, Industrialization and Inclusive Growth. Geneva: UNCTAD.

(2013). *Global Value Chains: Investment and Trade for Development. World Investment Report 2013*. New York; Geneva: United Nations; UNCTAD.

(2011). *Economic Development in Africa Report 2011*. New York; Geneva: United Nations, UNCTAD.

(2006). *Trade and Development Report*. New York; Geneva: United Nations, UNCTAD.

Utterback, J. (1994). *The Dynamics of Innovation*. Boston: Harvard Business School Press.

Vamvakidis, A. (2002). "How Robust Is the Growth-Openness Connection? Historical Evidence." *Journal of Economic Growth*, 7(1): 57–80.

Van Dijk, M., and M. Bell. (2007). "Rapid Growth with Limited Learning: Industrial Policy and Indonesia's Pulp and Paper Industry." *Oxford Development Studies*, 35(2): 149–169.

Vargas, M., and R. Alievi. (2003). "Learning Trajectories and Upgrading Strategies in the Footwear Productive System of the Sinos Valley/Rs." In Cassiolato, J. E. et al. (Eds.), *Systems of Innovation and Development – Evidence from Brazil*, pp. 352–375. Cheltenham, UK: Edward Elgar Publishers.

Velho, L. (2004). "Science and Technology in Latin America and the Caribbean: An Overview." UNU-INTECH Discussion Paper No. 04.

Vernon, R. (1966). "International Investment and International Trade in the Product Cycle." *Quarterly Journal of Economics*, 80(2): 190–207.

Vértesy, D. (2017). "Preconditions, Windows of Opportunity and Innovation Strategies: Successive Leadership Changes in the Regional Jet Industry." *Research Policy*, 46(2): 388–403.

(2011). "Interrupted Innovation: Emerging Economies in the Structure of the Global Aerospace Industry." *Innovation & Development*, 2(1): 193–194.

Viner, J. (1958). "Stability and Progress: The Poorer Countries' Problem." In Hague, D. C. (Ed.), *Stability and Progress in the World Economy*, pp. 41–65. London: Macmillan.

Wade, R. H. (2012). "Return of Industrial Policy?" *International Review of Applied Economics*, 26(2): 223–239.

(2003). "What Strategies Are Viable for Developing Countries Today? The World Trade Organization and the Shrinking of 'Development Space.'" *Review of International Political Economy*, 10(4): 621–644.

Wardley, P. (1991). "The Anatomy of Big Business: Aspects of Corporate Development in the Twentieth Century." *Business History*, 33(2): 268–296.

Williamson, J. (2012). "Some Basic Disagreements on Development." KDI High-Level Knowledge Forum on Expanding the Frontiers in Development Policy, Seoul.

(1990). "What Washington Means by Policy Reform." In Williamson, J. (Ed.), *Latin American Adjustment: How Much Has Happened*, pp. 90–120. Washington, DC: Institute for International Economics.

Williamson, O. E. (1975). *Markets and Hierarchies*. New York: Free Press

Windrum, P., M. Haynes, and P. Thompson. (2014). "Modular Encapsulation and Japanese Dominance of the Professional Camera Sub-Market, 1955-1974." DRUID Society Conference.

World Bank (2012). "China 2030: Building a Modern, Harmonious, and Creative High-Income Society." Washington, DC: World Bank.

(2010). "Exploring the Middle-Income-Trap." Washington, DC: World Bank.

(2005). "Economic Growth in the 1990s: Learning from a Decade of Reform." Washington, DC: World Bank.

(2002, 2004). "Review of Small Business Activities." Washington, DC: World Bank.

World Development Indicators (WDI). (various years). Washington, DC: World Bank.

World Economic Forum. (2007). "Global Competitiveness Report 2006–2007." New York: Palgrave Macmillan.

Xu, C. (2011). "The Fundamental Institutions of China's Reforms and Development." *Journal of Economic Literature*, 49(4): 1076–1151.

Yanikkaya, H. (2003). "Trade Openness and Economic Growth: A Cross-Country Empirical Investigation." *Journal of Development Economics*, 72(1): 57–89.

Yeung, H. W.-C. (2016). *Strategic Coupling: East Asian Industrial Transformation in the New Global Economy History*. Ithaca; London: Cornell University Press.

Yonekura, S. (1994). *The Japanese Iron and Steel Industry, 1850–1990: Continuity and Discontinuity*. New York: St. Martin's Press.

Yusuf, S., and K. Nabeshima. (2009). "Can Malaysia Escape the Middle-Income Trap? A Strategy for Penang." *World Bank, Policy Research Working Paper* No. 4971.

Zhu, H., Y. Yang, M. T. Tintchev, and G. Wu. (2006). "The Interaction between Regulation and Market and Technology Opportunities: A Case Study of the Chinese Mobile Phone Industry." *Innovation*, 8(1-2): 102–112.

Index